ARCHAEOLOGY OF MINNESOTA

ARCHAEOLOGY OF MINNESOTA

The Prehistory of the
Upper Mississippi River Region

GUY GIBBON

UNIVERSITY OF MINNESOTA PRESS
MINNEAPOLIS · LONDON

The University of Minnesota Press gratefully acknowledges financial
assistance provided for the publication of this book from the
Department of Anthropology, University of Minnesota.

Original maps created by Philip Schwartzberg, Meridian Mapping, Minneapolis
Vegetation data courtesy of Scott Anfinson, University of Minnesota

Published by the University of Minnesota Press
111 Third Avenue South, Suite 290
Minneapolis, MN 55401-2520
http://www.upress.umn.edu

Library of Congress Cataloging-in-Publication Data

Gibbon, Guy E., 1939–
  Archaeology of Minnesota : the prehistory of the upper Mississippi river region / Guy Gibbon.
  Includes bibliographical references and index.
  ISBN 978-0-8166-7909-6 (hc : alk. paper)
  ISBN 978-0-8166-7910-2 (pb : alk. paper)
1. Paleo-Indians—Minnesota. 2. Mississippian culture—Minnesota. 3. Indians of North America—
Minnesota—Antiquities. 4. Minnesota—Antiquities. I. Title.
  E78.M7G48 2012
  977.6'01—dc23   2012029387

Printed in the United States of America on acid-free paper

The University of Minnesota is an equal-opportunity educator and employer.

20 19 18 17 16 15 14 13 12   10 9 8 7 6 5 4 3 2 1

To the memory of Lloyd A. Wilford and Elden Johnson

CONTENTS

Histories of Minnesota typically begin with the explorations of French fur traders Groseilliers and Radisson along the western shores of Lake Superior in 1659 and 1660. Archaeology, the study of the human past through the recovery and interpretation of material remains, has discovered, however, that Native Americans lived in the region we now call Minnesota for at least 13,000 years before Groseilliers and Radisson's arrival. *Archaeology of Minnesota* is a story of their history.

In the previous sentence I use the expression "a story" rather than "the story" because all histories are written from a point of view. Histories of the United States, for example, are about great people, economic relationships with other countries, political struggles, the westward movement of the nation, and the Americanization of different ethnic groups, among many other themes. Likewise, archaeologists writing the history of Native Americans before European contact can opt to describe their surviving artifacts, reconstruct past subsistence and economic systems, or concentrate on evidence for past belief systems, among other avenues of inquiry. The message is that there are multiple ways of seeing the past, whether through written records or the archaeological record.

In *Archaeology of Minnesota,* I concentrate on the lifeways of the Native people who lived in the Upper Mississippi region before contact with European explorers. I use ideas developed by Lewis Binford in his many articles and books but especially in his *Constructing Frames of Reference: An Analytical Method for Archaeological Theory Building Using Ethnographic and Environmental Data Sets.* This way of seeing as I have developed it is explained in the Introduction, which also reviews the various ways that archaeologists organize the archaeological record of the state. Chapter 1 describes the present and past environments of the state, and chapters 2 through 8 present the state's archaeological cultures, from earliest to most recent. The conclusion summarizes long-term pattern in the development of precontact lifeways in Minnesota and explains the relevance of that pattern to understanding human life today.

As stressed throughout this book, information about the archaeology of the precontact period in Minnesota is more often than not difficult to access. Much of the most recent information is in cultural resource management (CRM) reports or, more likely, in someone's head—places that are hard to access. I am grateful to Scott Anfinson, Kent Bakken, George Holley, and Susan Mulholland, as well as two manuscript reviewers for the University of Minnesota Press, for reading and commenting on one or more chapters. Scott Anfinson, Minnesota state archaeologist; Patricia Emerson, head archaeologist at the Minnesota Historical Society; and Edward Fleming, curator of archaeology at the Science Museum of Minnesota, graciously acquired approval for the illustrations printed in this book. Research funds provided by the Department of Anthropology at the University of Minnesota paid for preparation of the maps and sketches. Todd Orjala and Kristian Tvedten from the University of Minnesota Press shepherded *Archaeology of Minnesota* through the publication process; their professionalism, humor, and patience are greatly appreciated. Finally, my wife, Ann, as always, was supportive of my effort throughout the writing process (which, as all writers know, involved large amounts of time present in body but not in mind). The book is dedicated with a warm heart to my two predecessors in the Department of Anthropology at the University of Minnesota, Lloyd A. Wilford and Elden Johnson.

The Tools of the Trade

A widely shared image of an archaeologist is someone who digs sites and studies artifacts—and I do dig sites and study artifacts. However, that image is only half true, for we are equally and in many ways more importantly involved in reconstructing the social, economic, and political systems—the lifeways—of past peoples. Said another way, archaeologists work in two worlds: the present world with its surviving archaeological record, and the past world of the people whose remains form that record. As archaeologists, we adopt different methods when studying each of these two quite different worlds. Since confusion between these two sets of methods can cause confusion when building pictures of life in the past, I begin my review of Minnesota archaeology with a discussion of several key tools I use in each of these worlds in this book.

TOOLS FOR ORGANIZING THE ARCHAEOLOGICAL RECORD

Minnesota's precontact archaeological record consists of the material remains of the many people who lived within the present boundaries of the state before European contact. Since that period spanned 13,000 years, the state's precontact archaeological record is made up of hundreds of thousands (if not millions) of artifacts (portable objects used, modified, or manufactured by human beings), features (nonportable evidence of past human activities, such as a house basin or garbage pit), animal and plants remains, and other items that are present in the ground, in private collections, and in the storage facilities of museums and universities. The arrowheads and pieces of pottery that farmers pick up in their fields and that collectors find eroding out of riverbanks are part of this record too. To make sense of these items, archaeologists need tools to group them together in meaningful space-time units for study.

Each unit should coincide with the past community or group of interrelated communities that made the artifacts and features that archaeologists recover. That is the ideal. However, in archaeology, as in life, ideals are just that, ideals. As we will see, there are many reasons why it is more often than not difficult to associate a group of artifacts, even from the same field or riverbank, with a particular community in the past.

Three approaches to grouping portions of the archaeological record together in space and time have been used by Minnesota archaeologists: a method proposed in the 1930s by W. C. McKern, an archaeologist who became director of the Milwaukee Public Museum; a system proposed in the 1950s by Harvard archaeologists Gordon Willey and Philip Phillips; and a system introduced in the 1970s by Leigh Syms, a Canadian archaeologist, for use in the Northeastern Plains and northern Lake Superior basin. Like many grouping systems in science, these approaches use nested categories based on evermore inclusive degrees of similarity of artifacts and other traits to organize the archaeological record. In biology, for example, life-forms are grouped together within a species, genus, family, order, class, phylum, and on upward to a kingdom. Grouping systems in archaeology are constructed as well to show evermore inclusive relationships. Since all three approaches—McKern's, Willey and Phillips's, and Syms's—have been used to classify Minnesota's archaeological record, it is helpful to have a passing familiarity with each of them, for they are used as organizing devices in this book and in the articles, reports, and books included in the bibliography at the end of this book.

McKern's Midwestern Taxonomic Method groups archaeological traits (characteristics of the archaeological record, such as a type of pottery or the presence or absence of a type of grinding stone) by degree of formal similarity (that is, by how similar they look) into five evermore inclusive classes: foci, aspects, phases, patterns, and bases.[1] The smallest unit is the focus, which is composed of a mostly recurring set of traits, such as a particular type of pottery, projectile point, house form, and economic pursuit, like wild rice harvesting. Increasingly higher-level classes—the aspect, phase, pattern, and base—contain ever fewer traits in common, but the traits are sufficiently distinctive to distinguish archaeological units on like levels from one another, just as groups of plants or animals can be distinguished as similar at the order, class, and phylum level in the classification of life-forms. The mix of traits defining each class is ultimately determined by an archaeologist's subjective judgment of the degree of similarity between components—and differences in subjective judgments have led to confusion. An example is when one archaeologist defines a focus by the presence of a type of pottery and another archaeologist includes a large number of traits. Does the presence of the pottery in a field indicate the presence of an instance (called a component; see below) of the focus, or must the other traits be present too?

In all three approaches, a component is a set of similar types of artifacts and features within a site that are ideally the product of a single occupation by members of the focus. I say *ideally* here, for it is often difficult to separate out repeated seasonal occupations by the same group over a series of years at the same site. A site, which is a spatial concentration of artifacts and features, can contain one to many components. In McKern's method, similar-appearing components in different sites make up a focus.

Lloyd A. Wilford, the founding father of modern archaeology in Minnesota, used McKern's method in his 1941 and 1955 pioneering classifications of Minnesota's precontact archaeological record.[2] Many of his studies of the archaeology of different regions of Minnesota also used McKern's terminology. As an example, he assigned a component at the Humphrey site in southern Minnesota to the Blue Earth focus of the Oneota aspect, Upper Mississippian phase, and Mississippian pattern.

In contrast to McKern's method, which is based solely on degree of trait or content similarity, the Willey and Phillips system is based on the variables of space, time, and content.[3] Similar components within a fairly limited area called a locality are grouped together to form a phase. Chronological sequences within a locality (a local sequence) are formed by the succession of these components and phases. In ever-wider areas (regions and culture areas) and longer-term time trajectories (regional sequences and periods), phases are grouped together to form a tradition, traditions to form a culture, and cultures to form a stage. Thus, a culture is composed of a number of related traditions that span to varying degrees a period of time within a large but circumscribed area. The broadest level of synthesis in the Willey and Phillips system is the stage, which is organized around a defining economic pattern and its accompanying technologies. Thus, what is considered a component of the Blue Earth focus in McKern's system is now a component within the Center Creek locality of the Blue Earth phase of the Oneota tradition.

Syms's hierarchical system of assemblage, complex, composite, configuration, and pattern corresponds roughly to Willey and Phillips's system of component, phase, variant, tradition, and culture, as later modified by Donald Lehmer, who added the concept of a variant between phase and tradition.[4] Unlike the two earlier systems, a defining characteristic of Syms's system is the explicit association of an ethnographic reality with each classificatory unit. Thus, an assemblage is the "surviving materials, features, and evidence of activities of a single residential group over a short period of time at one site," and a complex is "the total expression of a number of assemblages left by the same group" over a short time span.[5] Here, the Humphrey site component becomes an assemblage within a Blue Earth complex of the Oneota configuration.

Unlike the McKern and Willey and Phillips taxonomic systems, Syms's system for organizing the archaeological record recognizes that mobile societies may have a core area where most of their activity takes place, secondary areas where they move at times during the year (to visit a spring fish spawning ground, for example), and tertiary areas that they visit more rarely. Because of this high degree of movement, assemblages of different complexes or composites can be present in the same region during the year, though the assemblages may not have been formed during the same season of the year.

To conclude, the commingling of these three different approaches to organizing Minnesota's archaeological record can be a source of confusion that we have to be aware of when reading articles, reports, and books about the state's precontact archaeological record. Is Oneota an aspect, a tradition, or a configuration? And does the use of one term or another really make a difference? It certainly does. An aspect is a group of traits at a certain level of abstraction; a tradition, a grouping of traits that have space-time connotations; and a configuration, a grouping of people (not artifacts) at a certain level of abstraction.

Although the McKern and Willey and Phillips taxonomic systems were devised to organize the archaeological record, archaeologists still generally assume as in Syms's system that a component or assemblage represents the camp or village of a people, such as a band, who "normally reside together in a face-to-face association," and a phase represents a society that consists of one or more communities, which in this example would be a group of interrelated bands.[6] In both cases the assumption is that these are culturally and linguistically homogeneous societies. As Willey and Phillips remind us, however, "Ethnography offers abundant examples of different societies sharing a material culture that would be impossible to differentiate archaeologically."[7] Roger Owen proposes, too, that simple societies like these are more often linguistically and culturally hybrid social units, rather than culturally and linguistically homogeneous societies.[8] Be aware, then, that the social reality behind the taxonomic terms that archaeologists use must be determined, rather than assumed. In addition by assuming these equivalences before examination or analysis, we blind ourselves to the many other sociocultural and natural processes that can produce pattern in the archaeological record, such as whether and how trash is removed from an encampment and the movement upward at different rates of artifacts of different sizes in sediments during freeze-thaw cycles. Both of these processes produce patterns of their own that can confuse the interpretation of the contents of an archaeological site. I return to these issues throughout the book.

Before I move on, it is important to mention three other peculiarities of the archaeological record that make its study less than straightforward. First, the record is only partial, for organic materials like cloth and wood do not normally survive for long periods in the ground. A hunter's quiver, bow, and arrows, for example, all deteriorate, leaving only the arrow's stone projectile point for study. The record is partial, too, for another reason, for only a small number of sites have been excavated and studied. Many are buried deeply beneath the surface of the ground or have been destroyed by historic period farming or

Years AD/BC	Southeast	Southwest
AD 1650–1200	Oneota Tradition	
	Mississippian Tradition Silvernale Phase (AD 1050–1200)	*Plains Village Tradition* Great Oasis and Cambria Phases (AD 950–1200)
	Terminal Woodland Initial, Mature, and Final Late Woodland (AD 500–1200)	*Terminal Woodland* Lake Benton Phase (AD 700–1200/1300)
	Initial Woodland Early Woodland, Havana-Hopewell Middle Woodland, Late Middle Woodland (500 BC–AD 500)	*Initial Woodland* Fox Lake Phase (200 BC–AD 700)
500–3000 BC	*Late Archaic*	
3000–7500 BC	*Middle Archaic*	
7500–10,500 BC	*Late Paleoindian/Early Eastern Archaic*	
10,500–11,200 BC	*Early Paleoindian*	

Figure I.1. Archaeological periods (in italic) and complexes in precontact southern Minnesota.

construction projects. Second, components within a site are nearly always mixed because of rodent burrowing or other ground-churning processes. Therefore, it is often difficult to impossible to associate the numerous flint chips, standardized artifacts like stone knives and scrapers, and animal bones with a particular component within a site that has two or more components. And third, artifacts and other materials in a site do not come already dated. They have to be arranged in time using methods like radiocarbon dating and style changes that are evident in the various depth levels at a site. Even today, our dating of the content of most sites remains hypothetical at best.

Rather than offer a standardized categorization of the archaeological record of precontact Minnesota, I use the terms currently used by archaeologists to avoid adding to an already confusing situation. For the most part, the system in use today is a truncated version of the Willey and Phillips system. It has temporal (regional sequence, period), spatial (locality, region), and content (phase, tradition, culture) dimensions but neglects the concept of stages. The "for the most part" refers to the use of Syms's terminology for some archaeological materials in far northern Minnesota that are more extensive to the north in Canada, and to a greater use of the concept of a complex as an intermediate term between a phase and a tradition or culture, a practice that is gaining acceptance among Minnesota archaeologists. Figures I.1–I.3 summarize the terminology used in this book for southern, central, and northern Minnesota in that order.[9]

Years AD/BC	Headwaters Lakes Locality	Mille Lacs Locality
AD 1650–1200	*Late Terminal Woodland* Psinomani Complex	
	Middle Terminal Woodland Blackduck Complex (AD 600/800–1200)	*Middle Terminal Woodland* Kathio Complex (AD 800–1300)
	Early Terminal Woodland (AD 400–600/800)	*Early Terminal Woodland* St. Croix and Isle Phases (AD 500–800)
	Initial Woodland Elk Lake Complex (1000 BC–AD 400)	*Initial Woodland* Rum River Phase (200 BC–AD 500)
	Late Archaic (3000–1000 BC)	*Late Archaic* (3000–200 BC)
3000–7500 BC	*Middle Archaic*	
7500–10,500 BC	*Late Paleoindian/Early Plains Archaic*	
10,500–11,200 BC	*Early Paleoindian*	

Figure I.2. Archaeological periods (in italic) and complexes in precontact central Minnesota.

Years AD/BC	Rainy River Locality
AD 1650–1350	*Late Terminal Woodland:* Psinomani Complex
AD 1350–1000	*Late Terminal Woodland:* Rainy River Composite
AD 1100–800	*Middle Terminal Woodland:* Blackduck Complex
AD 1000–500 BC	*Initial Woodland:* Laurel Complex
500–3000 BC	*Late Archaic*
3000–7500 BC	*Middle Archaic*
7500–10,500 BC	*Late Paleoindian*
10,500–10,900 BC	*Early Paleoindian*

Figure I.3. Archaeological periods (in italic) and complexes in precontact northern Minnesota.

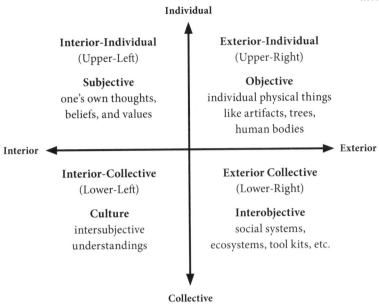

Figure I.4. A four-quadrant perspective on human beings and their societies. Adapted from Wilber 2000, 65.

TOOLS FOR STUDYING PAST LIFEWAYS

Archaeologists use taxonomic terms like *phase, tradition, locality,* and *period* to impose order on the many thousands of artifacts and features that make up the archaeological record in a region. Since that record is the result of many sociocultural and natural formation processes, they create research programs (or ways of seeing) to learn about the people who formed the archaeological record.[10] The working assumptions of the way of seeing adopted in this book are based most centrally on ideas developed by Lewis Binford, John Bodley, Morton Fried, and Ken Wilber.

A tool for helping us understand the relationships between past sociocultural systems and the archaeological record, as well as the tasks and problems of archaeological analysis, is Wilber's four-quadrant or integral approach to understanding human beings and their societies.[11] As Figure I.4 illustrates, the upper-left quadrant is composed of the interior thoughts and experiences of individual human beings; the lower-left quadrant, of the intersubjective understandings or culture of groups of people; the lower-right, of the exterior of social systems (including the system's interconnected material culture); and the upper-right, of the exterior of individuals and things, including individual artifacts and their constituent elements. Although a fully integral study of a human community is the study of all four of these quadrants, I concentrate in this book on the lower-right quadrant, which is the realm of visible systems of social organization, that is, the basic structure of a society (in this book whether band, tribe, or chiefdom), and the size of its social units, primary economic activity (foraging, horticulture, or intensive farming),

---

Characteristics of band-level social organizations

- Bands tend to be foragers (hunters and gatherers of wild foods).
- Bands tend to share resources (especially food) because of the uncertainty of the food quest and the problem of food storage.
- Bands tend to be small (fewer than 100 people) kin-based groups (that is, all members of the group are related to each other by kinship or marriage ties).
- In bands, nuclear families (a kinship group consisting of parents and children) tend to move seasonally from one food resource to another throughout the year (i.e., to be fairly mobile). The band splits into nuclear families to gather food and hunt apart from other groups during much of the year but merges for special religious and social occasions.
- In bands, the most important ceremonies are typically concerned with an individual's life crisis rites of birth, puberty, marriage, and death.
- Bands tend to have a simple and meager material culture (in large part because of their mobility).
- In bands, housing usually consists of insubstantial dwellings or temporary shelters (again because of mobility).
- Bands tend not to have full-time supported specialists (tribes may have a few).
- Bands tend to live more leisured lives than horticulturalists and agriculturalists.
- Bands tend to be egalitarian (i.e., contrasts in prestige are minor and are based on age and gender; band leaders and shamans (part-time religious specialists) are only "first among equals."
- Bands lack formal law in the sense of a legal code that includes trial and enforcement.
- Band territories tend to have vague boundaries.
- In bands, people tend to shift band membership several times in a lifetime.
- In bands, division of labor is generally based on age and gender. Men typically hunt and fish while women gather and collect. (Just which group supplies the most food varies from one group to another, and often from one season or year to another.)
- Bands make social distinctions based on age (old people generally receive great respect).

Figure I.5

and political sources of social power, among other features. However, think of what an archaeology based on one of the other quadrants or on all four quadrants might be like. That gives some idea of what I am not looking at in this book.[12]

Among the tools I use in studying the exterior of the social systems of precontact people in Minnesota is Bodley's concept of scale of culture.[13] The scale of culture of a community is based on how people in that community organize social power, which he defines as an "individual's ability to get what he or she wants, even when others might object."[14] All of the study area's precontact social systems fall within his domestic scale of culture, which he defines as characterized "by small, kinship-based societies, often with only 500 people, in which households organize production and distribution."[15]

Characteristics of tribal-level social organizations

- A tribe has evidence of nonintensive food production (horticulture, for instance, rather than farming) and the use of simple tools (hoes and digging sticks) to grow crops.
- People who live in tribal-level societies typically have a diet of domesticated plants (and possibly animals) supplemented by hunted and gathered wild foods.
- Tribal peoples typically live in small, sedentary villages that have no more than several hundred residents (and more often 30 to 150 people).
- Houses in tribal societies are often more substantial than among mobile band-level groups, because villages tend to be occupied year-round.
- Another characteristic of tribal societies is small-scale warfare, which is nearly always of the ambush, skirmish variety. Consequently, their villages are often surrounded by palisades or other defensive devices.
- Unlike bands, some tribes have marked gender stratification, with an unequal distribution of resources, power, prestige, and personal freedom between men and women (attributed, perhaps, to the importance of warriors).

Figure I.6

Since the study area's precontact social systems were all at a domestic scale of culture, I use four different strategies to differentiate, examine, and think about them. The first strategy is the familiar distinction between band-based and tribal societies, both of which are at Bodley's domestic scale of culture. I believe that this is an important empirically supported distinction in the study region. In brief, bands tend to be foragers who capture and gather wild foods using residential mobility as a major subsistence strategy. They are typically small, egalitarian, kin-based groups with a simple and meager material culture due in large part to their mobility. Tribes tend to be collectors who live in small, sedentary villages from which task groups venture out to gather resources. Their diet is typically domesticated foods supplemented by hunted and gathered wild foods.

Traits characteristic of bands and tribes, and of chiefdoms, a more complex type of social organization that influenced Minnesota's Native American populations between about AD 900 and 1250, are listed in Figures I.5–I.7. As I describe in the lifeway descriptions below, Minnesota's Native American societies switched suddenly from a band-level to a tribal-level social organization during that same time period, perhaps due to the direct or indirect influence of large-scale chiefdoms in Illinois and other states south of Minnesota.

As introduced so far, bands and tribes are presented as though they are static societies frozen in time. In contrast my focus in this book is on identifying long-term processes of change in Minnesota's precontact band-based and tribal societies.[16] To accomplish this

---

Characteristics of chiefdom-level social organizations

- A chiefdom is a ranked society in which one's position and power are determined by how closely related one is to the chief and his lineage or corporate group.
- The chief lacks a consistently available and effective means of physical coercion. In other words, a chiefdom lacks an army or police to enforce the chief's will by physical means.
- The chief has at his disposal two levels of administrative control, those associated with the settlement and mound center of his residence, and the smaller settlements administered by lesser chiefs, who are often his relations.
- Sufficient wealth is controlled by the ruling elite, who often employ craft specialists, at least on a part-time basis.
- In chiefdoms, political and religious powers are closely intertwined, so much so that the chief and his family are revered as almost godlike.
- The elite try to convince their followers to produce more and more food surplus by investing in any activity that increases food production.
- Chiefdoms are an extraordinarily competitive type of social organization.

Figure I.7

goal, I first summarize the archaeological record for a particular period in chapters 2 through 8 and then draw inferences about the lifeways of the people whose material remains form that record.[17] In the conclusion I place these long-term historical trajectories in the context of the history of human societies throughout the world and argue that the identification of historical trajectories like these should be of interest to all of us.

The second strategy I use to examine precontact social systems is Fried's still useful notion that a tribe is a mode of social organization forced into existence when band-level groups interact with hostile or at least competitive groups having larger-scale social organizations.[18] The third is a frames of reference approach proposed by Binford.[19] Binford's approach to the study of hunter-gatherer lifeways is complicated and difficult to comprehend in detail if for no other reason than the richness and abundance of the ideas and data he packs into *Constructing Frames of Reference*. Consequently, I present a simplified summary here, geared to the concerns of this study of Minnesota archaeology.

Like all approaches to the study of human lifeways, Binford's approach is based on a set of fundamental assumptions about the underlying forces (processes, ideas) that explain or give insight into human lifeways and the reasons for their change through time. Three of the most basic are the following: (1) "[H]uman actors attempt to maximize their energetic returns in contexts of energy expenditure; in short, they commonly optimize"; (2) "Humans also seek to synchronize the flow of free energy into the human system relative to the human [seasonal] demand curve for food and other energy sources, such as firewood"; and (3) "Humans tend to organize their labor and their activities in a way that reduces the risk associated with accessing critical resources, and they tend to organize into cooperative social units in order to minimize any uncertainty associated with the dynamics of their social and ecological environments."[20]

Since environments differ profoundly around the world—from cold polar ice fields to warm, steamy tropical jungles to hot, arid deserts—hunter-gatherer food-acquiring systems, social organization, and division of labor between men and women differed profoundly during the early historic period, and would have differed profoundly in the prehistoric past too. Said more plainly, hunter-gatherers around the world have never shared a single, homogeneous lifeway but have had a bewildering number of lifeways rooted in differences in environment, level of sociocultural complexity, and culture. From a Minnesota perspective, this means that the details of hunter-gatherer social systems in precontact central Illinois, southern and northern Minnesota, and central Manitoba were assuredly different. It is a goal of archaeological research to determine what these differences were and why. Binford's *Constructing Frames of Reference* provides a reasoned argument for what these differences would have been and why, and the why is firmly anchored in the nature of global environments.

In Binford's words, most basically, "water and solar radiation are . . . the two major variables whose interaction determines the irregular and complicated pattern of biotic production observable across the surface of the globe"; "solar radiation is distributed globally in a pattern of gradual reduction as the distance from the equator increases"; and "rainfall is somewhat irregularly distributed as a result of the temperature and related movement of circulating air masses in response to different pressure levels" caused, for example, by encounters with topographical features like landmasses, bodies of water, and differences in surface elevation.[21] As a rule, though, primary plant biomass increases with rainfall, which accounts for the distribution of prairie and forest in Minnesota at present and in the past.

In *Constructing Frames of Reference*, Binford explores the associations of a large number of environmental variables with features of hunter-gatherer lifeways as recorded in a sample of 390 historic-period hunter-gatherer groups from around the world and as predicted by a model (the Terrestrial Model) based on his assumptions about the principles (processes) that underlie hunter-gatherer lifeways. These variables include measures of regional temperature, available solar energy, water availability to plant communities, net primary plant productivity, accessible animal foods, length of growing season, water balance conditions, net aboveground productivity, biomass, vegetation type, elevation, and characteristics of drainage systems.

Given these associations and model predictions, what pattern of hunter-gatherer adaptations might we expect to find in precontact Minnesota? If we assume—and rightly so, I think—that the state was initially colonized by small numbers of pioneering foragers, we would expect to see its land surface eventually covered by the contiguous home ranges of ever-growing numbers of daughter communities supplemented perhaps by new colonizing populations from outside the state.[22] According to Binford's data, this ever-growing number of foraging bands can lead to population packing, which results in smaller home ranges, pressure on resources, and a greater concentration on second-order foods, like fish and plants.[23] Resource intensification in turn is associated with the adoption or invention of new equipment appropriate to the new resource tasks, a changing division of labor between men and women, a less mobile lifeway, and adjustments in social organization in response to these changes. In many areas these trends lead to the sudden emergence of new, more-settled lifeways that rely on domesticated plants and animals or the harvesting of an abundant natural resource, like marine mammals or wild rice.

Following Binford's suggestion in *Constructing Frames of Reference,* I use a computer modeling tool developed by University of Wisconsin–Madison climatologist Reid Bryson to reconstruct the climatic history of Minnesota for the past 13,500 years.[24] By inputting current climatic information for particular geographical locations (indicated by longitude and latitude) in the state, I can use the modeling tool to approximate what past temperatures and rainfall and snowfall rates, among other climatic variables, may have been like in those locations. This is a critical tool for the approach I adopt in this book, for Binford's predictions about social content and change depend on the availability of regional paleoclimatic data.

Chapters 2 through 8 explore in some depth the range of ideas summarized above when applied to Minnesota's precontact environments and archaeological record. This approach provides new insights into the content and sequence of the state's archaeological cultures, though there remain many problems of detail, which I return to in the conclusion. A glimpse of this pattern as it unfolded in Minnesota is apparent in the sequence of lifeways summarized below, which is my fourth strategy.

At this early stage in my use of a frames of reference approach, I use the following nine lifeways as tools for thinking about the results of subsistence intensification through time in precontact Minnesota.

Pioneer Forager (circa 11,200–10,500 BC). According to our analysis, the earliest people to enter Minnesota were small numbers of Early Paleoindians whose subsistence focus was hunting. Since they were the only hunter-gatherer groups in the state, they were able to "free wander" the rapidly changing Late Glacial landscape in pursuit of large- and medium-sized quarry. Given their free-wandering lifeway in Minnesota's

Late Glacial landscape, their sites are, for the most part, small, artifact-poor, and nonaccumulative.

Coniferous Forest Game Hunter (circa 10,500–3000 BC). By the Late Paleoindian period, the Pioneer Forager lifeway was replaced through the coniferous forests of northern Minnesota by a Coniferous Forest Game Hunter lifeway. These hunter-gatherers were also very mobile foragers with a strong hunting subsistence focus, but they now lived within home ranges. Still, their home ranges were large enough for them to concentrate on their preferred quarry. The number of Coniferous Forest Game Hunter groups in northern Minnesota was low. Their sites remain small and marked by the presence of the material culture of mobile hunters, but many sites were regularly reoccupied during subsistence-settlement cycles. This lifeway persisted through the Late Paleoindian, Early Archaic, and Middle Archaic periods in this region.

Deciduous Forest Game Hunter (circa 10,500–7500 BC). Similar in characteristics to the Coniferous Forest Game Hunter lifeway, the Deciduous Forest Game Hunter lifeway was an adaptation to the early postglacial deciduous forests of southern Minnesota. This lifeway persisted through the Late Paleoindian–Early Eastern Archaic and Middle Archaic periods in this region, or until eastward-expanding tallgrass prairie replaced deciduous forest.

Early Pedestrian Bison Hunter (circa 10,500–3000 BC). As prairies entered the state from the west, an Early Pedestrian Bison Hunter lifeway similar in basic characteristics to the two previous Game Hunter lifeways appeared that was focused on the exploitation of bison herds. This lifeway expanded across southern Minnesota and into northeastern Minnesota during the Prairie period, a dry period I discuss in chapter 3. This lifeway persisted in the broad expanse of Minnesota's prairies during the Late Paleoindian–Early Eastern Archaic and Middle Archaic periods.

Proto–Wild Rice Harvester (circa 3000 BC–AD 1200). The Proto–Wild Rice Harvester lifeway emerged when subsistence intensification began in response to population packing brought about by ever-growing numbers of bands. Proto-Wild Rice Harvesters largely occupied the mosaic of coniferous-hardwood forests and pine stands in the central and northern regions of the state. The content of their sites shows evidence of the increased exploitation of second-order foods, such as fish and wild rice. This lifeway persisted through the Late Archaic, Initial Woodland, and early portion of the Terminal Woodland periods in this area.

Proto-Horticulturalist (circa 3000 BC–AD 1000). The Proto-Horticulturalist lifeway is the counterpart of the Proto–Wild Rice Harvester lifeway. It was centered in the southeastern, deciduous forest quarter of the state where domesticated plants could be grown most easily. Like Proto–Wild Rice Harvesters, these were band-level hunter-gatherers who supplemented their subsistence base with second-order foods, including some domesticated plants, like sunflower, amaranth, and squash. This lifeway persisted through the Late Archaic, Initial Woodland, and Terminal Woodland periods in this area.

Late Pedestrian Bison Hunter (circa 3000 BC–AD 1000). As in the Proto–Wild Rice Harvester and Proto-Horticulturalist lifeways, the Late Pedestrian Bison Hunter lifeway was characterized by increased exploitation of second-order foods and a more regular occupation of some seasonal settlement sites. This lifeway persisted in the western tallgrass prairies of the state through the Late Archaic, Initial Woodland, and Terminal Woodland periods.

Intensive Wild Rice Harvester (circa AD 1250–1650). By AD 1250, if not earlier, tribal groups emerged suddenly in the coniferous forests of central Minnesota and gradually spread northward. They now lived in relatively sedentary village clusters. Although they are still considered hunter-gatherers, they relied heavily on wild rice, the "corn of the north." The primary reason for the emergence of this lifeway has not been firmly established, but I suggest that it was in reaction to the presence of larger-scale tribal groups in southern Minnesota. This lifeway was present during the latter portion of the Terminal Woodland period in this area.

Horticulturalist (circa AD 1000–1650). Tribal groups appeared equally suddenly, if somewhat earlier, in southern Minnesota. The primary reason for the initial emergence of these groups (Silvernale, Cambria, and Great Oasis) seems to be tensions related to the emergence of chiefdom-scale societies in Illinois and other states south of Minnesota. This lifeway is characteristic of the Mississippian period in southern Minnesota.

As I mentioned in the preface, there are many ways to examine, or "see," the past. The way of seeing used in this book is very much in the tradition of the *longue durée* approach to the study of history in that its focus is on long-term patterns of change in the organization of societies in a region. I believe that this emphasis is of importance in archaeological research today, for the details of lifeways at various scales can be more informatively filled in once this background is better understood. I also believe that an understanding of long-term patterns of change in social organization in a region like Minnesota—as compared to a discussion limited to a description of the archaeological cultures of a region—has most to contribute to our understanding of the broader patterns of development of human societies that took place throughout the world in the postglacial period. These patterns included additional chiefdom, city-state, emperor, and capitalist global scales of culture.[25]

CHAPTER 1

Environments of Minnesota

LAND OF TRANSITIONS

For archaeologists, Minnesota is both a perplexing and an intriguing state to work in. Its vegetation cover grades into boreal coniferous forest to the north, tallgrass prairie to the west and southwest, and deciduous forest to the east and southeast. Famous for its ten thousand lakes, the state is also crossed and bordered by streams that flow in these same directions. Streams in the southern and southeastern part of the state, like the Minnesota, Blue Earth, St. Croix, and Root, flow into the south-flowing Mississippi River. Streams on the Coteau des Prairies in the southwestern corner of the state, like the Rock, flow southwestward into the Missouri drainage. And streams to the north, like the Rainy, Red River of the North, Big and Little Fork, and St. Louis, drain either northward into Hudson Bay or eastward into Lake Superior. Phrased another way, Minnesota is the only state having drainage to the Gulf of Mexico, through the Gulf of the St. Lawrence, and to the Arctic Ocean. Because of this confluence of major waterways and ecological communities, Minnesota was a melting pot of prehistoric cultures—a peculiarity of its history that I explore in this book.

THE LAND IN THE 1850S

At 86,943 square miles, Minnesota is the twelfth largest of the fifty states. Bordered by Canada on the north, Iowa on the south, Wisconsin and Lake Superior on the east, and the Dakotas on the west, the state is about 400 miles long and 250 miles wide. It is a relatively flat state, as is apparent in the difference between its highest point (Eagle Mountain at 2,301 feet above sea level) and its lowest point (at Lake Superior at 602 feet above sea level), both of which are in northeastern Minnesota.[1]

Besides its snowy, cold winters, Minnesota is famous for its "ten thousand" lakes and numerous rivers and streams.[2] Today, the total surface water area of the state including wetlands is about 20,526 square miles. About 4,000 square miles of this surface water are deepwater lakes and rivers, and 14,537 square miles are wetlands (in the 1850s there were about 29,062 square miles of wetlands). Minnesota's 21,200 miles of drainage ditches are just one measure of the effort made to drain its surface water. Some lakes in the southern, agricultural part of the state, such as Great Oasis, have been completely drained for farmland.

Of Minnesota's 11,842 lakes ten acres or more in size, nine of the ten largest—Red Lake (both Upper and Lower, 288,800 acres), Mille Lacs Lake (132,516 acres), Leech Lake (111,527 acres), Lake Winnibigoshish (58,544 acres), Lake Vermilion (40,557 acres), Lake Kabetogama (25,760 acres), Mud Lake (in Marshall County, 23,760 acres), Cass Lake (15,596 acres), and Otter Tail Lake (13,596 acres)—are in the northern two thirds or north woods part of the state. The four counties that have no natural lakes (Mower, Olmsted, Pipestone, and Rock) are all in the lower two tiers of counties. Its largest border lakes are Lake Superior (31,820 square miles), in the northeast, and Lake of the Woods (1,485 square miles), in the north. Minnesota's 6,564 natural rivers and streams flow a combined 69,200 miles, with that part of the Mississippi River entirely within the state the longest river at 680 miles (the Minnesota River is about 370 miles long).

And what about those cold, snowy Minnesota winters? When residents of Florida or Arizona think of Minnesota, the first images that spring to mind are of blizzards and long, snowy, cold winters, rather than beautiful lakes and northern forests. Like its lakes and streams and transitional plant and animal communities, Minnesota's climate and weather are intimate parts of its character. The state's climate, which is characterized by warm, humid summers, cold, dry winters, and a steep south–north temperature gradient, is determined by its geographical location near the center of North America, its long, narrow shape, and the coming together of three air masses over its land surface. Cool, dry air flows in from the northwest; relatively dry, warmer air, from the west; and humid, warm air, from the south. When the air masses clash across the state, the result is moisture in the form of rain or snow, tornadoes, and sudden temperature inversions.

Although Minnesota's climate can be regionally variable, average temperatures increase from northeast to southwest, and average precipitation increases from northwest to southeast. The frost-free growing season ranges from 140 to 160 days in the south to fewer than 120 days in the north, with a gradient in between (in a normal year, the average temperature is 2° to 3°F cooler for every 100 miles of northward travel). That differences like these in climate had a direct effect on the lifeways of Minnesota's precontact hunter-gatherers is apparent in Map 1.1, where the line between the five-month and six-month growing season effectively marks the archaeological division in the late prehistoric period between maize-growing (corn-growing) communities in

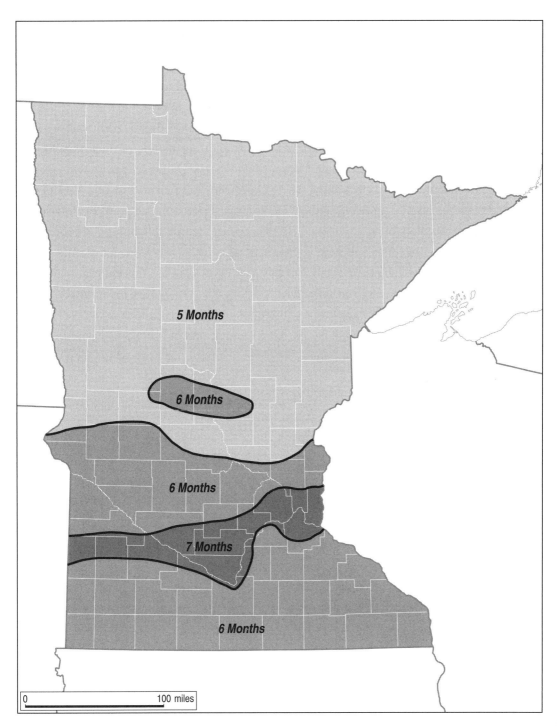

5 Months

6 Months

6 Months

7 Months

6 Months

0   100 miles

Map 1.1. Length of growing season in months in Minnesota in the late twentieth century.
The formula for determining the length of the growing season is GROWC, which counts the number
of consecutive months in which the mean monthly temperature exceeds 8°C (Binford 2001, 73).

southern Minnesota and communities that continued to rely on the hunting and gathering of wild food resources in central and northern Minnesota. This climatic division is used to structure the content of chapters 4 through 8.

Northern lakes, like Lake of the Woods and the border lakes, tend to freeze over in mid- to late-November and to be ice-free by late April. Even Lake Superior occasionally freezes over in very cold winters. Southwestern lakes freeze over by early December and are ice-free by early April. All of this is important information for those traveling by canoe or planning to plant maize. For precontact horticulturalists, the growing season in the northern two-thirds of the state was probably too short to grow the varieties of corn and beans then available as dependable crops. Superimposed on this pattern of climate are thunderstorms, an occasional tornado, and seasonal floods, with flooding occurring along the larger southern rivers on average one to two years out of ten.

Although a welter of seemingly dull facts and figures, the shifting patterns of temperature and moisture determined the pre-1850s distribution of plant and animal communities in Minnesota, and in turn the distribution of hunter-gatherer lifeways. Thus, understanding the distribution of Native American lifeways in Minnesota before European contact requires knowledge about the physical environments in which they lived.

MINNESOTA'S MAJOR BIOTIC PROVINCES

Minnesota has been divided into different combinations of geographical subdivisions, depending on the interests of the people making the subdivisions. Familiar examples are maps that show varying rates of farmland production across the state, weather patterns, and popular (and not so popular) tourist destinations. I summarize two other ways of subdividing the state that archaeologists find useful: major biotic provinces and archaeological resource regions.

At historic contact Minnesota was a mosaic of forests, lakes, and prairies.[3] To simplify this review, descriptions of the state's native vegetation and wildlife recorded by the first government land surveyors in the nineteenth century are used to divide Minnesota into three major biotic provinces: mixed hardwood forest, deciduous forest, and tallgrass prairie. I add a fourth province, the boreal coniferous forest, because it was the dominant land cover in the state thousands of years ago when Native Americans first entered this land and now covers a vast area north of Minnesota. Since plant communities reflect regional climatic patterns and since animal species are better adapted to some plant communities than to others, biotic provinces are associations of climate and plant and animal communities. Map 1.2 shows the location of the boreal coniferous forest, mixed hardwood forest, deciduous forest, and tallgrass prairie provinces in the mid-nineteenth century.

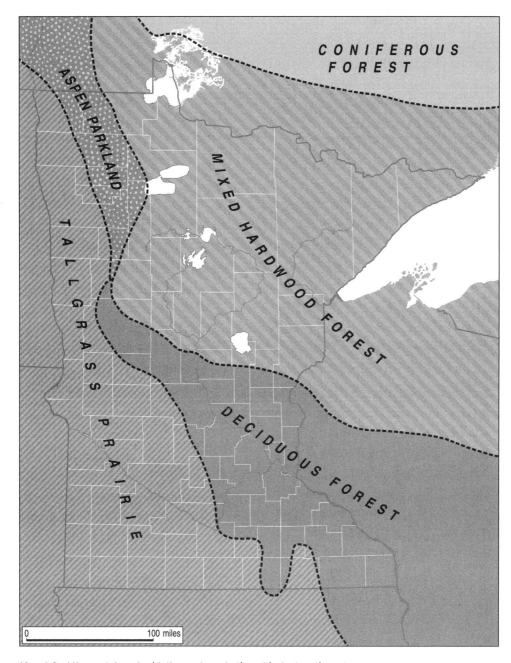

Map 1.2. Minnesota's major biotic provinces in the mid-nineteenth century.

Boreal Coniferous Forest. The boreal coniferous forest is the most northern of the four provinces.[4] It is also called the spruce-fir-moose-caribou biome, a more descriptive label from the perspective of Native American hunter-gatherer societies. Although boreal forest once covered large areas of Minnesota, it stretches today across northern North America from Alaska to Newfoundland and northward to the tree line. Referred to over much of its area as the subarctic, it is known for its long, cold winters, deep snow cover, and short, warm summers. It is a recently deglaciated land of thin soils, exposed bedrock, and immature drainage. An intricate maze of bogs, lakes, and rivers remains as a heritage of this withdrawal of glacial ice. Its forest cover is taiga, or boreal coniferous forest, composed of often dense stands of black and white spruce, white birch, jack pine, balsam fir, and tamarack. Poplar, cedar, and willow are also present, as are white pine, red pine, and hemlock. The latter species are intrusive members from the mixed hardwood province to the south and occur in greatest densities along the southern edge of the boreal forest.

Game animals associated with the boreal forest include moose, caribou, black bear, wolf, lynx, wolverine, marten, fisher, red fox, porcupine, beaver, and snowshoe hare. Fish are abundant in lakes and rivers. The most important of these are bass, pike, pickerel, whitefish, lake trout, sturgeon, smelt, perch, bullhead, catfish, sucker, and freshwater drum. Turtles, frogs, and clams are also present in some lakes and rivers.

Mixed Hardwood Forest. Most Minnesotans call the mixed hardwood forest the north woods.[5] Although a distinctive biotic province in its own right, it is also a broad transition zone between the much larger boreal forest and deciduous forest provinces, where boreal forest plants and animals increase in frequency to the north, and deciduous forest plants and animals become more common to the south. While all of the boreal forest trees are present, this province is dominated by still greater quantities of white and red pine, cedar, alder, yellow birch, beech, elm, hemlock, aspen, basswood, and sugar maple, especially to the south. All of the boreal forest animals are present, too, but caribou, wolverine, and lynx are rare, while moles, mountain lion, and bobcat are more common. White-tailed deer are common where deciduous trees are abundant.

The climate in the mixed hardwood forest is intermediate as well. While winters are still long and cold, summers are somewhat longer and warmer than in the north. Although the land was also heavily glaciated, its soils are richer in organic content and tend to be deeper than those in the north. It retains, however, extensive lakes and bogs, again a heritage from the passing of the last glacier.

Deciduous Forest. An increasingly narrower northwestward extension of the deciduous forest province separates the mixed hardwood forest and prairie biotic provinces in Minnesota.[6] Also called the oak-deer-maple biome, this province is characterized by broadleaf trees that drop their leaves in winter, like oak, hickory, maple, beech, walnut, butternut, elm, ash, basswood, and cottonwood. Large numbers of a wide variety of animals were present at historic contact. Although white-tailed deer were the primary game animal, black bear, elk, opossum, raccoon, cottontail rabbit, squirrel, gray fox, bobcat, mountain lion, wolf, mink, otter, beaver, muskrat, and woodchuck were hunted, too. Occasional buffalo and badgers inhabited areas of open grassland. The climate of the province is still more moderate, with shorter winters, less snowfall, and longer, hotter summers. Soils are deeper and richer, and drainage systems are much more mature than in the northern provinces.

Tallgrass Prairie. The fourth major biotic province is the prairie.[7] Also called the grass-oak-bison biome, it contained prairie vegetation and animal associations. Typical mammals included buffalo, elk, skunk, badger, jackrabbit, ground squirrel, gopher, and coyote. While generally thought of as a region of sweeping tallgrass prairie with scattered copses of oak and hickory, forests were present along stream valleys, around lakes, and on some plateaus and low hills. The most common tree species were oak, sycamore, cottonwood, elm, hackberry, maple, basswood, and beech. Winters and summers are similar to those of the deciduous forest province. Plains buffalo, elk, jackrabbit, gophers, and badgers were among the most common mammals in the prairie biome.

MINNESOTA'S ARCHAEOLOGICAL RESOURCE REGIONS

Archaeologists find it useful in their studies to partition the state using a wider range of criteria that may also have been important to precontact hunters and gatherers. The most commonly used of these systems is one proposed by State Archaeologist Scott Anfinson. It divides the state into five primary archaeological resource regions—northwest, northeast, central, southwest, and southeast—and nine secondary regions (Map 1.3).[8] Anfinson's resource regions are based on hydrologic features (presence or absence of lakes, lake morphology, and lake depth) in addition to the distribution of plant and animal communities. These variables have been more or less stable for the past 5,000 years (the Late Holocene), the period during which most sites in the state's archaeological database were formed. Since the description of each region is data packed (and thus a challenge to read right through), readers may find it more convenient to refer back to these descriptions when reading about different regions of the state in later chapters.

Northwestern Minnesota

As the last glaciers moved northward across the state's northern border between 12,000 and 11,000 BC, the outflow of the accumulated meltwater was blocked by the Canadian ice mass to the north and by a moraine dam to the south near Browns Valley. Unable to flow northward or southward, the water pooled, forming Glacial Lake Agassiz.[9] At

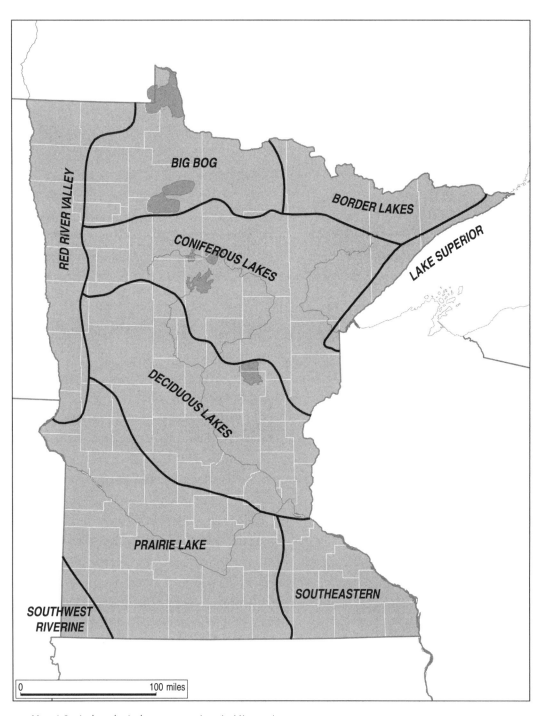

RED RIVER VALLEY

BIG BOG

BORDER LAKES

LAKE SUPERIOR

CONIFEROUS LAKES

DECIDUOUS LAKES

PRAIRIE LAKE

SOUTHEASTERN

SOUTHWEST RIVERINE

0   100 miles

Map 1.3. Archaeological resource regions in Minnesota.

its greatest extent the lake covered about 123,520 square miles of north-central North America. Its legacy in Minnesota is a huge, flat lake bed interrupted only by the incised valleys of meandering streams and by the former shorelines of the lake. Beach ridges are typically linear swells of sand and gravel 13 to 17 feet high and 500 feet or more in width. These ridges run in roughly parallel bands for miles across the surface of the region. The eastern arm of the lake bed stretches eastward to International Falls and the headwaters of Rainy River. Its southern lobe stretches south to Lake Traverse, which is the headwater of the Red River of the North.

The southern lobe, which extends into eastern North Dakota and southeastern Manitoba, is bordered on the east by the Herman ridge and in the north by the Campbell beach, both remnants of the last glacial advance. Since all of this part of northwestern Minnesota is within the Red River drainage basin, it is called the Red River Valley region. It contains Clay, Kittson, Norman, and Wilkin Counties and parts of Marshall, Pennington, Polk, Red Lake, Roseau, and Traverse Counties. Many west-flowing rivers intersect the north-flowing Red. While lake basins are absent, there were numerous shallow marshes in the 1850s, many of which dried up by late summer. Most of these marshes are now drained. While there are no bedrock outcrops in the Red River Valley region, cobble deposits in beach ridges in the eastern part of the lobe were sources of toolstone. These deposits are most easily accessible where rivers cut through the beaches.

After the final retreat of Glacial Lake Agassiz from this lobe at about 8200 BC, the land was covered by tallgrass prairie. River-bottom forests (elm, ash, and cottonwood) were present along the Red River and its major tributaries, and an irregular band of aspen-oak forest, or aspen parkland, spread along the lobe's northeastern edge. Like a rainbow, the aspen band arced across the northern prairie in Canada and extended southward toward the Rocky Mountains. The major Late Holocene food resource was bison, which were present along the Red River in large herds. Large elk herds were also reported in the early 1800s. Near the eastern edge of the region, deer were available, while in the northeast, moose and even woodland caribou were present. Some fish and mussels were available in the Red River and its major tributaries. Waterfowl were seasonally abundant on the shallow marshes, and plant foods would have included prairie species (such as prairie turnip), marsh plants (like cattails), berries, and nuts from the riparian forests.

Today, the long eastern (or Beltrami) arm of Glacial Lake Agassiz is appropriately called the Big Bog, for it is covered by vast wetlands and patterned bogs (tree-covered islands of vegetation).[10] The Big Bog is a fairly recent development. Following the retreat of Glacial Lake Agassiz from the area, wet prairie and patches of aspen and oak woodlands covered the area. About 2500 BC, in response to a cooler, wetter climate, extensive peatlands began to build up over most of the eastern two-thirds of the Big

Bog region. They followed a developmental progression from cattail marshes, to sedge meadows and heath bogs, to sphagnum moss. Bog conifers, such as spruce, tamarack, cedar, and balsam, grew on higher ground. This large and sparsely occupied area of the state remained a watery barrier between the Headwaters Lakes region of the Mississippi River to the south and Canada to the north for thousands of years.

The Big Bog region of northwestern Minnesota contains Lake of the Woods County and parts of Beltrami, Clearwater, Koochiching, Marshall, Pennington, Polk, Red Lake, and Roseau Counties. Although 6 to 8 feet of lake sediment and up to 100 feet of glacial drift cover most of the bedrock, outcrops of Precambrian bedrock occur around Lake of the Woods, along the Rainy River, and in eastern Koochiching County. Lakes and transecting rivers are rare in the heart of the Big Bog, but lakes and streams are present around its borders. Several large, shallow remnants of Glacial Lake Agassiz (Red, Thief, and Mud Lakes) are on its western edge, and its southwestern corner is drained by the headwaters of rivers that flow west to the Red River. North-flowing rivers, which intersect the west-flowing Rainy River along the northern edge of the region, include the Roseau, Warroad, Rapid, Little Fork, and Big Fork. Late Holocene game animals included deer, moose, caribou, beaver, and black bear. Some bison were present in the west. Fish were plentiful in Red Lake, Lake of the Woods, and the major rivers, and waterfowl were seasonally abundant. Wild rice was present in the region, too, though it was not as abundant as in the central lakes regions to the south.

Northeastern Minnesota

Northeastern Minnesota is the most rugged part of the state, with the state's highest (2,301 feet above sea level) and lowest (602 feet above sea level) elevations. Its rocky and ice-scoured surface is a result of a complicated glacial history in which erosion rather than deposition was a dominant process. As a consequence, glacial drift is relatively thin or absent over wide areas, and lakes pool in bedrock cavities, unlike the state's southern and western lakes, which are embedded in glacial drift. Because of different bottom profiles and water chemistries, the fish species in the two sets of lakes are different, and large stands of wild rice are not common in northeastern lakes. The resource region's Late Holocene vegetation was dominated by pine and spruce, with some inclusions of aspen and birch. Game animals included deer, moose, caribou, beaver, and bear. Waterfowl were seasonally abundant, especially on interior lakes.

Like northwestern Minnesota, this large-scale resource region is divided into two distinctive parts, an interior Border Lakes region and a Lake Superior region. The Border Lakes region is famous for its interconnected complex of tightly packed lakes and rivers.[11] The Pigeon River drains rivers in the eastern part, and the Rainy River those in the central and western parts. The region covers northern Cook, Lake, and St. Louis Counties and the small portion of eastern Koochiching County that includes Nett Lake and the eastern area of Rainy Lake. It also extends northward into Ontario where Quetico Provincial Park is today. High-quality toolstone outcrops are present at locations associated with the Gunflint and Vermilion iron formations.

The eastern Lake Superior region stretches along Lake Superior.[12] It includes the eastern edges of Carlton, Cook, Lake, and St. Louis Counties, and extends northward along Lake Superior into Ontario as far as Thunder Bay. Unlike other regions of Minnesota, the Lake Superior region has rocky cliffs with many small bays and points. Abundant Precambrian bedrock exposures are present, making waterfalls common, as the short, steep streams and rivers cascade down the 900- to 1,500-foot drop to Lake Superior. In contrast, the southern tip of the region is the flat plain of Glacial Lake Duluth, which is drained by the St. Louis and Nemadji Rivers. Lakes are rare in the Lake Superior shore highlands, though brown trout lived in the major streams below cataracts, and large fish populations were present in Lake Superior. Game animals were less common than in the Border Lakes region.

Central Minnesota

The state's largest resource region, central Minnesota is covered by extensive wetlands, many deep lakes (some reaching depths of more than 95 feet), and gently rolling hills. The topography of the region is a patchwork of hilly moraines, till (glacial drift), outwash, and glacial lake plains, another legacy of the Wisconsin glaciation. The tops of the most prominent of the moraines, the Alexandria Moraine, which extends from Douglas County north into Mahnomen County, and the Itasca Moraine in Becker and Hubbard Counties, are about 900 feet above the bed of Glacial Lake Agassiz to the north. Only the plain of Glacial Lakes Upham and Aitkin lacks lakes. In some areas glacial sediment is 490 feet thick. Large lakes include Bemidji, Leech, and Mille Lacs, one of the state's largest lakes. Wild rice beds were extensive throughout most of central Minnesota, and fish and waterfowl were abundant in its many lakes and rivers.

This resource region, too, can be usefully divided into two regions based on differences in vegetation and watersheds. A more northern Coniferous Lakes region includes portions of Aitkin, Beltrami, Carlton, Cass, Clearwater, Crow Wing, Hubbard, Itasca, Kanabec, Koochiching, Lake, and St. Louis Counties. The Coniferous Lakes region incorporates much of what has been called the Headwaters Lakes region of Minnesota, for the Mississippi River crosses much of the area, flowing through or near several large lakes as it leaves its source in southeastern Clearwater County. The path of the Mississippi has changed significantly over the past 15,000 years, though by the beginning of the Late Holocene period (about 2500 BC) it began to follow what is essentially its modern route. The western part of the region is drained by rivers flowing into the Red River, while the northeastern part is drained by the St. Louis River, which flows into Lake Superior. The southeastern part is drained by rivers flowing into the St. Croix River and eventually the Mississippi. Precambrian outcrops are found in the northeast, along with taconite deposits that contain some high-quality toolstone, in particular, cherts, jasper, and taconite itself.

Pine trees (white, jack, and red) dominated the Late Holocene vegetation of the Coniferous Lakes resource region, though there were significant inclusions of deciduous trees (elm, maple, basswood, ash, oak, aspen, and birch). Peat bog vegetation covers the glacial lake plains in the southeast portion. Late Holocene game animals included deer, beaver, moose, and black bear.

The more southern Deciduous Lakes region includes most of central and east-central Minnesota, including Anoka, Benton, Cass, Chisago, Crow Wing, Hennepin, Isanti, Mille Lacs, Morrison, Ramsey, Sherburne, Stearns, Todd, Wadena, Washington, and Wright Counties and parts of Becker, Dakota, Douglas, Kandiyohi, Kanabec, Meeker, Otter Tail, Pine, Pope, and Swift Counties. The region could be extended eastward into west-central Wisconsin. The Mississippi-Sauk River flows through the eastern and central parts of the region, and the Lower St. Croix River forms the eastern boundary. Other important waterways include the Crow, Rum, and Snake Rivers. Streams flowing west into the Red River drain the western part. Bedrock outcrops are limited to occasional granite rock exposures in the center and eastern edge of the area.

In the 1850s the vegetation in the southern and westerns parts of the Deciduous Lakes resource region was dominated by Big Woods species (elm, maple, and basswood) with many large incursions of prairie and oak woods. Since the development of extensive Big Woods forests was a recent event (after AD 1500), much of the Big Woods area was probably oak forest during the Late Holocene.[13] Oak forest was still dominant in the eastern portion of the region in the 1850s. A mixed deciduous-coniferous forest dominated by pine was present in the northern sector. Late Holocene game animals included deer throughout the region, small herds of bison and elk in the south and west, and beaver, black bear, and even moose in the north and east.

Southwestern Minnesota

Thick ice-age deposits of sand, gravel, and clay also cover southwestern Minnesota. The Coteau des Prairies (Buffalo Ridge), an elongated block of bedrock, dominates the resource region's topography. The plateau stretches westward into eastern South Dakota, where it reaches an elevation of more than 2,100 feet. Two prominent belts of high, hilly terrain on its eastern flank are late-glacial moraines. The outermost belt, the Bemis Moraine, forms the high crest of the plateau and is an impressive topographic barrier in this corner of the state. Southwest of the moraine is a lake-free, gently rolling surface of drift not covered by late surges of the Wisconsin glacier. These different surface histories divide the section into two distinct regions, the Southwest Riverine and the Prairie Lake.

Located in the extreme southwestern corner of Minnesota, the Southwest Riverine region includes all of Rock County, large parts of Pipestone and Nobles Counties, and small portions of Lincoln and Murray Counties. Although Minnesota's smallest region, it is part of a larger, well-drained topographic unit that includes parts of northwestern Iowa and southeastern South Dakota. Rock River, which flows south to connect with the Missouri River system, is the region's major drainageway. Many small but deeply entrenched creeks, such as Split Rock and Pipestone, flow to the southwest. While bedrock outcrops of Sioux Quartzite are common in the western part of the region, there are no outcrops of toolstone of good flaking quality. Concentrated exposures of catlinite, a soft, clay-rich stone produced from chemically weathered quartzite, were mined by native Minnesotans to make pipes, plaques, and other items. Although not glaciated by Late Wisconsin ice surges, extensive loess deposits caused by late glacial winds cover earlier glacial drift.

Before farming changed the land's surface, the Southwest Riverine resource region was covered by tallgrass prairie. Trees were scarce due to regular prairie fires and occasional droughts, though some woody vegetation was present along the major streams and at favorable topographic breaks. The largest woods were river-bottom forests dominated by elm, ash, and cottonwood along the Rock River in south-central Rock County. Major game animals included bison, elk, and smaller upland mammals. The only common game bird in the Late Holocene may have been sharp-tailed grouse, for waterfowl were not abundant due to the absence of lakes and multiple large rivers. Seasonally available plants included the prairie turnip (*Psoralea esculenta*) and ground plum (*Astragalus caryocarpus*).

The much larger Prairie Lake region covers most of southwestern and south-central Minnesota. It includes all of Big Stone, Blue Earth, Brown, Carver, Chippewa, Cottonwood, Faribault, Freeborn, Jackson, Lac qui Parle, Le Sueur, Lyon, McLeod, Martin, Nicollet, Redwood, Renville, Scott, Sibley, Stevens, Swift, Watonwan, and Yellow Medicine Counties and parts of Douglas, Grant, Kandiyohi, Meeker, Nobles, Otter Tail, Pipestone, Pope, Rice, Steele, Traverse, and Waseca Counties. The region extends into northeastern South Dakota and north-central Iowa.

The interior topography of the Prairie Lake region is the typical swell and swale topography of a ground moraine. Hilly end moraines are found along its northern, eastern, and southern edges. The major topographic features are the broad valley of the Minnesota River, which bisects the area southwest to northeast, and the scarp of the Coteau des Prairies highland in the west. The Minnesota River valley was the main channel of Glacial River Warren, which intermittently drained Glacial Lake Agassiz. Prairie "pothole" lakes are numerous and vary greatly in size. All of the lakes are shallow, with none exceeding 30 feet in depth. During severe droughts, most of these shallow lakes dry up. Besides losing their aquatic plants and animals, dry lakes are ineffective firebreaks. Many streams and rivers crisscross this part of southwestern Minnesota. Many of the larger rivers, such as the Minnesota, Redwood, Cottonwood, and Des Moines, follow the path of earlier glacial meltwater channels. All of these streams and rivers eventually flow into the Mississippi River.

Bedrock outcrops are rare in the Prairie Lake region, especially deposits of good-quality toolstone. In the eastern section, occasional outcrops of Paleozoic rocks near the confluence of the Blue Earth and Minnesota Rivers include some deposits of high-quality chert. In the western section, there are numerous outcrops of Sioux Quartzite in Cottonwood County. Granites and poorly consolidated Cretaceous rocks, such as shale, are found in the Minnesota valley.

During the precontact portion of the Late Holocene period (circa 2500 BC to 1650), the Prairie Lake region was covered with tallgrass prairie. Trees were uncommon in the western section. Exceptions were narrow river-bottom forests and oak woods along the major river valleys and small patches of woodland in fire-protected areas (peninsulas, islands, and isthmuses) at major lakes. The Minnesota River valley contained the principal wood resources for the western part of the region. The eastern part contained extensive Big Woods vegetation (elm, maple, and basswood) in the north and patchy oak parkland with large prairie openings that became more numerous as one moved westward in the more southern portion of the area. While the modern prairie-forest border was established about 4,500 years ago, the southern bulge of Big Woods vegetation is a recent phenomenon, as mentioned earlier. Oak woodlands were present all along the eastern edge of the Prairie Lake region until about 300 years ago.

Bison and an occasional large elk herd were the dominant upland game animals in the Prairie Lake resource region during the Late Holocene. White-tailed deer were present along the Minnesota River valley and in the eastern woodland fringe. The major animal-food differences between the two southwestern Minnesota regions are a result of the many shallow lakes in the Prairie Lake resource region and their absence in the Southwest Riverine resource region. The southwestern lakes contained extensive populations of aquatic mammals, such as muskrats, and waterfowl and fish, as well as edible plants, like water lilies and cattails. Though not extensive, wild rice was present, especially in the Minnesota River valley and in a few northern and eastern lakes. Upland plant resources included the prairie turnip, ground plum, and acorns in the oak woods.

Southeastern Minnesota

The Southeastern region of Minnesota has a stream-dissected terrain that was only lightly glaciated during the Pleistocene Ice Age (a thin mantle of Pleistocene deposit 3 to 33 feet thick covers the bedrock surface). The deep erosion of deposits covering the bedrock surface resulting from rivers flowing into the Mississippi River left a lake-free land surface with deeply entrenched flat-floored stream valleys and numerous bedrock exposures that contain high-quality toolstone. While no natural lakes are in its interior, valley-bottom lakes are present along the Mississippi River. Some, like Lake Pepin, which stretches from Red Wing to Wabasha, are quite large. Three major river systems, the Cannon, Zumbro, and Root, extend westward from the Mississippi into the region's interior. The wide Mississippi River valley, which is bordered by steep, scenic bedrock walls, is itself a complex of interconnected stream channels. Southeastern Minnesota includes Dodge, Fillmore, Goodhue, Mower, Olmsted, Wabasha, and Winona Counties and parts of Dakota, Freeborn, Rice, and Waseca Counties. The resource region continues into adjacent corners of Wisconsin and Iowa.

During the Late Holocene, forests of elm, ash, and cottonwood lined the river lowlands, and Big Woods forests of maple, elm, and basswood occupied the uplands near the Mississippi River. Patches of oak groves in the prairie, often described as oak barrens, were scattered across the western part of the region, while the middle of the region was a more open prairie. Subsistence resources included deer, elk, and scattered bison in the uplands and mussels, fish, and waterfowl in the rich bottomlands. Edible plants would have included water lilies and other aquatic flora and upland plants like the prairie turnip. Extensive oak woods were a rich source of acorns. The region's favorable climate and extensive bottomlands made it more suited for precontact corn (maize) horticulture than any other region in the state.

Minnesota's Paleoenvironments

Minnesota did not always have the landscape features, climate, and weather described in the preceding two sections. The state's topography and plant and animal communities were very different 4,500 years ago and earlier, in fact so different that we would not recognize the state if we were able to go back and wander through it. Since Minnesota's

Climatic Episode	Sub-Episode	Provisional End Date	Character
	Modern		Warmer
	....	AD 1915–1920	
	Neo-Boreal		"Little Ice Age"
	....	AD 1550	
Post-Sub-Atlantic			
	Pacific		Cooler
	....	AD 1150–1200	
	Neo-Atlantic		"Medieval Warm Period"
	....	AD 700–750	
	Scandic		
....		AD 300–400	
Sub-Atlantic			
....		ca. 950 BC	
Sub-Boreal			
....		2900–3000 BC	
Atlantic			Quite warm summers, cold winters
....		6700 BC	
Boreal			"Younger Dryas," colder
....		8400 BC	
Pre-Boreal			Rapid warming
....		10,800 BC	
Late Glacial			Very cold

Figure 1.1. Climatic episodes in the Holocene geological period. Adapted from Bryson 1998.

precontact native peoples lived in these "paleo" (older) environments for at least 8,000 years, I outline their features here and describe them in more detail in later chapters.

Geologists and climatologists divide the 13,000 years in which humans were present in the state in different ways. Geologists divide this time span into Late Glacial (11,200–10,500 BC), Early Holocene (10,500–7500 BC), Middle Holocene (7500–2500 BC), and Late Holocene (2500 BC to present) geological periods. I use this terminology to organize chapters 2 and 3 in this book. In this system of classification, Late Glacial refers to that period when glacial ice was withdrawing from Minnesota, Early Holocene to a warming then colder period before the Middle Holocene, which was a long period during which prairie expanded across the state in response to hotter and drier summers. The Late Holocene marks the emergence of a modern climate and pattern of vegetation distribution across the state.

Climatologist Reid Bryson divides the Holocene into seven climatic episodes that vary in summer and winter temperatures, amount of rainfall, number of yearly lightning strikes, and season of most precipitation, among other variables (Figure 1.1).[14]

Minnesota's changing climate resulted in shifts in the distribution of plants and animals within the state and, consequently, in the food energy resources available to hunters and gatherers. Although severe shifts in climate ended in the state with the close of the Atlantic climatic episode, more minor shifts, such as the Medieval Warm period (AD 700/750–1150/1200) and Little Ice Age (AD 1550–1915/1920), most likely still had an impact on hunter-gatherer lifeways.

WHAT KIND OF SETTING WAS MINNESOTA
FOR HUNTERS AND GATHERERS?

Cultural traditions are the result of the coming together of many influences, such as the flow of traditional lifeways, interaction with new neighbors, and technological and spiritual innovations. However, early Native Americans who, say, migrated northward from the central Mississippi valley to Minnesota would have had quite a different lifeway than relatives who migrated to Oklahoma. Environment matters, then. This is especially true for hunter-gatherers whose food energy comes from local and regional food resources. Given the fundamental importance of local and regional environments to hunters and gatherers, a reasonable question to ask, then, is, What kind of setting was Minnesota for hunters and gatherers?

Differences in environmental variables like available solar energy, the amount of water available to plant communities, length of growing season, available animal foods, and type of vegetation around the globe once resulted in a wide variety of different environments available to hunter-gatherers, each with its own unique combination of food resources. A global classification by S. R. Eyre lists thirty-one different types of vegetative communities, ranging from desert, to midlatitude semidesert scrub and woodland, to midlatitude short-grass prairie, to southern pine forests, to boreal forests, to polar tundra.[15] Each of these communities differs in type of vegetation, mean annual rainfall, length of growing season, size of expected prey, and location on the surface of the globe expressed in degrees latitude.

In preliminary review, Minnesota's environmental potential for hunters and gatherers is determined in large part following Binford by its position within a series of south to north climate-related thresholds above and below which changes in the behavior of hunter-gatherers regularly occur.[16] The growing season threshold occurs at an effective temperature (ET) value of 18° latitude, where effective temperature is defined as the amount of solar radiation available at any given location, the magnitude of which is directly related to the length of the growing season; above that value in a roughly southward direction are environmental settings with the potential for a twelve-month growing season; below that value in a roughly northward direction are

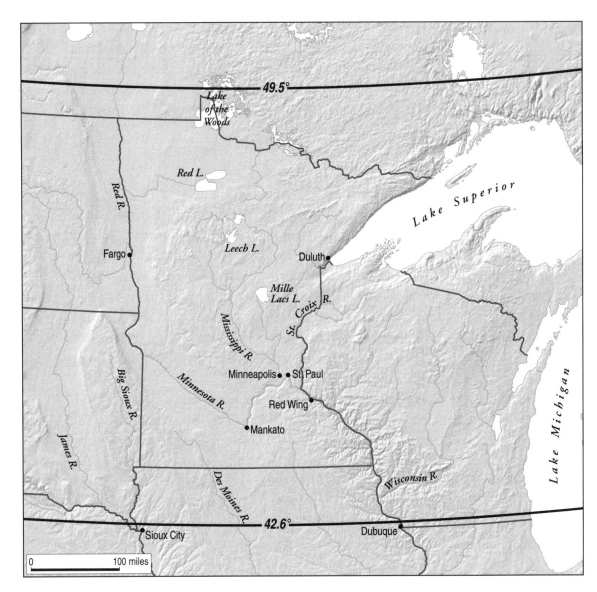

Map 1.4. Minnesota's geographical position between the climate-related terrestrial plant threshold and the subpolar bottleneck.

settings with shorter growing seasons. The storage threshold occurs at an ET value of 15.25° or at approximately 35° latitude, which roughly follows the state boundary that separates Tennessee from Mississippi and Alabama. In general the storage of food for consumption during times of the year when food energy was less abundant becomes of increasing concern in areas above that threshold.

Above the storage threshold, the terrestrial plant threshold occurs at an ET value of about 12.75° degrees and a latitude of 42.6°, which roughly corresponds to a habitat in which the temperature during the coldest month of the year is −4°C. In warmer settings than this, plant-dominated subsistence strategies can be expected. In cooler settings a plant-dominated subsistence strategy would not be expected, for accessible plant resources become less available. In Minnesota's region the threshold is marked by a horizontal line that stretches between Sioux City and Dubuque in northern Iowa and eastward across the southern border of Wisconsin (Map 1.4). The subpolar bottleneck occurs at an ET value of 11.53°, which is along Minnesota's northern border or slightly north of it. In Minnesota's region it corresponds with the southern edge of the boreal forest biomes, which have substantial biomass but very little species diversity.

The terrestrial plant threshold (or transition zone) is where a shift in diet occurs between terrestrial animal hunters to the north and terrestrial plant-dependent groups to the south. Major changes in hunter-gatherer adaptations also occur above the subpolar bottleneck in boreal forests due to a decrease in both diversity of plant productivity (despite relatively high biomass values) and amount of expected prey in terms of kilograms per square kilometer. Minnesota is positioned, then, in a setting where a subsistence focus on terrestrial animal hunting is predicted. Since these predictions are based on Late Holocene "modern" environmental values, the type of hunter-gatherer settings present in the state in earlier paleoenvironments remains to be established.

PALEOINDIAN AND ARCHAIC PERIOD

CIRCA 11,200 TO 500 BC

CHAPTER 2

First People

Paleoindian and Early Eastern
Archaic Adaptations

Today, it seems increasingly likely that small bands of mobile hunter-gatherers who drifted into or by Alaska from Asia between 20,000 and 14,000 years ago were the first human beings to enter the Americas.[1] Like all people who have lived in the Americas, they were physically modern *Homo sapiens*. Archaeologists call the time span within which most of these people lived the Paleoindian period and divide it into two subperiods, an Early Paleoindian (11,200–10,500 BC) and a Late Paleoindian (10,500–7500 BC). Besides a difference in age, Early and Late Paleoindian peoples lived in different, rapidly changing Late Glacial and Early Holocene environments, respectively, and made technologically and stylistically distinct kinds of stone weapon points. Each group also had a mobile forager lifeway, though a gradual increase in the numbers of foraging groups led by the end of the Early Paleoindian period to a concentration of a group's food resource activities within a territory hemmed in by the territories of neighboring groups.

Unlike many other areas in North America, such as the Southeast and Southwest, where the transition between Paleoindian and Archaic traditions is relatively brief, there is a long temporal overlap between Late Paleoindian traditions and the early portion of the Archaic tradition (the Early Eastern Archaic) in Minnesota. I recognize that overlap in the subtitle of this chapter, "Paleoindian and Early Eastern Archaic Adaptations."

LATE GLACIAL AND EARLY HOLOCENE ENVIRONMENTS

As I described in chapter 1, Minnesota did not always have Late Holocene (modern) surface features, plant and animal communities, climate, and weather. In this section I describe the land in the Late Glacial (15,000–10,500 BC) and Early Holocene (10,500–7500 BC) geological periods, the time span in which human beings first entered Minnesota.

The Wisconsin, or last, glacial period began about 60,000 years ago and drew to a close about 12,500 years ago (10,500 BC) in Minnesota.[2] Much of the state was covered with glacial ice throughout this period, although glaciation took place in a complex series of ice lobe advances and retreats. During the maximum southward extent of ice masses about 17,000 years ago, only an area in central Minnesota and the two corners of the state remained free of ice. Even these unglaciated areas, however, were unattractive for human habitation, for they were sparsely covered by vegetation and contained few animals. Two principal ice lobes covered large areas of Minnesota near the end of this period, the Superior Lobe, which crept southwestward out of the Lake Superior basin into east-central Minnesota, and the Des Moines Lobe, which first moved south through the Red River valley and then turned east into the Minnesota River valley (Map 2.1). These huge masses of expanding ice gradually depressed the land they covered from a few feet near their edges to several hundred feet at their northern cores.

When the glacial lobes began their retreat around 15,500 years ago, the resulting meltwater formed enormous rivers and lakes. Map 2.2A shows the location of major glacial lakes in Minnesota. The largest of these, Glacial Lake Agassiz, with a basin of almost 365,000 square miles, covered all of northwestern Minnesota at one time and was the largest glacial lake in North America.[3] Although enormously large, the basin itself was not entirely covered with water at any one time.

Glacial Lake Agassiz began expanding about 13,500 years ago as the Des Moines Lobe retreated northward into the Red River basin. During much of this period, its only outlets were lowland channels to the south, for glacial ice barricaded possible northern outlets. The size of its principal southern outlet, known as Glacial River Warren, is still visible today as the broad valley of the Minnesota River. As the ice continued to retreat, previously blocked northern outlets gradually opened, and Lake Agassiz began to drain northward, as the Red River of the North does today.

Lake Superior also fluctuated greatly in size and configuration during the Wisconsin glacial period.[4] During the height of the Ice Age, when great amounts of water were locked up in continental glaciers, water levels in the lake were quite low. As the ice retreated, the level rose again, as did much of the surrounding land when the weight of the ice was removed. Periodic eastward discharges from Glacial Lake Agassiz also had catastrophic effects on Lake Superior. The result was an intricate shift in lake levels, locations of outlets, and beach positions, which geomorphologists and archaeologists reconstruct to determine when specific parcels of land were above water and where they were in relation to the shore of the lake.

By about 14,000 years ago (12,000 BC), all of southern Minnesota and most of the central part of the state were free of glaciers and covered, for the most part, by an open boreal coniferous forest dominated by grasses and scattered conifer trees.[5] This early forest has no modern counterpart, for it contained small amounts of oak and other temperate-climate deciduous trees, such as black ash, and it lacked jack pine, a common tree in northern boreal coniferous forests today. This peculiar mix of trees was probably

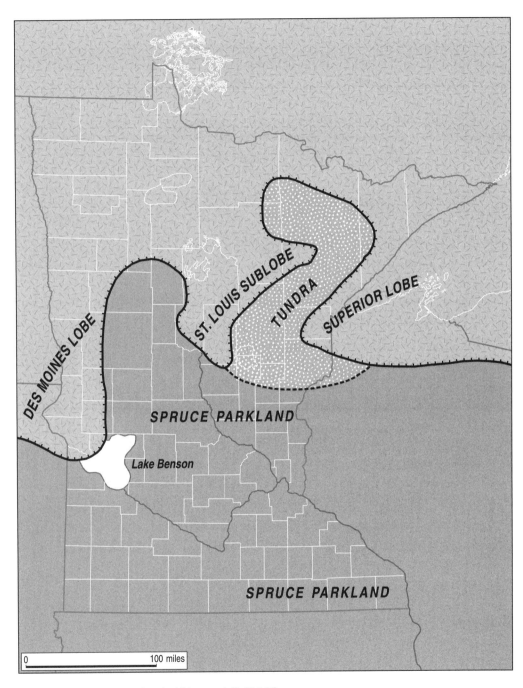

DES MOINES LOBE

ST. LOUIS SUBLOBE

TUNDRA

SUPERIOR LOBE

SPRUCE PARKLAND

Lake Benson

SPRUCE PARKLAND

0   100 miles

Map 2.1. Minnesota's major plant biomes at 12,000 BC.

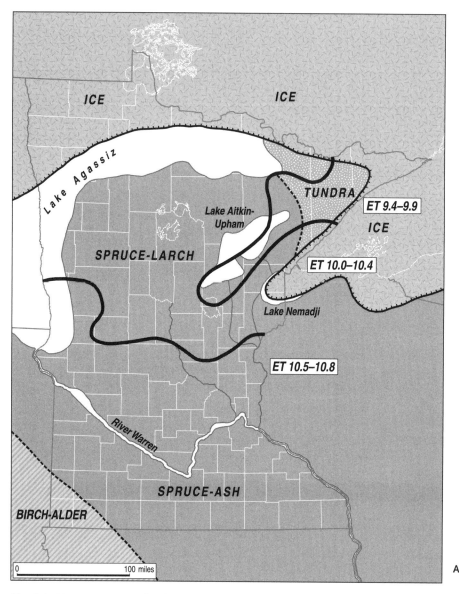

Map 2.2. Minnesota's major plant biomes at (A) 11,500 BC and (B) 11,000 BC. The thick black lines separate effective temperature values of 9.4 to 9.9 in the northeast corner of the state from values of 10.0 to 10.4 between the lines, and values of 10.5 to 10.8 south of the lower line.

the result of the different rates of migration of tree species from distant refuge areas and a more temperate, warmer climate in Minnesota than exists now in northern boreal coniferous forests in Canada. Many low-lying areas within the forest were probably filled with open water and marsh or swamp. Openings on higher ground were most likely covered with shrubs and grasses. In some areas, such as the southeastern corner of the state, the spruce forest seems to have contained large, relatively open swards of grassland. Ice was gone from the state by about 13,000 years ago (11,000 BC).

A deciduous forest dominated by birch, alder, elm, and other trees that shed their

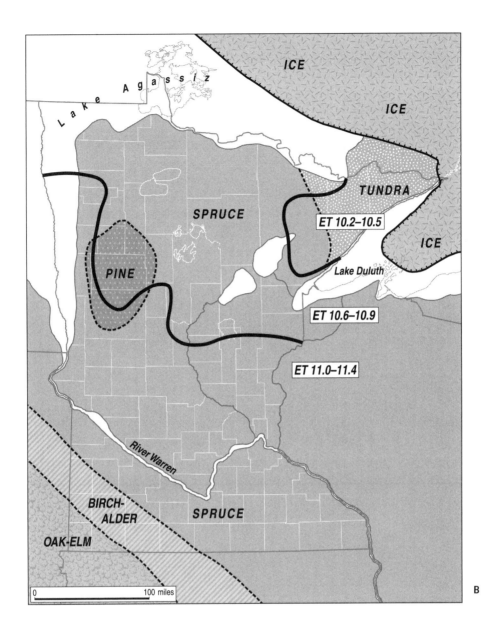

leaves at the end of the growing season entered the southwestern corner of Minnesota as early as 14,000 years ago and spread outward about 13,000 years ago (see Map 2.2B). At about the same time, that is, by about 13,000 years ago (11,000 BC), a new oak-elm forest penetrated the southwestern corner of the state and spread rapidly northward and eastward. Deciduous birch-alder and oak-elm forests swept across southern Minnesota during the Early Holocene (10,500 to 7500 BC) period, followed closely by prairie (Map 2.3).

The composition of the animal communities that occupied these Late Glacial–Early Holocene forests is not fully known, although fossilized bone provides some

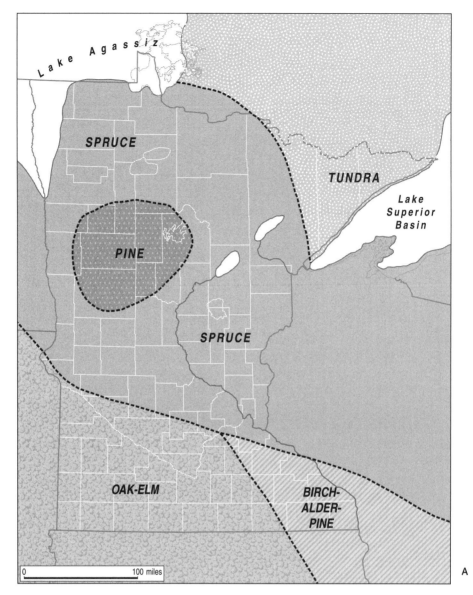

Map 2.3. Minnesota's major plant biomes at (A) 10,500 BC and (B) 8000 BC.
The thick black line separates effective temperature values of 11.6 to 11.9 north
of the line from values of 12.0 to 12.4 south of the line.

clues. The spruce forest was probably inhabited by now-extinct animal species, such as mastodon and giant beaver, and by many of the modern mammals that were common in the mixed northern coniferous/hardwood forest in the early historic period. Mastodon preferred feeding on the coarse vegetation of pine and spruce forests, for they found it difficult to find food in the winter in forests that drop their leaves in winter. More open areas near the ice may have contained herds of mammoth, barren-ground caribou, and musk ox. Animal communities in open prairie-like areas to the south included elk, mammoth, and now-extinct forms of large bison.

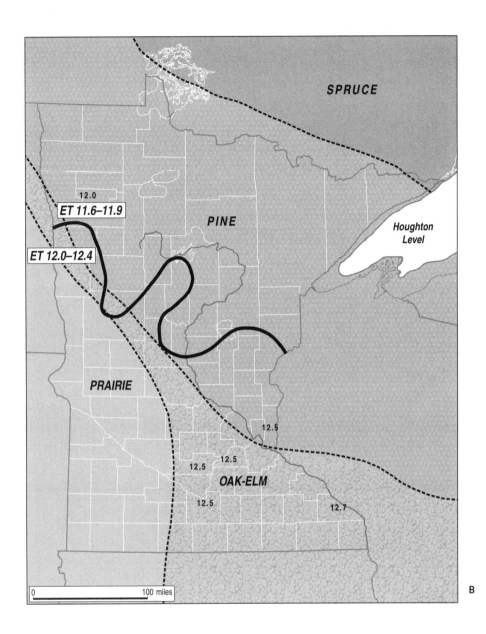

SPRUCE

12.0

ET 11.6–11.9

ET 12.0–12.4

PINE

Houghton
Level

PRAIRIE

12.5

12.5

12.5

OAK-ELM

12.5

12.7

0   100 miles

B

The reason for the extinction in the Americas of many large mammals like mammoth and mastodon at the end of the Ice Age remains a puzzle.[6] Their disappearance has been attributed to overkill by human predators and climate change. Since the extinction of all megafauna occurred abruptly at about 11,000 BC, a combination of these and other causes, like disease, seems a more likely explanation.

Modern species of animals probably inhabited the deciduous and mixed northern coniferous/hardwood forests that followed the spruce forest northward. White-tailed deer, moose, porcupine, weasels, fisher, otter, coyote, bobcat, red fox, timber wolf,

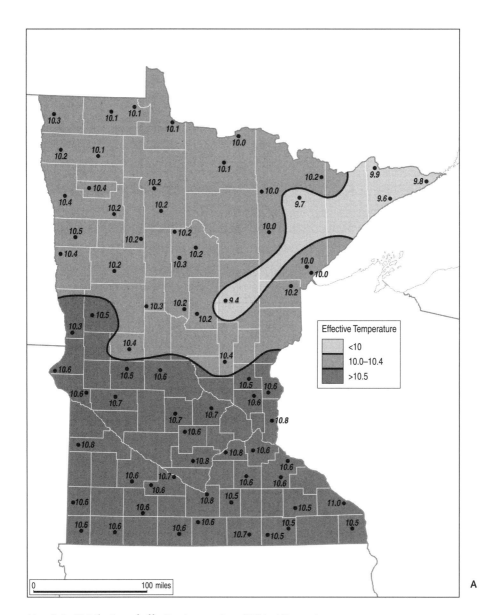

Map 2.4. Distribution of effective temperature (ET) in Minnesota at (A) 11,500 BC and (B) 11,000 BC.

black bear, muskrat, and beaver are familiar examples. A wide variety of birds, fish, and amphibians were also present. In fact the composition of the plant and animal communities of these forests and of the expanding southwestern grasslands seems very similar to their modern counterparts at historic contact, though the composition of these earlier biotic communities is not well known.

The climate in Minnesota during the Late Glacial period is not well known, but cold conditions existed year-round for 100 to 200 miles south of the ice front, as shown by the presence of relic permafrost features. These arctic-like conditions were especially prevalent in areas between lobes, such as the southern corners of the

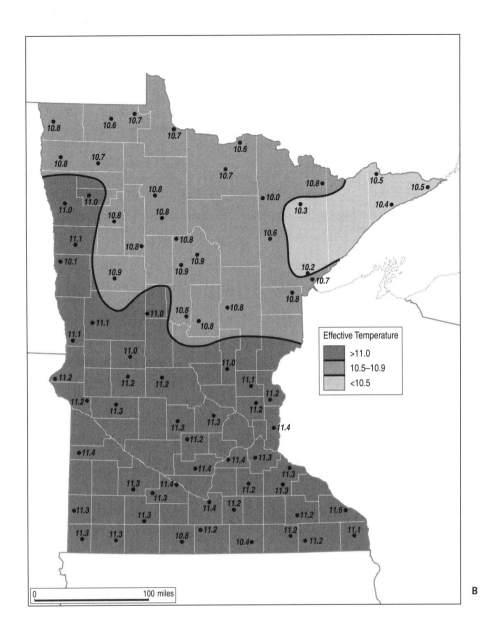

B

state. Map 2.4 shows the distribution of effective temperature (ET) at 11,500 BC and 11,000 BC, as approximated by Bryson's climatic modeling software. For comparison, the mean ET value of the southern edge of the Arctic Circle today is roughly 9.5 to 9.9, and of the boreal forest, 11.3; ET values between 10.0 and 11.0 are roughly in between these two environments.

Estimated mean January temperature in Fahrenheit in 11,000 BC for Baudette in extreme northern Minnesota is −16.6° (0.8°), for Brainerd in the central portion of the state, −9.6° (7.8°), and for Fairmont in southern Minnesota, −4.6° (12.8°) (with modern means in parentheses for comparison). Estimated mean July temperature in Fahrenheit

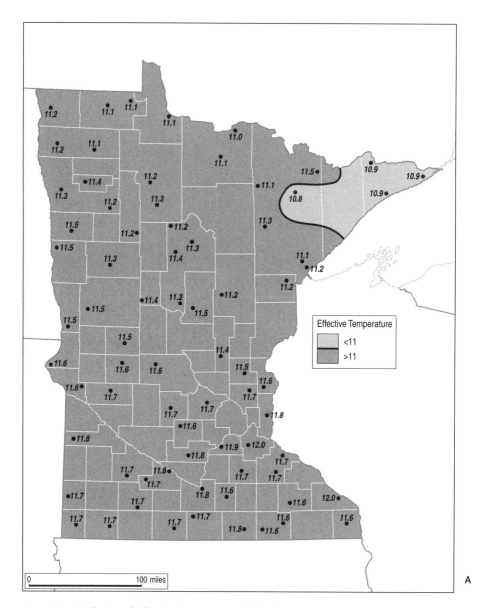

Map 2.5. Distribution of effective temperature (ET) in Minnesota at (A) 9000 BC and (B) 8000 BC.

in 11,000 BC is 58.2° (65.1°) for Baudette, 61.2° (68.1°) for Brainerd, and 63.2° (70.1°) for Fairmont. Estimated temperature is only part of the story, however, for strong winds near the glacial front would have had significant windchill effects. These same strong winds may have deeply buried archaeological sites under the accumulating deposits of loess.

By the Early Holocene period, temperatures throughout the state were rapidly warming, as shown by the distribution of effective temperature (ET) values in Map 2.5 for 9000 BC and 8000 BC. Estimated mean January temperature in Fahrenheit at 9000 BC and 8000 BC for Baudette are, respectively, −13.0° and −7.1°, −6.0° and −0.1° for Brainerd, and −1.0° and 4.9° for Fairmont. Estimated mean July temperatures for

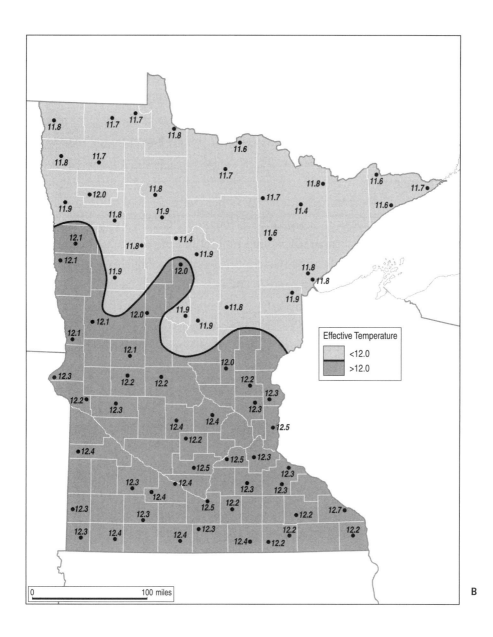

Effective Temperature
<12.0
>12.0

0   100 miles

B

the same dates are 62.8° and 70.0° for Baudette, 65.9° and 73.0° for Brainerd, and 67.9° and 75.0° for Fairmont.

Paleoindian and Early Eastern Archaic lifeways in Minnesota were an adjustment in part to these often harsh, rapidly changing Late Glacial and Early Holocene landscapes. Since the landscapes differed markedly from modern landscapes in distribution and usually in composition (in fact, the closest modern environments now exist far to the north in the Arctic and Subarctic of Canada), we must re-create them in our imagination to understand some of the seasonal activities of these early Native American people.

THE EARLY PALEOINDIAN ARCHAEOLOGICAL RECORD

The most defining characteristic of the Early Paleoindian archaeological record is the hemisphere-wide presence of lanceolate-shaped stone weapon points that have a distinctive large flake (flute) removed from the center of the point (Figure 2.1). This fluting technique appears to be related to the manner in which the point was hafted onto its shaft and how the weapon itself was used. Other characteristics of the period in Minnesota include a rapidly changing Late Glacial landscape that contained now-extinct Pleistocene (Ice Age) megafauna, like mammoth and mastodon, and the presence of small, highly mobile bands of Native Americans who occupied places for only brief periods between about 11,200 BC and 10,500 BC.

At present, Minnesota's entire Early Paleoindian sample of artifacts consists of seventy-three weapon points and two other possible artifacts, a scraper and a drill. Archaeologists have assigned the points to four named types—Clovis (or Clovis-like), Folsom, Cumberland, and Holcombe—and to an "unassigned" category.[7] Only one of these points (a Folsom from the Jim Regan site in St. Louis County) is from a controlled excavation in a single component context. Most are poorly documented as to exact find location, and most are in private collections, especially in two large eastern Minnesota collections centered on Freeborn and Pine Counties.

Clovis points and their close variants are perhaps the most widely distributed point type in North America. They have been found from coast to coast and from northern Mexico in the south to Canada and Alaska in the north. True Clovis points are well represented in Wisconsin, where 115 of 417 fluted points examined in a 2007 study were classified as Clovis.[8] These numbers suggest that Clovis points are underreported in Minnesota, where only 8 Clovis or Clovis-like points are known. A somewhat rare type, Folsom points are present in densest numbers in the Southwest and on the High Plains. Scattered specimens have been found as far eastward as Wisconsin

Figure 2.1. Early Paleoindian projectile points. *Left to right:* Clovis, Folsom, Holcombe.
Courtesy of the Wilford Archaeology Laboratory, University of Minnesota.

and Illinois in the upper Midwest. Folsom points are more numerous (17) in Minnesota than are either Clovis or Holcombe points, even though their contexts are just as vague. Fluted Folsom points seem to cluster in the southwestern half of the state. Folsom points on the Plains date to 10,900–9500 BC, with dates at the Folsom type-site clustering at 10,500 BC. They are thought to date to the same period in southern Wisconsin.

Holcombe points, which appear in both fluted and unfluted forms, are not well dated, but they are thought to date to 10,400 BC in Michigan, where they represent the final Paleoindian phase in that state. This type's unfluted form may be the earliest unfluted point type in southeastern Michigan and southern Ontario. At present, 11 fluted Holcombe or Holcombe-like points have been found in Minnesota, where they seem to have a northern concentration. The point type has also been found in northern Ohio, northwestern Pennsylvania, and Wisconsin. The last named fluted point type represented in Minnesota is a single Cumberland point found in the 1930s in Rock or Pipestone County in the southwestern corner of the state. Cumberland points are most common in the Tennessee and Cumberland River valleys and their adjoining highlands in the Southeast. They are more widely distributed in smaller numbers throughout the Mississippi basin and the southern two-thirds of the Midwest, with a few reported from the northern Great Lakes region. Thirty-six points in Minnesota's fluted point sample have not been assigned to type, which may be a reflection of the state's intermediate position between the Great Plains and the Great Lakes regions.

Only two non-point tools in Minnesota's sample, a spurred end scraper found near a Clovis point on the Timberline campground in Pine County, and a fluted drill found at the Williams Narrows site in Itasca County, may date to the Early Paleoindian period. I assume, however, that the weapon points were only one item in a more extensive artifact assemblage, for multiple-use tools, such as scrapers with graver spurs, bifaces, and cutting and scraping tools made on flakes or blades are frequently present artifacts on Clovis sites.[9] Other characteristics of the Clovis archaeological record are a general absence of decorative art; the almost exclusive use of high-quality toolstone, which was sometimes derived from sources hundreds of miles away from the sites where the tools are found; and small habitation spaces that lack site furniture and rarely include storage pits or the remains of habitation structures.

THE LATE PALEOINDIAN AND EARLY EASTERN ARCHAIC RECORD

The transition from the Early Paleoindian horizon to the Late Paleoindian horizon in the Upper Mississippi River region is marked in the archaeological record by the disappearance of fluted points, the appearance of stemmed points and some heavy stone tools, and the use of new toolstone materials, especially Hixton quartzite from west-central Wisconsin. Based on calibrated radiocarbon dates for Late Paleoindian and Early Eastern Archaic artifact assemblages in other parts of central North America, I date the period to 10,500–7500 BC.

Late Paleoindian and Early Eastern Archaic components in sites are most easily recognized by the presence of distinctive weapon point types, which occur in much greater numbers in Minnesota than do fluted spearheads. Since most of them have also been found out of context, such as on the surface of a plowed field or in a site with churned soil, their associations with each other and with other kinds of artifacts remain uncertain.

Late Paleoindian weapon points appear in a variety of forms, many of which occur in vertical sequence in stratified, dated deposits on the Great Plains. Most are long, leaf-shaped, and unfluted. Many also share fine oblique or collateral flaking across the blade faces, ground and thinned basal edges, and high-quality workmanship. Often called the Plano tradition on the Plains to differentiate them from Early Paleoindian and Archaic points, they form part of a continuous distribution throughout the Great Plains.[10]

At present, 232 Late Paleoindian points from Minnesota sites are assigned to a named type. Another 81 points are considered Late Paleoindian because of shape or technique of manufacture, or both, but are otherwise considered aberrant. The named types are Agate Basin (117 points), Alberta (16), Angostura (10), Browns Valley (12), Eden (7), Frederick (6), Hell Gap (26), Midland (4), Plainview (29), and Scottsbluff (5).[11] These are medium- to large-sized points that have a characteristic lanceolate shape, fine transverse to oblique pressure flaking on the faces, and moderate to heavy grinding around the lower edges of the blade. They are found in both lanceolate (Figure 2.2) and stemmed-lanceolate (Figure 2.3) forms. Points of these types are concentrated in the Great Plains, where they are associated with the hunting of bison. Alberta, Scottsbluff, and Eden points are part of a Cody complex that includes Cody knives. There are 53 Cody knives in the sample of Late Paleoindian artifacts.

There is some patterning in the spatial distribution of this sample of Late Paleoindian points. For example, Plainview points are absent in the northeastern section of the state, while Hell Gap points are most common in the northwestern, and Alberta points most common in the east-central regions of the state. Plainview, Agate Basin, Hell Gap, Scottsbluff, and Alberta points have all been found in northwestern Minnesota.

Fifty-four percent of 139 Late Paleoindian sites with good location information are associated with lake edges, and 38 percent with rivers. Most lake-edge sites are located on smaller lakes (not glacial lakes) but at no special location on these lakes (that is, not necessarily on islands, peninsulas, or inlets/outlets). The reason may be the presence of trees everywhere and the absence yet of a focus on wild rice. In the Red River valley, the

Figure 2.2. Late Paleoindian lanceolate projectile points. *Clockwise from top left:* Agate Basin, Plainview, Browns Valley, Hell Gap.

Courtesy of the Minnesota Historical Society. Printed with permission.

Figure 2.3. Late Paleoindian stemmed projectile points. *Left to right:* Hardin, Scottsbluff. Courtesy of the Minnesota Historical Society. Printed with permission.

majority of Late Paleoindian sites (e.g., Donarski, Greenbush) are on or near late-phase Agassiz beaches, especially the well-developed Campbell beach. In the eastern arm of the Agassiz basin, many sites (e.g., Plummer, Pelland) appear to be on or near the Emerson phase beaches, although the Patrow site is on the Herman beach.

Find spots of points, lithic workshops (e.g., Bradbury Brook, Greenbush Borrow), and seasonal camps (Cedar Creek) are the most common Late Paleoindian site types in Minnesota. Habitation sites (possibly in the Reservoir Lakes area), kill sites, and burials (Browns Valley) are still rare.

The only defined larger-scale Late Paleoindian taxonomic units in Minnesota are the Reservoir Lakes phase in the lakes area northwest of Duluth and the Lake of the Woods/Rainy River Complex farther west, both of which are thought to be part of a larger regional Late Paleoindian Interlakes Composite. Jack Steinbring describes the Reservoir Lakes phase as follows:

> This provisional phase is characterized by a recurring combination of Plano types, including clear, intermediate, and variant forms of Scottsbluff, Agate Basin, Eden, Hell Gap, and Plainview points, many of which are made from jaspilite. With them is associated a lithic industry which largely lacks polished and ground stone tools and employs a hard gray "shale" as the principal source material. The artifacts are normally massive and include choppers, crudely made bifaces, crescentic blades, adzes, long heavy picks, and a wide assortment of bold retouched flakes mostly in the form of scrapers. Many of the scrapers are prepared on long prismatic flakes, often along parallel edges and also at the end.[12]

Early Eastern Archaic points are notched or stemmed forms that appear in the mid-south and central Mississippi valley region by 9400 BC. If transitional forms like Dalton (thirty-six points), Hi-Lo (four), and Quad (seven) are included in this category, the Early Eastern Archaic starts as early as 10,700 BC in the Upper Mississippi River region. These are often heavily reworked lanceolate points with a concave base, basal ears, and fluting on some specimens (Figure 2.4). They are thought to be transitional forms between the Paleoindian and Archaic point traditions, for some points (especially early points) have a mixture of Paleoindian (fluting) and Archaic (beveling and serrated edges) traits. Classic, somewhat later dating Early Eastern Archaic point forms found in Minnesota include Thebes, St. Charles, Graham Cave Side Notched, and Kirk Corner Notched (Figure 2.5).[13]

Most Early Eastern Archaic points are from sites in southeastern and more generally southern Minnesota. Unlike Paleoindian weapon points, which generally are of large size and have distinctive lanceolate shapes, Early Eastern Archaic points are less distinctive compared to more recent Archaic and Initial Woodland points. As a result they have attracted less attention from archaeologists, and their distribution and relative abundance remain less clear.

In this north-central region of North America, Late Paleoindian and Early Eastern Archaic weapon points are usually associated with thin scatters of scrapers and other generalized artifacts in excavated components. In one study of Paleoindian stone tool assemblages on the Great Plains, weapon points accounted for 10 to 20 percent

Figure 2.4. Early Eastern Archaic early projectile points. *Left to right:* Dalton, Hi-Lo, Quad.
Courtesy of the Minnesota Historical Society. Printed with permission.

Figure 2.5. Early Eastern Archaic later projectile points.
Clockwise from top left: Thebes, St. Charles, Kirk Stemmed (2).
Courtesy of the Minnesota Historical Society. Printed with permission.

of the tool kit, side and end scrapers for 20 to 40 percent, and knives, blanks, and other tools for the remainder.[14] The basic tool kit seems fairly standardized everywhere: weapon tips, scrapers, and knives—the tool kit of mobile foragers who focused on the hunting of larger mammals, such as deer, moose, or bison, depending on environment.

On the Great Plains, successive Late Paleoindian tool assemblages contain ever more specialized tools. This trend may have been taking place in Minnesota, too. An example is the appearance of the distinctive asymmetrical Cody tanged knife, an artifact often associated with Alberta, Scottsbluff, and Eden points, as mentioned earlier. More common and perhaps more diagnostic of the material culture of Late Paleoindian people in the woodlands of Minnesota, however, are a wide range of heavy stone tools, like choppers, adzes, mauls, gouges, hammerstones, and picks (Figure 2.6). Most of these tools seem a technological elaboration for woodworking in forested environments. Associations or possible associations of Late Paleoindian points with heavy tools like these have been found across northern Minnesota and in adjacent forested areas.[15] A variety of large bifaces, worked and unworked flakes, wedges, and bipolar and non-bipolar cores are also in possible or probable association with these assemblages.

The material culture of the Late Paleoindian and Early Eastern Archaic societies that lived in Minnesota during the 10,500–7500 BC period undoubtedly included many other items that have not survived in the archaeological record. Examples are hardwood tools, wooden containers, cords and textiles, clothes, and wooden spear shafts. Small wigwam-like houses and, possibly, boats would have been part of this repertoire as well. The artifacts that have survived are an impoverished remnant of what once must have been a rich and varied, if easily portable, material culture.

The following three sites are examples of different types of Late Paleoindian sites in Minnesota. One is an apparent camp site (Cedar Creek), another, a quarry (Bradbury Brook), and the third, a burial (Browns Valley).

Figure 2.6.
Late Paleoindian trihedral adze and keeled scrapers from the Bradbury Brook site.
Courtesy of the Minnesota Historical Society. Printed with permission.

Cedar Creek is a multicomponent site located along Cedar Creek at its outlet from Cedar Lake on the southern beach ridge of Glacial Lake Aitkin.[16] Extensive wetlands are present in front of the beach ridge. Artifact assemblages from the Late Paleoindian period through the Historic period are present and mixed, so a Late Paleoindian component (or components) could not be stratigraphically isolated. However, Late Paleoindian weapon points of at least three types (one Browns Valley–like, three Agate Basin–like, one Plainview-like, and four untyped lanceolate points) were present, as were adzes and spokeshaves that may be Late Paleoindian in age. Some of the points were recovered from subsurface contexts. Site interpreters suggest the glacial ridge was a transportation route through the region's wetlands and lakes throughout prehistory. The disturbed stratigraphy of the Cedar Creek site is typical of many sites in central and northern Minnesota, where only a thin layer (1 foot or less) of soil overlays bedrock or glacial till.

Bradbury Brook is a single component, largely undisturbed siltstone quarry near the confluence of Bradbury Brook and the Rum River, a few miles south of Mille Lacs Lake.[17] Site features include several locations where siltstone was quarried from glacial cobbles and reduced to usable chunks of stone, a habitation area, and a deep pit about 5 feet across and 26 inches deep below the plow zone (Figure 2.7). The pit contained lithic debris and charred wood at the bottom, which was radiocarbon dated to 8500 BC. The stone tool assemblage included an Alberta point, trihedral adze, keeled scrapers, prismatic blades, scrapers (some with graver tips), anvil stones, hammerstones, and expedient flake tools. The quarry appears to have been used for only a brief period of time.

Browns Valley is a multicomponent site (Late Paleoindian, Plains Village) on a gravel ridge between Lakes Traverse and Big Stone in the valley of Glacial River Warren in Traverse County.[18] The site contained a Late Paleoindian U-shaped, red ochre–stained burial pit that began about 4½ feet below the surface. The pit was disturbed during gravel removal in 1933. A large stone near the bottom of the pit may have been placed on top of the burial, which was that of a thirty-five- to thirty-nine-year-old male.[19] Gravel removal had disturbed much of the pit, causing human bones and artifacts to tumble down the slope or become mixed with other pieces of gravel during gravel removal. Four projectile points, including several Browns Valley points, two sandstone abraders, and two knives may have been associated with the burial, although the abraders and knives could as well be associated with the later Plains Village component. Two calibrated radiocarbon samples on bone date the burial (and presumably the points) to 8000 BC.[20] A statistical comparison of Paleoindian and Asian skeletal populations by J. F. Powell and D. G. Steele concluded that Paleoindian skeletons, including Browns Valley, have closer morphological (physical) ties to South Asian (Australian-Melanesian)

Figure 2.7. The Bradbury Brook quarry site.
Courtesy of the Minnesota Historical Society.

and European populations than to North Asian (China and Japan) or more recent Native American populations, as represented in their sample.[21] Browns Valley is the only recorded Paleoindian burial in Minnesota.

PALEOINDIAN AND EARLY EASTERN ARCHAIC LIFEWAYS

In Lewis Binford's reconstructed development of hunter-gatherer lifeways through time (the Terrestrial Model), a small number of ethnic groups first enter a large region like Minnesota, where they are able to free-wander from one unoccupied habitat to another. Eventually, the splitting off of daughter communities and the influx of new migrants fill the region with bands of hunter-gatherers. To avoid conflict and perhaps to accommodate the nearby presence of related families, hunter-gatherer groups begin concentrating their food acquisition activities within bounded but still large areas (home ranges), with which they become identified. Unlike their pioneering ancestors, they can no longer free-wander from one habitat to another.

As home ranges become packed together and populations grow, hunter-gatherers are usually forced to intensify their food acquisition efforts, since their ability to move around in search of preferred foods is restricted. In regions where the pioneering foragers were terrestrial animal hunters, intensification efforts usually involve the exploitation of second-order foods, such as fish and terrestrial plant remains, where these resources are available. If the numbers of hunter-gatherers and the tempo of resource intensification in a region continue to increase, more complex lifeways based on domesticated foods or abundant natural resources, like sea mammals, may suddenly emerge. To oversimplify what is often a complicated sequence of processes in reality, I have found it useful in the study of Minnesota prehistory to divide the developmental trajectory of Binford's Terrestrial Model into four phases: (1) the appearance of pioneer foragers in a region, (2) the filling up of the region by socially circumscribed but not packed foraging groups, (3) the crossing of a packing threshold beyond which hunter-gatherer groups have to intensify their food acquisition efforts, and (4) the sudden emergence of a more complex lifeway based on agriculture or the focused exploitation of an abundant natural resource, like marine mammals or wild rice.

Within the framework of the model, the playing out of these processes depends on the nature of the natural environment and its change through time, available technology, and the complexity of neighboring social groups.[22] As a consequence, while lifeways and their tempo of change exhibit regularities throughout the world, they will necessarily differ with regularity in regions with different natural resources. Binford's 2001 *Frames of Reference,* which relies for its conclusions on a study of 390 ethnographic (historic) hunter-gatherer groups and his Terrestrial Model, is an insightful exploration of what these differences will be and why.

The sequence of phases in the development of hunter-gatherer lifeways laid out in *Frames of Reference,* as I reconstruct it, agrees closely with my understanding of what took place in precontact Minnesota during the Paleoindian–Early Archaic period. According to this understanding, the first pioneering phase of the sequence coincides with the Early Paleoindian period (11,200–10,500 BC). As outlined in the first section of this chapter, the region's rapidly changing Late Glacial land surface was dominated during this period by the lingering presence of the massive Laurentide continental glacier in the far north, postglacial lakes, very cold meltwater streams that carried a heavy load of rock flour from the melting glacier, great blocks of remnant glacial ice, and open spruce parkland that was dominated by a needle-leaf evergreen forest. Temperatures were cold, and winter snowfall was about twice the amount we experience today.

According to my present interpretation of the model as it applies to Minnesota, the first pioneering families to enter the state were highly mobile Early Paleoindians whose subsistence focus in this Late Glacial boreal environment would have been the hunting of terrestrial animals because of the lack of suitable plant remains and as yet abundant aquatic resources. Since they were the only hunter-gatherers in the state and initially entered in small numbers, they moved from one food patch to another in pursuit of large- and medium-sized terrestrial game animals in order to maintain their subsistence security. Their numbers remained small, and the amount of uninhabited area was too large for them to attain the minimum population density that would compel the creation of bounded home ranges. I refer to this lifeway as the Pioneer Forager lifeway.

The presence of a free-wandering, game-focused lifeway at this time is supported by the predominance of single-find projectile points, the use of high-quality toolstone from widely scattered sources, a hunter's tool kit (as known more securely from other areas), the absence of long-term habitation sites, and the presence of mastodon and mammoth kills in nearby states, such as Lange-Ferguson in western South Dakota, Kimmswick in eastern Missouri, and the Schaefer and Hebior sites in southeastern Wisconsin. A possible association of a mastodon and Clovis point has also been discovered at the Boas site near the northeastern edge of the driftless area in southwestern Wisconsin.[23]

By describing this lifeway as free-wandering, I do not mean to imply that hunter-gatherer groups necessarily roamed freely across the countryside. Some may have seasonally exploited the same areas for many years. Rather, groups could free-wander if they chose to because of the small number of hunter-gatherer groups present. Likewise, a focus on game hunting does not mean that terrestrial plants, aquatic resources like fish, and small animals were not also part of the diet. The presence of white-tailed deer, rabbit, turtle, and other smaller animals in possible association with mammoth and mastodon kills, such as at Lange-Ferguson and Kimmswick, provide some support for the view that these were opportunistic foragers whose subsistence focus just happened to be game animals. Rather, it is more useful to think of their diet as being something like 70 percent land animals, 20 percent aquatic resources, and 10 percent terrestrial plant remains. As we will see, these percentages change markedly once resource intensification becomes a way of life in the more recent Woodland period. It is unclear at present whether these early hunter-gatherers were warm-weather ("snowbird") foraging parties in the northern portion of their summer range or colonizing parties pushed northward due to population growth in more resource-rich southern staging areas.

As predicted by the model, both increasing numbers of hunter-gatherer groups and regionalization seem to have taken place in the second half of the period. The presence of these trends is supported by increasing numbers of projectile points through time and their distribution (while eight Clovis points are concentrated in the southern two-thirds of the state, seventeen later Folsom points have a southwestern concentration, and twelve Holcombe points a northern concentration).

A consequence of the highly mobile lifeway of these pioneer foragers and their subsistence focus on larger game animals is the near invisibility of their remains in the archaeological record. The presence of a Folsom point in a cultivated field on a hill overlooking a large wetland in the Sherburne National Wildlife Refuge is typical for the period. Although the point is only one artifact in a mixed collection of artifacts, it suggests the presence of a small hilltop campsite from which a small number of Folsom hunters or perhaps a family watched for game. Sites of the lifeway are for the most part scattered, small, artifact-poor, generally nonaccumulative, and located in upland positions overlooking places where game might congregate. This pattern of campsite location and content continued in large areas of Minnesota for thousands of years up to the Woodland period. At about that time, the state's hunter-gatherers began living at least seasonally in more frequently occupied camps and hamlets along lakes and streams. These more recent habitation sites were positioned to maximize the acquisition of a wider variety of resources, such as water, firewood, fish, and wetland plants, rather than to facilitate the search for food on an encounter basis.

The second phase in the sequence begins with the onset of the Late Paleoindian–Early Eastern Archaic period (10,500–7500 BC) and continues on through the Middle Archaic period (7500–3000 BC), a period I discuss in chapter 3. During the Late Paleoindian–Early Eastern Archaic period, which coincides in Minnesota with the Early Holocene geological epoch, major climatic and vegetation changes took place throughout the state, as stressed earlier. Deciduous forests dominated the southern portion of the state, while pine forests replaced the earlier boreal spruce forest in the north by 9400 BC (see Map 2.2). Early Eastern Archaic points seem confined for the most part to the southern deciduous forest zone, although this remains largely conjecture at present. In contrast partially contemporary Late Paleoindian points are widespread throughout all forests. By 8000 BC, tallgrass prairie began spreading eastward across Minnesota, too, in a time-transgressive manner, as illustrated in Map 2.3.

Even though there are many more finds of artifacts and sites from this period than for the earlier Early Paleoindian period, we are still unable to outline the lifeways of Late Paleoindian–Early Eastern Archaic hunter-gatherers with assurance and in detail. However, on a general level it seems that populations remained sparse and highly mobile, as indicated by their archaeological remains, which consist for the most part of small scatters of stone artifacts. Like the stone tool assemblages of the Early Paleoindian people before them, their assemblages are almost always limited to tools for processing meat, hide, and bone. It seems that a small, sparse, highly mobile population of terrestrial animal hunter-gatherers with a very simple, highly portable material assemblage continued to occupy the thousands of square miles of Minnesota's varied terrain.

Still, there are (possible) trends that characterize this period. Examples are a further increase in population growth, increasing material culture diversity, and a gradual anchoring of annual activities within home ranges bounded by the home ranges of other hunter-gatherer groups. Although these groups continued to position their residential sites in the landscape to facilitate the search for game on a daily encounter basis, they now "mapped on," I believe, to the resources of the home range in an annual settlement-subsistence cycle. In addition, these societies were adjusting to the changing Early Holocene mosaic of woodlands and a progressively warmer climate. The diversity of projectile point styles throughout the state, a focus on local toolstone and infrequent use of exotic stone, the continued presence of a hunter's tool kit and of small, elusive sites, and the much greater presence in the archaeological record of Late Paleoindian–Early Eastern Archaic remains compared to Early Paleoindian remains provide support for these trends.

In this study these new home range–focused lifeways of this phase are called Coniferous Forest Game Hunter and Deciduous Forest Game Hunter for groups that focused on hunting terrestrial forest animals, and Early Pedestrian Bison Hunter for groups that focused on hunting bison in the grasslands. Because of the continuing focus on large game animals, ethnographic comparison suggests that males still did most of the hunting and that group size during the most dispersed time of year was between twelve and twenty-one people. As earlier, smaller animals, birds, fish, and plants were part of the diet. The increasing number of sites and artifacts indicates that the human population was growing but had not yet reached a packing threshold beyond which game hunting as a subsistence focus was no longer a viable option.

WERE THERE PEOPLE IN MINNESOTA BEFORE THE PALEOINDIANS?

Although fluted points are the oldest confirmed artifacts in the state, people could have lived in the state earlier, for the earliest fluted points date somewhat after the continental ice sheet began to retreat. A sprinkling of sites across the Americas, such as Schaefer and Hebior in southeastern Wisconsin, the Meadowcroft Rockshelter in Pennsylvania, and Monte Verde in Chile, show that people may have—and increasing numbers of archaeologists would say "most likely" or even "surely"—lived in the

Americas a thousand years or more before the appearance of fluted points.[24] At present, there is no good, confirmed archaeological evidence for the presence of pre–fluted point makers in Minnesota, but earlier artifacts could be present and unrecognized—and several archaeologists and geologists have claimed that pre-Paleoindian artifacts have been found in the state. Therefore, let's review several claims for pre-Clovis people in Minnesota.

Frances Eliza Babbitt, a Little Falls schoolteacher, claimed to have found "glacial man" in Minnesota in the winter of 1878–79.[25] Similar claims have been made over the years for other areas of the state. Several prominent newspapers, for example, announced the discovery of three Neanderthal skulls along the Minnesota-Ontario border (the Gold Island burials) in the early 1970s. Since Neanderthals became extinct at least 25,000 years ago, this would have been a startling discovery indeed. Professor A. E. Jenks made an equally spectacular newspaper splash with his announcement of the discovery of "Pleistocene Man" near Pelican Rapids in the 1930s. But these two claims, like the others, have not withstood the test of close scrutiny. Either the recovered material has proven to be more recent than originally thought, or the context in which it was found cannot be accurately dated.

Were there people in Minnesota before the Paleoindians? The evidence remains scanty and ambiguous. Perhaps the best-documented possibility still remains Babbitt's Little Falls discovery. Apparent implements of white quartz were first found at Little Falls in 1877 by Professor N. H. Winchell on a slope between the modern floodplain and an older glacial terrace of an ancestral Mississippi River. These possible implements, which were found in association with chipped fragments of the same material in a water-sifted sand deposit, were angular and "perfectly unwaterworn," unlike other stones in the deposit, which were distinctly waterworn.

Babbitt's discovery was more significant than Winchell's, for the quartzes she found were apparently systematically clustered in an undisturbed geological stratum overlain by 12 to 15 feet of stratified gravel and sand outwash and underlain by sand, coarse waterworn gravel, and glacial till. Besides being unweathered, too, her quartzes were only present in this one layer, with thin, small pieces in one place, triangular-shaped fragments in another, and clusters of materials determined to be in the process of manufacture in others. In 1881 she also found a sharply angular and completely unwaterworn block of quartz, 12 to 18 inches across, in the stone rubble at the top of the till. She considered the block a core from which the smaller implements could have been struck. Experts of the day, including F. W. Putnam, curator of the Peabody Museum, unanimously declared the quartzes to be the "unmistakable products of intention."

Babbitt felt that the ancient flint workers had entered the glacial floodplain for the purpose of quarrying the quartz outcrops in the winter, when the volume of meltwater would have been reduced and the quartz-bearing slate bedrock more accessible. She reasoned that the floodplain was formed from meltwaters from the receding glacier as the last ice age drew to a close. This interpretation was supported by Winchell, then Minnesota State Geologist, and Warren Upham, his assistant at the time, who argued that the site had been on a rocky island in the glacial floodplain.[26] The island had been eventually buried by proglacial streams following an increase in the amount of meltwater.

Unfortunately, a relative eventually tossed out Babbitt's extensive collection of quartzes, and perhaps only a few specimens sent to Putnam are available for study today. A study in 1975 by Joan Carothers of the terrace in which the quartzes were found, however, has refined the date at which the terrace was formed. Carothers was able to associate the Little Falls terrace with another on the Anoka Sand Plain that has been radiocarbon dated to about 17,000 years ago.[27] The Little Falls quartzes may, then, date to Late Wisconsin times.

Were Babbitt's quartzes actual implements manufactured by people who predate the Paleoindians? The question remains unanswered. Since the evidence was discarded, we can no longer verify her claim with the sophisticated techniques established in archaeology in the past half century. Only future excavation and, perhaps, the rediscovery of Putnam's specimens will determine whether Babbitt's quartzes are pre-Paleoindian artifacts.

Since the presence of pre-Clovis people in the Americas remains one of the most hotly debated—and undecided—issues in American archaeology, every field archaeologist working in the state should assume as a matter of procedure that people lived in Minnesota before the Paleoindians. I support this cautionary approach with two old adages: "It's better to be safe than sorry" and "You don't see what you're not looking for."

Were there people in Minnesota before the Paleoindians? I don't know. However, a recent claim for the discovery of pre-Paleoindian remains near Walker in central Minnesota could help answer that question. Since in-depth, professional reports have not yet been prepared for this site, I adopt (given the long history of similar claims in Minnesota) a cautionary wait-and-see attitude at this writing.

CHAPTER 3

Prairie Everywhere
Middle and Late Archaic Adaptations

Archaic societies replaced Paleoindian societies and were followed by pottery-making Woodland peoples. This is a minimal definition of the term *Archaic,* for the content and size of these societies varied widely across the continent, and archaeologists define the concept according to different sets of criteria.[1] For some, the term refers to small, mobile groups of people with simple social structures and a diffuse hunter-gatherer economy. From this perspective, these societies are an evolutionary stage or level of social complexity intermediate between migratory big game–hunting Paleoindians and later, more sedentary Woodland horticulturalists. Other archaeologists apply the term to early Native American societies that did not grow their own food, make pottery, or construct earthen burial mounds. In this view, Archaic assemblages are distinguished from earlier Paleoindian assemblages by the presence of unfluted, nonlanceolate notched and stemmed projectile points, and from more recent Woodland assemblages by the absence of pottery, earthen burial mounds, and domesticated plant foods.

In recent years both of these sets of criteria have been questioned. The sharp shifts in human adaptive strategies that separate Archaic cultures as a stage from earlier big game hunters in the first view have become blurred, as stressed in chapter 2. In addition, pottery, earthen burial mounds, and domesticated plant foods have been found in contexts in some areas of eastern North America that previously had been accepted as Archaic. These discoveries negate the second view.

I define an Archaic complex in Minnesota as one that lacks both Paleoindian projectile points and pottery and that dates roughly before 500 BC. Components of an Archaic complex are usually identified by the presence of certain kinds of notched and stemmed projectile points that date between about 9400 BC and 500 BC. If point types in the transitional Dalton point cluster are considered Archaic, the age range is 10,700 BC to 500 BC.

The Archaic has traditionally been divided into Early, Middle, and Late periods. That tradition is followed here to emphasize material culture changes during this long time span, although many of the original reasons for this tripartite division no longer seem valid. As evident in the previous chapter, the Early Archaic in Minnesota can no longer be viewed as a transitional phase between Paleoindian and Archaic lifeways (for Late Paleoindian and Early Eastern Archaic social groups were contemporary in part, and both seem to have had a terrestrial animal hunter lifeway), and, as we will see, the Late Archaic can no longer be considered transitional to Woodland economies firmly based on domesticated plant foods. In addition, the ages assigned to these periods are only approximate, for they remain poorly dated, and transitions to and from an Archaic material culture seem to have occurred at different times in the separate archaeological regions of the state.

MIDDLE AND EARLY LATE HOLOCENE ENVIRONMENTS

As defined here, the Middle and Late Archaic periods (7500–500 BC) in Minnesota roughly coincide with the Atlantic, the Sub-Boreal, and the early half of the Sub-Atlantic climatic episodes, and the Middle and Early Late Holocene geological periods. Environmentally, the Middle Archaic was a dynamic period during which the prairie-forest border migrated far to the northeast of its present position and then receded to its approximate modern position (Maps 3.1–3.3, Map 1.2).[2] These severe vegetation dislocations were the result of the Atlantic climatic episode (also called the Holocene Climatic Optimum, the Hypsithermal, and the Prairie period, among other names), during which warm and dry westerly winds blew across the state. At its most severe, annual rainfall may have been 20 percent less than modern levels, and the average temperature 5°F warmer than today. From the perspective of a modern Euro-American farmer, the period would be a disaster, for summer drought increased, shallow lakes dried up, and the annual discharge of water in rivers declined significantly. The mean annual discharge of the Mississippi River, for example, declined 40 to 60 percent, and the river probably shifted from a braided to a meandering stream.[3] As one measure of higher Middle Holocene temperatures, Maps 3.4 and 3.5 show the far northern position of the dividing line between effective temperature (ET) values below and above 12.0 during the period (compare the position of the dividing line in these figures with those in Maps 2.4 and 2.5).

Eventually, even deciduous woods became restricted to major river valleys, the edges of large lakes, and other less xeric (dry), fire-protected areas throughout much of the state. At its most eastward position by about 5800 BC, the prairie-forest border in north-central Minnesota was more than 100 miles northeast of its modern position. By

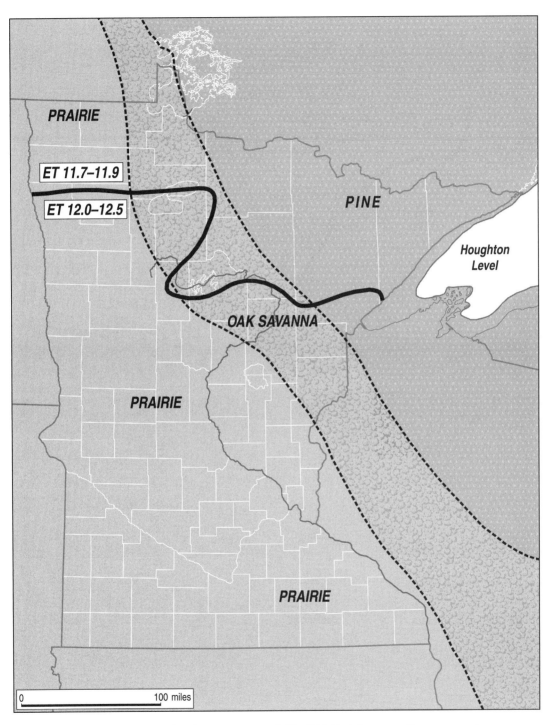

Map 3.1. Minnesota's major plant biomes at 6800 BC. The thick black line across the map separates effective temperature values of 11.7 to 11.9 north of the line from values of 12.0 to 12.5 south of the line.

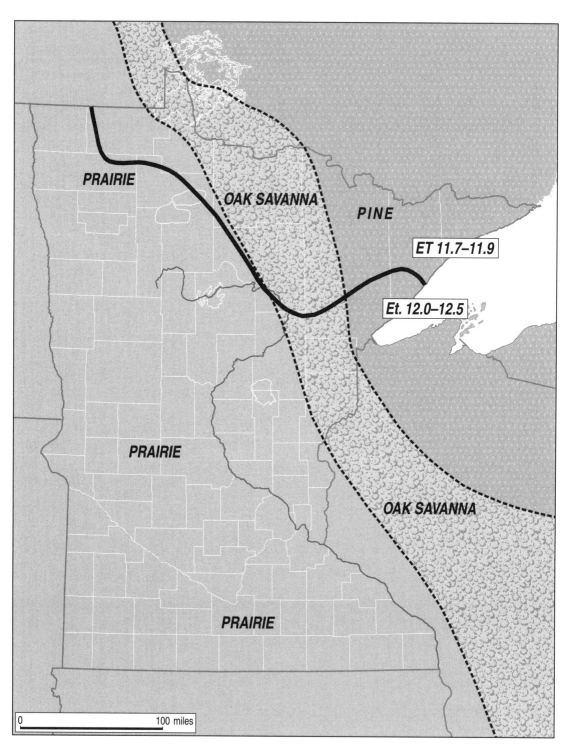

Map 3.2. Minnesota's major plant biomes at 5800 BC. The thick black line separates effective temperature values of 11.7 to 11.9 north of the line from values of 12.0 to 12.5 south of the line.

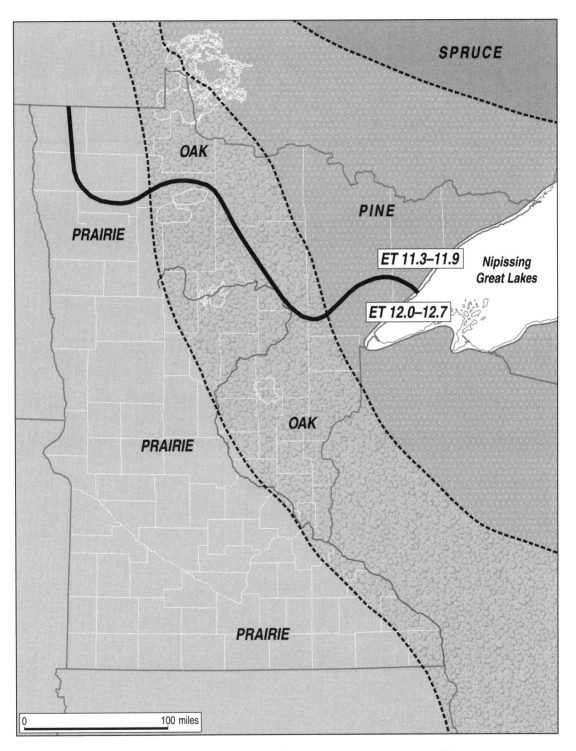

Map 3.3. Minnesota's major plant biomes at 4000 BC. The thick black line separates effective temperature values of 11.3 to 11.9 north of the line from values of 12.0 to 12.7 south of the line.

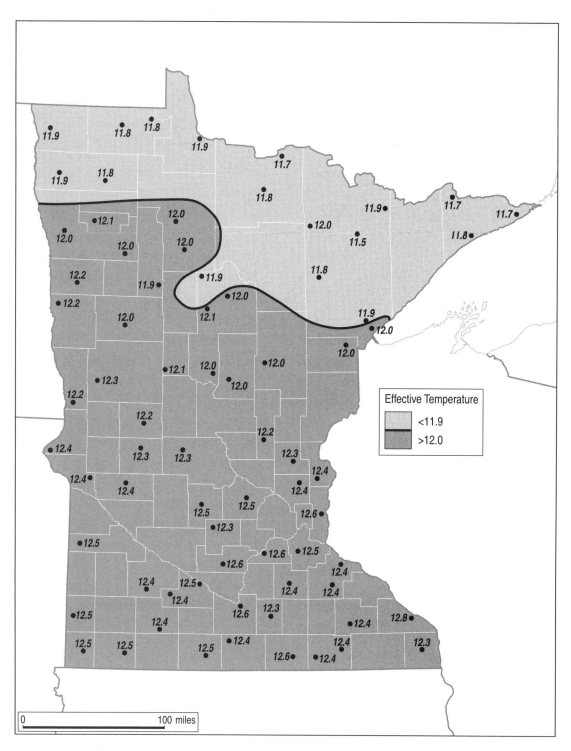

Map 3.4. Effective temperature (ET) in the Middle Holocene at 7000 BC. The black line separates ET values of 11.9 to 11.7 north of the line from values of 12.6 to 12.0 south of the line.

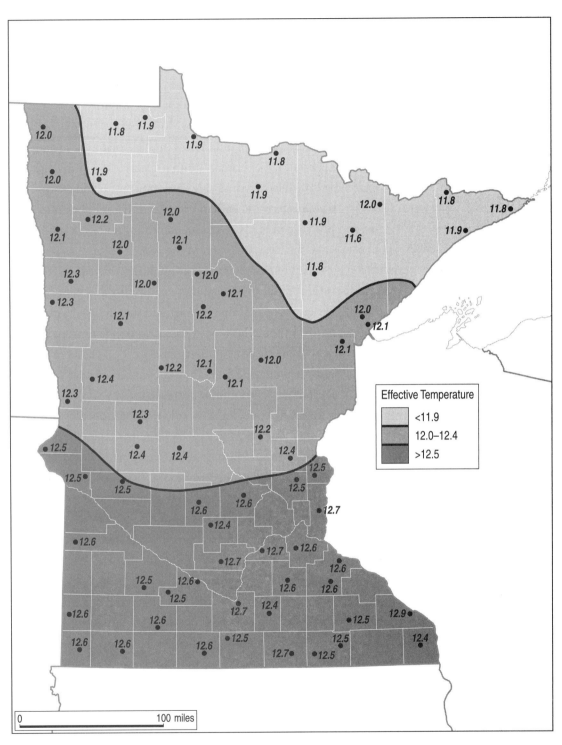

Map 3.5. Effective temperature (ET) in the Middle Holocene at 4000 BC. The upper black line separates ET values of 11.8 to 11.9 north of the line from values of 12.0 to 12.4 between the two lines, which are then separated by the lower black line from ET values of 12.5 to 12.7 south of this line.

about 4900 BC, however, the climate had become cooler and wetter, and prairie gradually retreated, reaching its modern borders between 2500 BC and 1200 BC.

As in earlier periods, the use of terms like *prairie, deciduous forest,* and *coniferous forest* disguises a varied mosaic of more specific and usually overlapping habitats. For instance, the prairie biome was not a sweeping, flat plain of tall, waving grass. A wide variety of landforms, including glacial lake beds, steep bluffs, rolling till plains, morainic hills, and beach ridges and swales, created differences in soil moisture that affected the distribution of prairie grasses and, therefore, of animal species. The thin, dry soils of the uplands were covered by little bluestem and side oats, moister uplands with deep fertile soils were covered by big bluestem and Indian grass, and the wet lowlands were dominated by bluejoint and prairie cordgrass. Wetland communities dominated by rushes and sedges, such as pothole marshes, also dotted the prairie in places. The result was a dry but complex prairie ecosystem of plants and animals that varied widely in food resources for foragers. To add to this complexity, these communities changed in size and distribution as the Middle Holocene became warmer and then moister after 4900 BC. As the prairie spread and the climate became warmer, wetlands and shallower lakes shrank (and became marshes or dried up in many cases), groundwater levels dropped, and dry habitat communities increased. As the state became cooler and moister, wetlands increased, and dry habitat communities decreased.

Other changes influenced the foraging strategies of Middle Holocene people, too. For example, as the last remnants of stagnant glacial ice melted, the landscape began to stabilize, and the opening of a northern Glacial Lake Agassiz outlet greatly reduced the flow of water that coursed through the valley of the Minnesota River. As the water warmed, warmwater species of fish increased in number as they moved northward through the extensive streams and interconnected lake basins of the state. Waterfowl probably also began to appear in large numbers. As they returned to the state annually, they established migratory patterns that have lasted for thousands of years.

As cooler and especially moister conditions returned to the state after 4900 BC, the forest gradually moved westward, often in jumps, with oak woodland advancing across morainic ridges and with oak-poplar-brush prairies or woodland filling prairie openings. When these fire-hardy woodlands became sufficiently dense and extensive enough to form effective fire barriers, mesic (temperate) forests began to develop in their lee. The result was a continually changing prairie-forest mosaic under the influence of broadscale climatic and local conditions.

The modern diversity of the mixed forest, and perhaps the floristic tension zone along its southern edge, dates to this expansion. However, the composition of the developing deciduous and mixed forests in the western Great Lakes region was not the same everywhere. East–west gradients existed that had some effect on the food resources available for human exploitation. Beech, eastern hemlock, maple, hickory, and ash trees were more abundant to the east, and pine, birch, and oak to the west. The east–west gradient in the north was from a mixed forest of pine with some maple trees in the east to forests of pine with increasing numbers of birch trees in northwestern Minnesota. Travelers moving westward across the western Great Lakes would have found beech becoming scarce first, then eastern hemlock, maple, pine, and finally birch before they walked through oak scrub and onto the tallgrass prairies of northwestern Minnesota.

By 1200 BC, the major vegetation zones had with a few exceptions reached their 1850s position. Climatic oscillations continued to occur throughout the Sub-Atlantic and Post-Sub-Atlantic, but they were minor compared with the impact of the warm, dry westerlies of the Atlantic climatic episode. One major difference between the distributions of vegetation then and in Minnesota in the 1850s was the absence of the Big Woods, the bulge of elm-oak forest that covered a large area of south-central Minnesota in the early Euro-American settlement period. Although oaks, aspen, and willow had initiated the invasion of the prairie in this area at the end of the Middle Holocene dry period at about 2500 BC, the expansion of Big Woods trees (elm, basswood, ironwood, sugar maple, ash, hickory, and butternut) did not occur until about 300 years ago.[4]

Another difference was the absence of northern Minnesota's extensive peatlands, which did not develop until after 1000 BC, near the end of the Late Archaic period.[5] The peatlands developed when the cooler, wetter conditions of the Late Holocene slowed the decomposition of plant materials on poorly drained lake plains, especially on the bed of Glacial Lake Agassiz. Today, these peat beds are about 10 feet thick.

THE MIDDLE ARCHAIC ARCHAEOLOGICAL RECORD

In Minnesota, Middle Archaic artifacts and sites are sparse or remain unrecognized at the moment, even though this time period (7500–3000 BC) is well represented by sites and by growing populations farther south.[6] In fact, there is some confusion in Minnesota archaeology about how non-Paleoindian artifact assemblages dating to this period should be classified. The problem in part is the presence of an early Archaic time gradient, with the earlier appearance of Early Eastern Archaic assemblages to the south correlated with the earlier appearance of deciduous forests in that area. That such gradients existed at the time seems supported by a similar gradient in far northern Minnesota, where Late Paleoindian assemblages may have persisted to 6000–5000 BC.

As in earlier Paleoindian and Early Eastern Archaic periods, the main diagnostic Middle Archaic artifacts are distinctive weapon points. In general, Archaic points of all kinds are less well made than Paleoindian points. Indeed, it seems that high-quality stone working declines overall outside the Paleoindian tradition. Correlates of this trend are an increasing use of local chert and of heating poor-quality toolstone when chipping it, a process that improves its workability.

Like Early Archaic points, Middle Archaic points are generally smaller than Paleoindian points and contain notches on the base or side. Another difference is that Archaic points with their beveled, resharpened edges seem designed for cutting as well as penetration, compared to the long, narrow penetration points of the Paleoindians. This difference has been explained by a shift in game hunted, with Archaic points used primarily in the capture of smaller game, like deer, and Paleoindian points used primarily in the capture of larger mammals, such as bison and mammoth. This explanation remains problematical in Minnesota, however, for Middle Archaic hunters in the expanding prairies of the period almost certainly hunted more bison (and most likely more big game) than their woodland Paleoindian and Early Archaic predecessors.

In Minnesota Middle Archaic points fall into early and late point types. They also sort by their presumed region of greatest presence outside Minnesota, here simply referred to as Eastern Woodlands and Plains for convenience (Figure 3.1).[7] As the dates in the figure indicate, some types overlap into the earlier Early Archaic and later Late Archaic periods, when they may be more common.

When used as thrown weapons rather than as knives, Middle Archaic points, like other Archaic points, were most likely attached to wooden dart shafts that were propelled by an atlatl. An atlatl is a composite tool having two parts, a handle and a mechanism like a hook for the attachment of the dart foreshaft.[8] Experiments demonstrate that an atlatl provides more thrust to the dart and substantially increases the distance of a throw compared to a spear, which may have been the primary weapon used during the Late Glacial and Early Holocene periods. Fitting perforated stone or shell weights onto the atlatl shaft increased hurling force. Handles were sometimes made of stone and other materials as well. Artifacts that probably served as atlatl weights and handles, such as polished and ground boatstones, bannerstones, and gorgets, are common identifying traits of the late Middle Archaic and Late Archaic archaeological record in the American Midwest.

Extensively excavated site components that date to the 7500–6500 BC period are lacking in the expanding early Middle Holocene prairies in Minnesota, so direct evidence of the content of these components is missing. However, components exist in nearby states that illustrate what the content of these components might look like. The

Eastern Woodlands
EARLY PHASE (7500–3800 BC)
LeCroy Bifurcated Stem (7500–6700 BC)
Fox Valley Truncated Blard (6200–5500 BC)
Osceola (3700–1200 BC)
Raddatz Side Notched (3700–1200 BC)
Eva I (6000–4000 BC)
Morrow Mountain I and II (5000–4000 BC)

LATE PHASE (3800–3000 BC)
Matanzas Side Notched (3800–1200 BC)
Etley (3800–1200 BC)
Benton Stemmed (3500–2000 BC)
Elk River Stemmed (3500–2000 BC)

Plains
EARLY PHASE (7500–3800 BC)
Simonsen (6300–5400 BC)
Graham Cave Side Notched (9400–6300 BC)
Oxbow (4100–3300 BC)
LATE PHASE (3800–3000 BC)
McKean (3800–1800 BC)
Table Rock Stemmed (3800–1200 BC)

Figure 3.1. Stone weapon point types present in Minnesota in the Middle Archaic period. Traditional dates for their presence as a type in North America are given in parentheses, though their ages in Minnesota remain uncertain.

best known of these sites is Cherokee Sewer on a floodplain of the Little Sioux River just south of Cherokee, Iowa.[9] The earliest archaeological horizon at Cherokee Sewer, Horizon III, which dates to circa 7600–7200 BC, contained extensive evidence of an early winter, multifamily bison-processing campsite. Approximately eight bison *(Bison bison)* were found in association with a Late Paleoindian tool assemblage. Artifacts of stone included weapon points, bifaces, end scrapers, utilized and retouched flakes, a chopper, and a utilized cobble. Among bone artifacts were chopping tools, a deer antler tine, and a worked beaver incisor. Hearths and a possible boiling pit, which may have been used to render fat and marrow from broken-up bone, were also present.

Late Paleoindian bison kill sites that could date to this early Middle Holocene period may also be present in the expanding prairie in southwestern Minnesota. An example is a site in Chippewa County where Scottsbluff points were found in apparent association with bison bones. A Browns Valley point also appears to be associated with bison bone at the Petersen site in Lincoln County, and extensive exposures of bison bone in stream cuts have been reported from Watson Sag just north of Montevideo in an area where a Browns Valley point and other Late Paleoindian points have been found. Several Late Paleoindian points were also found with the dismembered remains of bison at another bog site near Granite Falls in Yellow Medicine County. The contents of these sites indicate that Late Paleoindian projectile points likely continued in use in Minnesota during the initial stages of the expansion of prairie across the state.

Based on artifacts in the lowest horizon at Cherokee Sewer, Anfinson has proposed a Cherokee phase for the expanding early Middle Holocene prairies of Minnesota.[10] The phase would represent the first full-grassland adaptation in the state that features a focus on bison hunting (an Early Pedestrian Bison Hunter lifeway), though small game and perhaps plant gathering were part of the adaptation too. He cites the Goodrich site in south-central Minnesota and the Patrow site in Itasca County as examples of sites that have components of this phase.

Anfinson has also suggested that the artifact assemblages of Native Americans who lived in the prairies of the state between 6500 and 3800 BC are sufficiently similar to group them within an Itasca phase.[11] The type-site of the phase, and the most thoroughly reported Middle Archaic site in Minnesota, is the Itasca Bison Kill on Nicollet Creek near Lake Itasca in southeastern Clearwater County.[12] At the time of the kill, the site was part of an oak savanna that was expanding northeastward in front of the northeastward expanding prairie. The site consists of two separate areas about 200 feet apart. The lower of the two, in a boggy creek, contains the remains of a now-extinct species of bison and an assemblage of tools (projectile points, knives, choppers, and an end scraper) consistent with what one would expect to find at a hunting and meat-processing station. The other area is a small campsite on a hill overlooking the bog.

Other Middle Archaic bison-hunting and meat-processing sites with similar stone tool assemblages have been found within the advancing prairie. The best-known examples are Granite Falls in Yellow Medicine County in Minnesota, Horizon II at Cherokee Sewer in northwest Iowa, and the Rustad Quarry site in southeastern North Dakota. Artifacts in Horizon II (6200–5900 BC) at Cherokee Sewer include side-notched and isosceles unnotched projectile points with straight to concave bases, ovate and triangular bifaces, choppers, end scrapers, hammerstones, and a milling stone.[13] Radiocarbon dates for the horizon are closer to 6000 BC than to 7000 BC, which may indicate that the age of the similar-appearing Itasca Bison Kill is also closer to 6000 BC than to 7000 BC.[14]

Middle Archaic sites dating to the peak of the Prairie period in Minnesota most likely resemble Horizon I (5500–5200 BC) at the Cherokee Sewer site, which archaeologists suggest was occupied by a small hunting band of fifteen to thirty people. Hearths and medium-sized side-notched weapon points were present in the horizon. As during other phases of the dry period, the drought does not seem to have greatly affected the way of life of prairie dwellers in western Iowa.

In other areas of Minnesota, known Middle Archaic components remain sparse, perhaps because they are usually small and deeply buried, occur in rarely surveyed landscape features, like uplands or along the rim of now silted-over lakes, or have been mistakenly assigned to more recent cultural horizons. Instructive examples are the Granite Falls and Rustad sites, which were both deeply buried in alluvial fans.

Known early Middle Archaic sites in south-central and southeastern Minnesota and in the mixed hardwood forests to the north are little more than surface scatters of stone artifacts. Components are infrequent, small, and shallow, and midden buildup is minimal. These features and their sparse occupational debris suggest that low population levels, high mobility, and, in general, one-time occupancy characterize the settlement pattern of these early foragers. Components of the period are frequently found around the edges of lakes, especially at outlets, and along stream banks.

In the forested northeastern corner of the state, early Middle Archaic assemblages remain largely unrecognized, perhaps because of a lingering Late Paleoindian typological base and a possible blending of Late Paleoindian and early Middle Archaic tool types.[15] Sites in eastern Manitoba, northwestern Ontario, and northern Wisconsin also suggest the presence of a similar late forest-adapted Late Paleoindian tradition that, if not part of or at least contemporary in part with early Middle Archaic assemblages in these regions, closely preceded them.

An interesting problem in early and middle Middle Archaic Minnesota is the apparent absence of some tool types present in contemporary assemblages to the south. Examples are the bannerstone, which is a weight apparently used to increase the thrust of an atlatl, which appears in the midsouth between 7000 BC and 5000 BC, and the full-grooved axe, which appears after 5000 BC. In Illinois, milling stones, polished stone axes, and hammerstones appear at the deeply stratified Modoc Rock Shelter in Illinois by about 6000 BC. The apparent absence of similar tools during this period in Minnesota could mean that the scattered surface finds of similar appearing tools have been mistakenly dated to the late Middle Archaic (circa 3800–3000 BC) or Late Archaic periods. It is also possible that many of these tools were unsuited to the bison-centered prairie lifeway of the period, for they may be associated with the exploitation of woodland environments in these other areas.

This suite of ground stone tools (bannerstones, plummets, and fully grooved and three-quarter grooved axes) does not seem to appear in any quantity in Minnesota until the late Middle Archaic period (circa 3800–3000 BC). Copper artifacts also first appear during this period, as do a host of new weapon points or at least points that now appear in greater abundance, including Osceola, Raddatz Side Notched, McKean, Table Rock Stemmed, Matanzas Side Notched, and Etley.[16] Since this time period coincides with the appearance of a moister (early Late Holocene) climate in Minnesota, I discuss these late Middle Archaic assemblages in the next section of the chapter.

Burials are thought to date to the Archaic period in Minnesota if they satisfy one or more of the following criteria: the burial is not associated with pottery or a burial mound; associated artifacts are typologically Archaic; the burial mode is considered Archaic (usually secondary non-mound burials in pits that extend into the subsoil); and associated radiocarbon dates fall within the range of the Archaic period. At the time of this writing, sixteen burials in the state are considered possibly Archaic, though only four have been radiometrically dated.

Only one of the burials—the Pelican Rapids–Minnesota Woman (21OT03) burial near Pelican Rapids in Otter Tail County in western Minnesota—is securely Middle Archaic in age.[17] The skeleton was discovered 10 to 12 feet below a roadbed by highway workers in 1931. Jenks, who excavated what was left of the site in 1932, thought the individual may have drowned accidentally in Glacial Lake Pelican sometime during the Ice Age.[18] The nearly complete skeleton is now known to be the remains of an adolescent female thirteen to fifteen years old at the time of death, which was in about 6700 BC.[19]

Like the earlier Browns Valley (21TR01) individual, the Pelican Rapids adolescent is not considered cranially distinct from later Archaic and Initial/Early Woodland individuals.[20] Susan Myster suggests that the similarity among these individuals' skulls indicates "a significant degree of genetic homogeneity and continuity between Paleoindian, Archaic, and Initial/Early Woodland traditions" in this region of north-central North America for about 6,500 years. This implies as well an in situ evolution of regional prairie-centered populations in Minnesota from earlier Paleoindian populations, a generalization that Myster extends as well to Archaic populations in the southeastern corner of the state.[21]

These fragments of information suggest that Middle Archaic (7500–3800 BC) site types in Minnesota include base camps, short-term camps, kill sites, lithic scatters, burials, quarries, and workshops.

THE LATE ARCHAIC ARCHAEOLOGICAL RECORD

Defining characteristics of the Late Archaic in Minnesota include the following: the appearance of different sets of diagnostic weapon point types, whose presence varies in space and time in the state; the presence of exotic raw materials, including native copper and marine shell, and of unusual artifacts, such as birdstones, gorgets, and Turkey Tail bifaces; the presence of communal burial sites; a continuing absence of ceramics (by definition in Minnesota); an increasingly modern early Late Holocene environment; and calibrated radiocarbon dates that fall between 3000 and 500 BC.[22] Evidence

Upper Mississippi River Valley
  LARGE SIDE NOTCHED CLUSTER
    Godar (3200–1800 BC)
    Madison Side Notched (2500–250 BC)
    Osceola (3700–1200 BC)
    Raddatz Side Notched (3700–1200 BC)
  DURST CLUSTER
    Durst Stemmed (1200–600 BC)
  LATE ARCHAIC STEMMED CLUSTER
    Karnak Stemmed (circa 2000 BC)
  TURKEY TAIL CLUSTER
    Turkey Tail (2000/1500–500 BC)
  TERMINAL ARCHAIC BARBED CLUSTER
    Delhi (1300–200 BC)
    Buck Creek Barbed (1500–600 BC)
  EARLY WOODLAND STRAIGHT STEMMED CLUSTER
    Fox Valley Stemmed (1500–100 BC)
    Kramer (1000–300 BC)
    Robbins (1000–1 BC)
  MOTLEY EXPANDING STEM CLUSTER
    Motley (800–600 BC)
    Atalissa (1500–1 BC)
    Tipton (1500–500 BC)

Northeast
  MATANZAS CLUSTER
    Matanzas Side Notched (3800–1200 BC)
    Brewerton Eared Notched (3000–1500 BC)

Central Mississippi River Valley
  TABLE ROCK CLUSTER
    Table Rock Stemmed (3000–1000 BC)
  ETLEY CLUSTER
    Etley (3800–1200 BC)
  NEBO HILL CLUSTER
    Nebo Hill Lanceolate (1600–1000 BC)
    Sedalia Lanceolate (2000–1000 BC)
  WADLOW CLUSTER
    Wadlow (2000–1000 BC)

Northern Plains
  MCKEAN CLUSTER
    McKean (3800–1800 BC)
    Duncan (3200–1100 BC)
    Hanna (1800–1200 BC)
  OXBOW CLUSTER
    Oxbow (2700–1000 BC)

Southeast
  EVA CLUSTER
    Eva II (4000–2000 BC)
  BENTON CLUSTER
    Benton Stemmed (3500–2000 BC)
    Elk River Stemmed (3500–2000 BC)
  LEDBETTER CLUSTER
    Ledbetter Stemmed (2500–1000 BC)
  DICKSON CONTRACTING STEM CLUSTER
    Gary (1500 BC–AD 100)
    Little Bear Creek (1500–500 BC)

Figure 3.2. Stone weapon points present in Minnesota in the Late Archaic period.

for major climatic discontinuities (as in the earlier Late Glacial and Early Holocene periods) is absent in the Late Archaic period.

Stone weapon points in the Late Archaic period tend to be side-notched and stemmed forms, which may overlap into earlier Middle Archaic or more recent Initial Woodland periods. Studies of the point collection at the Minnesota Historical Society indicate that thirty-two point types in the collection likely were present during the Late Archaic period. Other Late Archaic point types may be present in the state but remain unrecognized. Figure 3.2 associates the types by region of greatest presence and possible origin.[23]

Late Archaic material culture in Minnesota is more diverse than the material culture of earlier periods. Part of this diversity was the result of an expanded use of some

Figure 3.3. Late Archaic three-quarter grooved axes.
The smaller axe is 12 centimeters long.
Courtesy of the Minnesota Historical Society. Printed with permission.

tool types that had been present but rare earlier. An example is the flaked stone milling stone, which now becomes common in the archaeological record. Diversity was also the result of a series of new technological innovations that apparently begin to appear in the state in the late Middle Archaic, such as the rubbing and polishing of igneous and metamorphic rocks to form what archaeologists call "ground stone" tools. Examples are ground manos, metates, and axes (Figure 3.3). Other types of ground stone tools that probably first appear at this time are grooved axes for woodworking and spear-thrower (atlatl) weights called bannerstones. Since most of these artifacts are surface finds, their temporal associations remain uncertain. Harpoons, gorges, hooks, grooved net sinkers, and other specialized fishing gear are found now, as are celts, which seem to have been used as weights on fishing and birding nets (Figure 3.4). These are the first clearly identifiable fishing implements in the archaeological record of the state.

Nonetheless, Late Archaic artifact assemblages in Minnesota lack the abundance and diversity of tools, including plant-processing gear, that are now typical of sites in

Figure 3.4. Late Archaic ground stone celts.
The longest celt is 9.5 centimeters long.
Courtesy of the Minnesota Historical Society. Printed with permission.

the midsouth. In the central Mississippi valley region, for example, chipped stone adzes and celts, stone beads, atlatl weights, plummets, grooved axes, tubular pipes, steatite vessels, choppers (used as vegetable dicers), pestles, mortars, and pit steaming as a cooking device are present in abundance by about 3800 BC (the late Middle Archaic period in Minnesota) and characterize the Late Archaic period there. Conch shell was widely traded, and fiber-tempered pottery was present in the southeastern United States as early as the third millennium BC.

In the Prairie Lake region of southwestern Minnesota, Late Archaic components may be present at a small number of sites, including Pedersen, Mountain Lake, and Fox Lake. Anfinson has grouped these components into a Mountain Lake phase, which he dates between 3800 and 200 BC.[24] The type-site, Mountain Lake, is on a prominent hill that once was an island in a now-drained lake south of the town of Mountain Lake. Excavations at the site have recovered small lanceolate points in a stratigraphically distinct preceramic horizon that have a straight to concave base and contracting

Figure 3.5. Mountain Lake Archaic projectile points.
Courtesy of the Science Museum of Minnesota.

lower edges that resemble incipient stemming (Figure 3.5). These points, which are considered diagnostic of the phase, resemble Late Paleoindian forms but are smaller and more poorly made and are almost always made of local material. Some stemmed point forms may also be associated with the Mountain Lake phase. In general, Mountain Lake phase projectile points seem to share a family resemblance with contemporary forms to the east rather than to the west.

To the north, Late Archaic sites are more abundant than Late Paleoindian sites in the Red River valley and the Glacial Lake Agassiz basin. Early Late Archaic remains are primarily known from surface finds of copper artifacts and of diagnostic Oxbow (Parkdale Eared) and McKean points, although McKean points seem absent in the southern Glacial Lake Agassiz basin. The Canning site, which is in Norman County in the Red River valley, contains a McKean (Hanna) component that appears to be the archaeological remains of a winter bison-processing camp dating between 3000 and 1500 BC.[25] The component consisted of a discrete bed of bone, tools, burnt earth, and charcoal features covered by about 3 feet of sediment.

The early Late Archaic in northern Minnesota is most often characterized by the presence of copper artifacts. However, ground and polished stone objects, such as huge gouges that may have been used to manufacture dugout canoes, are also present in a stratigraphically distinct preceramic horizon. The Late Archaic component at Fish Lake West in the Reservoir Lakes area northwest of Duluth is composed mostly of hard, shaly artifacts, such as choppers, adzes, and bifaces, forms absent in the Late Paleoindian component at the Fish Lake East site. The lithic styles and hammered copper artifacts in this component are shared with the Riverside site in Michigan, the McCollum site in Ontario, and the Petaga Point site near Mille Lacs Lake in Minnesota.[26]

The Late Archaic archaeological record is poorly known in the deciduous forest region of southeastern Minnesota, but it may be a regional expression of the Durst phase (900–700 BC) of southwestern Wisconsin, for Durst Stemmed points are abundant in this region of Minnesota.[27] Other artifacts in Durst assemblages include simple stone knives, flake tools, and bone awls. No copper or polished stone tools have been found in these assemblages.

The most striking and distinctive late Middle Archaic and early Late Archaic technological innovation was the use of native copper to make a wide variety of mostly large, utilitarian implements. Among the most diagnostic and typical of these copper artifacts are spear points with sockets, stems, and other hafting devices; fishing implements, such as harpoons, gorges, and hooks; spuds, celts, adzes, gouges, wedges, chisels, and other wood-working tools; and general processing tools, like awls, drills, spatulas, and a variety of knife forms (Figure 3.6). Pendants, tubular and spherical beads, C-shaped bracelets, and other ornaments were also made in smaller numbers from native copper.

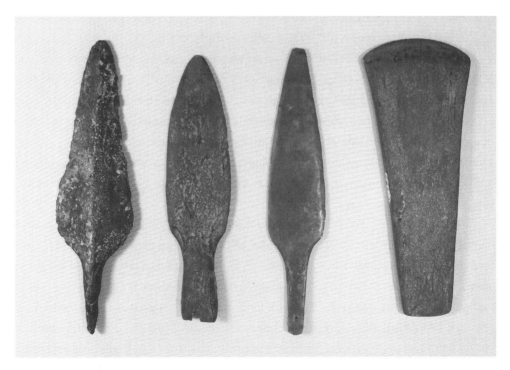

Figure 3.6. Old copper artifacts.
Courtesy of the Minnesota Historical Society. Printed with permission.

Since these particular types of copper artifacts seem to have a limited distribution in space and time, archaeologists assign them to an Old Copper complex.[28] Old Copper artifacts are widely distributed throughout the upper Great Lakes region and westward into central Canada, though they are most abundant in northeastern Wisconsin. Their precise dating in Minnesota remains conjectural, for nearly all are surface finds or were discovered accidentally in nonarchaeological excavations, such as the digging of a cellar. For the most part, they are thought to date between 3800 and 1200 BC, even though some artifacts in the rough form of Late Paleoindian points could date to the early Middle Archaic period or even earlier. After 1200 BC, copper, except for an occasional knife or awl, was mainly used to make items of personal adornment, such as beads and ear ornaments.

The majority of the sixteen burials assigned to the Archaic period at the time of this writing are likely Late Archaic in age. I concentrate here on two of those burials, Sauk Valley Man and the Voight site, both of which have associated radiocarbon dates. Other possible Late Archaic burials in the state include the Runck burial (21BW07) in Brown County, the Peterson Lake burial (21GR04) in Grant County, the Pelican Lake burial (21PO03) and Rooney Mound site (21PO13) in Pope County, the Eck burial (21HE92) in Hennepin County, the Red Ocher burial (21BK9001) in Becker County, and the Pelican Rapids burial (21OT79) in Otter Tail County.[29]

The Sauk Valley Man (21OT01) burial was discovered in a gravel pit in 1935 and has since been radiocarbon dated to about 2900 BC. A study of the skeleton by physical anthropologists found that the male, who was about forty to fifty years old at death, had arthritis, moderate to heavy wear on the teeth, no dental caries, and extremely robust postcranial bones "evidencing enthesopathies at areas of muscle attachment [enthesopathy is a disorder of bone attachments] and osteoarthritis [a common degenerative joint disease]."[30] In the original study, Jenks and Wilford estimated that the individual was about 5 feet 6 inches tall.[31]

The Voight site (21WN15), which is on a terrace of the Mississippi River in Winona County, has a calibrated radiocarbon date of 684 BC.[32] The excavated portion of the site contained four pits each with one to four individuals, red ocher, and worked bone and stone, but no pottery. Two subadults were buried in burial pit 1, and a young female with an unborn or stillborn child in the pelvic area, in pit 2, which also included a piece of unworked copper, shell, and animal bones (including two probable bird claws). A young adult female in an upright or seated position, three clam shells, and red ocher were in pit 3. Burial pit 4 contained one to three adult males and one, probably female, adolescent, along with red ocher, and two quartzite points or knives, one of which was with a burial. A clam shell was beside one skull. Included in the dirt fill of the pit were three possible bone gouges or awls, two pieces of deer antler with smoothed and worn tips, two possible fleshers, two other worked bones, a worked beaver incisor, a drilled canine tooth, and other small animal bones. No caries were present in the teeth of two females examined by physical anthropologists.

MIDDLE AND LATE ARCHAIC LIFEWAYS

As the two preceding sections of this chapter document, the archaeological records of the Late Archaic and especially the Middle Archaic in Minnesota remain underexamined and poorly understood. My reconstruction of the lifeways of hunter-gatherers during these periods remains conjectural, then, and largely based on trends predicted by Binford's Terrestrial Model, as I understand them. Nonetheless, samples of these archaeological records seem remarkably consistent with the projections of the model.

The three lifeways I believe were present in Minnesota during the Middle Holocene and earlier Late Paleoindian–Early Archaic period—Coniferous Forest Game Hunter, Deciduous Forest Game Hunter, and Early Pedestrian Bison Hunter—are those of classic hunter-gatherers who use mobility as their primary strategy for maintaining subsistence security (thus the difficulty in locating and sampling their archaeological record). In Late Glacial boreal and more recent environments in Minnesota to the end of the Middle Archaic–Middle Holocene period, the Terrestrial Model projects the following: subsistence throughout Minnesota was primarily dependent on terrestrial mammals; food storage was minimal, as food produced each day was consumed daily and groups moved frequently from one food patch of the habitat to another (this is what archaeologists call an immediate return subsistence system); mobility was used as the primary strategy for maintaining subsistence security; residential sites were positioned in the landscape to facilitate the search for food on an encounter basis; a minimal group size was favored (since food was only minimally stored, larger group sizes would result in greater mobility costs in the search for adequate food energy—and Minnesota was not a food-rich area compared to areas to the south); an ethnic group's home range was quite large; and demographic packing was not yet a problem.

Binford's Terrestrial Model and correlations among his sample of 390 historic hunter-gatherer groups and environmental variables project what some of the details of these lifeways may have been like. I concentrate here on the size of home ranges and foraging areas, degree of mobility, group size, division of labor, and type of political leadership. Other characteristics of foraging groups are discussed in chapters 4, 5, 6, and 8.

If we assume that hunter-gatherers are opportunistic foragers who adjust to environmental situations by maximizing energetic return and minimizing subsistence insecurity, then Binford's Terrestrial Model and his study of ethnographic data should provide useful approximations of the size of the area utilized exclusively by an ethnic group, the degree of mobility of that group, and the size of the social units that made up that group at various times in yearly cycles, among other values of hunter-gatherer variables like type of political leadership, division of labor, and nature and complexity of technology.

Let's start with size of home ranges and of foraging areas within those ranges. In general, foragers in unpacked situations who have an emphasis on terrestrial animal subsistence tend to have very large home ranges compared to hunter-gatherers with some other subsistence emphasis. According to Binford's formula for the size of the home range utilized exclusively by an ethnic group, home ranges in the state ranged between 5,800 and 25,000 square miles.[33] For modeling purposes, he estimated the foraging area that a dispersed family group was able to exploit on a daily basis within this larger ethnic area to be a circle with a total area of about 87 square miles.

Since food resources in Minnesota were less abundant in general than in states to the south, we can anticipate that the mobility level of social groups in the state was high. Using his ethnographic data base and Terrestrial Model, Binford also provides estimates of number of moves per year (five to thirty-two), distance per move (13 to 27 miles), and the total number of miles transversed by a group during an average annual round of residential movement (more than 186 miles) for foragers in general who are primarily dependent on terrestrial animals. Among northern groups in boreal environments the estimates are thirteen to fifteen moves per year of a distance of 19 to 34 miles, for a total distance moved per year on average of between 350 and 450 miles. The latter figures may be good estimates for Minnesota's Late Glacial boreal forest and northern forests during the early and middle Holocene epochs (Paleoindian through Middle Archaic periods). In general, too, there is usually considerably more spatial separation between daily foraging areas among groups primarily exploiting terrestrial animal resources than modeled for people not primarily dependent on terrestrial animals. In Minnesota it seems likely that transportation aids, like canoes or dogs, were already being used during this period.

Most hunter-gatherer groups disperse and aggregate in a patterned manner throughout the year. Binford identifies three kinds of common social units among hunter-gatherers and provides estimates of the optimal size range of these social units for groups whose focus is terrestrial animals. The smallest social unit is made up of families or households that work largely independently of similar social units during the most dispersed phase of their annual settlement-subsistence cycle. These groups tend to range in numbers between 9 and 38 people, with most groups ranging between 12 and 21 people. A somewhat larger social unit is made up of people who live together in a camp during the most aggregated phase of the settlement-subsistence cycle. These groups are variable in size, but they tend to consist of less than 70 people. The largest social unit among hunter-gatherers is made up of people who gather annually or at least every several years for reasons other than subsistence-related activities. These groups tend to range in size between 34 and 592 people. The latter aggregation of people may be considered an ethnic group, which is defined as "an association of on-the-ground hunter-gatherer groups that are economically and reproductively integrated within a wider system."[34]

In general, the sizes of social units of all three types are larger for sedentary peoples in politically complex societies and for plant-dependent people in high-productivity settings than for mobile foragers. Although hunter-gatherers dependent on terrestrial animals tend to have very large home ranges and dispersed-phase social units compared to peoples dependent on terrestrial plants or aquatic resources, the size of their ethnic groups is small, and their population density per home range is quite small (less than 1.59 persons, but mainly between 0.57 and 1.0, per 39 square miles, which is below the packing threshold). In northern boreal forests the size of social units during the most dispersed phase of the settlement-subsistence system optimally ranges between 12 and 22 people (which is relatively large), between 36 and 57 people during the most aggregated phase, and between 126 and 230 people at periodic regional aggregations.

Binford also mentions that a small seasonally dispersed social unit among groups that use residential mobility as their primary strategy in hunting terrestrial animals usually consists of six or fewer families that reside together in six or fewer household-sized units; that these family units are not necessarily sheltered together, though they sometimes are; and that the size of the social unit tends to increase as the length of the growing season decreases.[35] These conclusions are generalizations for "average" situations and, therefore, should be prefaced with "other things being equal."

Significant organizational differences also exist between terrestrial hunting and plant-dependent people, with the strategy and tactics involved in hunting terrestrial animals accounting for a substantial amount of the organized variability among these hunter-gatherer ethnic groups. For instance, among classic foragers, while males and females are both food producers, they are involved in different but complementary subsistence tasks, with males tending to work more in the food procurement aspect of life (64 to 91 percent in general, and 100 percent from terrestrial animals) than women. In Binford's Terrestrial Model, which applies to classic foragers before resource intensification, a seasonally dispersed social unit generally engages in an average of two foraging expeditions per day, one female and one male, with females having an average of three adults per work party, and men an average of two to three adults in a hunting party. While the total modeled foraging area of a typical group at any one time is a circle bounding about 87 square miles, the foraging radius of a female foraging party is about 4.2 miles, and of a male party about 6.2 miles in any particular day.

In general these are egalitarian groups with local autonomy and "show me" leaders whose leadership is dependent on performance, which is crucial to subsistence security in higher latitudes. In Binford's words, "Knowledge and its tactical use in planning for the capture of both terrestrial and aquatic animals, coupled with skill in using the [available] technology, are the two essential qualities that a leader must possess."[36]

By the Late Archaic period in Minnesota (3000–500 BC) new lifeways appear throughout the state in conjunction with (but probably not dependent on) the establishment of modern climate and vegetation patterns. These lifeways are the Proto–Wild Rice Harvester lifeway (circa 3000 BC–AD 1200), the Proto-Horticulturalist lifeway (circa 3000 BC–AD 1000), and the Late Pedestrian Bison Hunter lifeway (circa 3000 BC–AD 1000). These lifeways represent the third phase of the proposed four-phase sequence of lifeways in precontact Minnesota. The characteristic feature of these lifeways is ever-increasing resource intensification in a socially packed environment.

The Proto–Wild Rice Harvester lifeway emerged when subsistence intensification began in response in large part to population packing brought about by ever-growing numbers of bands in the mosaic of conifer-hardwood forests and pine stands in the central and northern regions of the state. The content of site components associated with the lifeway shows evidence of the increased exploitation of second-order foods, such as fish and wild rice. The lifeway persisted through the Late Archaic, Initial Woodland, and early part of the Terminal Woodland in this central-northern area of Minnesota. The Proto-Horticulturalist lifeway is the southern counterpart of the Proto–Wild Rice Harvester. It was centered in the southeastern, deciduous forest quarter of the state. Second-order foods included fish, mussels, and domesticated plants, like sunflower, amaranth, and squash. This lifeway persisted through the Late Archaic, Initial Woodland, and Terminal Woodland in this area. As in the Proto–Wild Rice Harvester and Proto-Horticulturalist lifeways, the Late Pedestrian Bison Hunter lifeway was characterized by increased exploitation of second-order foods and a more regular occupation of some seasonal settlement sites. This lifeway persisted in the western tallgrass prairies of the state through the Late Archaic, Initial Woodland, and Terminal Woodland periods.

According to Binford's research, resource intensification among terrestrial animal hunters occurs when the density of persons exceeds 1.59 individuals per 39 square miles.[37] He defines intensification as "any tactical or strategic practice that increases the production of food per unit area."[38] Hunter-gatherers are able to increase resource production in many ways. Among these are investing more labor in food-acquiring activities, shifting exploitation to species occurring in greater concentration in space, shifting subsistence dependence from animals of larger body size to aquatic species or plant species (or some combination of all three food sources), developing storage strategies, and growing domesticated plants in small gardens. Production-related processes like these play out at different tempos and in different environment-based specifics in different regions of the world and even in different habitats in a large state like Minnesota.

Long-term trends that may have accompanied the playing out of these production-related processes in Minnesota include a reduction in both home range size and the overall mobility of social units, a decrease in subsistence-related weapons as packing reduced dependence on large game resources, an increase in the numbers of people in an ethnic group (and thus greater demand for food), an increase in the number of ethnic groups as overall population in the state increased (further reducing home ranges and intensifying packing), the adoption of a "delayed return" subsistence strategy in which foods are stored or otherwise kept in reserve (as compared to the immediate return system practiced earlier), and an increase in the size of small, dispersed social units at least in part as a response to an increase in the bulk processing of foods like fish and wild rice for storage.[39] As some characteristics of the environment became irrelevant or less important, others became more relevant and important as intensification increased. In Binford's terms, the effective environment—the components of the gross environment that human groups most closely interact with—shifted during this phase of resource intensification.[40] In their research, archaeologists have to be sensitive, of course, to this shift in environmental emphasis, for work station locations and functions were shifting, too.

In archaeological research, we rely on trends like these to provide visible signs in the archaeological record of the process of intensification. Typical signs of intensification include a shift in exploitation from one type of biotic community to another (in this case from terrestrial animals to aquatic resources); evidence of reduction in the size of food procurement areas (perhaps evident in the food remains in sites); an increase in subsistence diversity; evidence of increased exploitation of food resources that require a greater investment of labor to procure and process; an increase in labor in the form of technological aids, such as traps and facilities for food procurement; changes of social group sizes at all levels of observation; evidence of greater sedentism (evident perhaps in longer stays at seasonal camps and more investment in the construction of dwellings); the appearance of larger residential camps in new strategic locations to better exploit a changing array of food resources; evidence of food storage; change in household size, since household size is responsive to intensification through labor unit expansion; the appearance of larger seasonal camps; and evidence of claims by social groups to ancestral rights to an area, most evident in the appearance of visible clusters of aboveground burial mounds.

In Minnesota the Late Archaic exhibits the onset of this process of resource intensification. Social groups still followed in general the settlement-subsistence practices of their Middle Archaic ancestors. Terrestrial game hunting based on an encounter strategy remained important, for upland campsites are still common. However, evidence of diversification is abundant as well in the form of new technologies, like fishing gear and plant-processing equipment, the presence of the remains of domesticated plants at several southern sites, and the first appearance of communal (if not aboveground) burial sites.

As later chapters will show, the tempo and characteristics of resource intensification were quite uneven and different in the state's five major resource regions. Of special interest is the presence of climate-based latitudinal "bottlenecks" just south and north of the state, which give the archaeology of Minnesota a distinctive and, I believe, unexpected flavor.

INITIAL WOODLAND PERIOD

CIRCA 1000–500 BC TO AD 500–700

CHAPTER 4

Southern Deer Hunters, Gardeners, and Bison Hunters

Initial Woodland Adaptations in Southern Minnesota

For many years the commencement of a new cultural tradition in the Eastern Woodlands, the Woodland, was defined by the first appearance of pottery containers, earthen burial mounds, and agriculture. Information gathered within the past thirty years has clearly demonstrated that these once diagnostic traits had already made their first appearance in areas of the Eastern Woodlands in the earlier Late and even Middle Archaic. Both indigenous and tropical plants appear in a variety of contexts throughout the midcontinent at least by the Late Archaic, and earthen burial mounds have been reported from a number of Middle Archaic sites south of Minnesota. Fiber-tempered pottery makes its first appearance in otherwise Archaic contexts by at least 2500 BC in Georgia, Florida, and other southern states.[1] Today, the commencement of the Woodland cultural tradition in Minnesota is simply defined by the first appearance of pottery containers. This commencement in the state does not coincide with the appearance of new lifeways but with the continued intensification of food resource activities initiated in the Late Archaic period.

In the American Midwest, the Woodland tradition is divided into Early, Middle, and Late periods. These divisions are based for the most part on socioeconomic developments that occurred in Illinois, Ohio, and other lower-tier midwestern states. In the northern Midwest, the same developments were delayed in their appearance, often by hundreds of years, occurred only in attenuated forms, or did not appear at all. Furthermore, unique adaptations and artifacts appear in the prairies, deciduous forests, and mixed hardwood forests of Minnesota that have no specific counterparts in the traditional lower-tier zone to the south. As a result, I prefer the use of the terms Initial and Terminal Woodland rather than Early, Middle, and Late Woodland as organizing concepts to describe Woodland developments in Minnesota for all resource regions of the state except for the Southeastern region. Although awkward at times, these concepts stress the unique accomplishments of Native Americans in Minnesota rather than their marginality to events and processes that occurred in more resource-rich environments to the south.

THE INITIAL WOODLAND ARCHAEOLOGICAL RECORD IN SOUTHEASTERN MINNESOTA

The Southeastern resource region coincides closely with that corner of the state east and south of St. Cloud. This corner with its milder climate, patches of deciduous forests, oak parkland, and prairie, and major river systems more closely resembled the heartland of the Midwest in Illinois, Indiana, and Ohio during the Initial Woodland period than did other regions of the state. To facilitate review, I divide the archaeological record of the Initial Woodland in southeastern Minnesota into three periods, Early Woodland (500–200 BC), Havana-related Middle Woodland (200 BC–AD 200), and Late Middle Woodland (AD 200–500). Since little systematic research has been carried out in southeastern Minnesota on the archaeological record of this period following Lloyd Wilford's pioneering effort, the dates and the content of these periods remain tentative.

Early Woodland, 500–200 BC

The most easily recognizable diagnostics of the Early Woodland period in southeastern Minnesota are thick-walled (often thicker than 1 centimeter) La Moille Thick pottery and, perhaps, somewhat more recent Black Sand–like pottery.[2] The surface of La Moille Thick is cordmarked, with distinct vertical to oblique cordmarking on the exterior surface, and horizontal to oblique cordmarking on the interior surface (Figure 4.1). La Moille Thick may be associated with a variety of straight-stemmed weapon points, the most common of which are Kramer points. Black Sand series vessels are decorated with narrow trailed lines (Black Sand Incised) or, less commonly, with finger or fingernail impressions (Sisters Creek Punctate). These latter ceramics are associated with weapon points with rounded, contracting stems, like Waubesa Stemmed (Figure 4.2).

La Moille Thick pottery resembles Marion Thick and other thick pottery types that are thought to be the earliest pottery in lower-tier midwestern states.[3] In the central Illinois valley, the Marion phase is dated from about 800 BC to 400 BC. However, thick ceramics like later Black Sand–like ceramics seem to have spread out to the north and west in a time-transgressive manner, with more distant phases more recent in time, which has implications for the dating of La Moille Thick pottery in Minnesota.

La Moille Thick pottery has been found at only five sites in the state: the La Moille Rockshelter in Winona County, the Schilling site on Grey Cloud Island in Washington County, the Kunz site in northeastern Watonwan County, the NSPII site in Goodhue County, and the Enno Schaeffer site in Faribault County.[4] Three of the five sites (La

Figure 4.1. A La Moille Thick pottery vessel from the La Moille rockshelter in Winona County. Courtesy of the Wilford Archaeology Laboratory, University of Minnesota.

Figure 4.2. Stemmed projectile points. *Left to right:* Kramer, Waubesa, Adena.
Courtesy of the Minnesota Historical Society. Printed with permission.

Moille, NSPII, and Schilling) are in the Mississippi River valley, and the other two (Kunz and Enno Schaeffer) in the Blue Earth River watershed on the western edge of southeastern Minnesota. Kunz is on the Watonwan River, a western tributary of the Blue Earth River, and Enno Schaefer is on the Blue Earth River, which joins the Minnesota River at Mankato. Thus, all known La Moille phase sites have a strong riverine orientation.

At present, site types include open-air camps (of some sort) and a rockshelter, the La Moille Rockshelter. La Moille was a deeply stratified rockshelter in the bluffs along the Mississippi River in Winona County before complete destruction by highway construction. When excavated by Wilford in 1939, the 15 feet of stratified deposit in the rockshelter contained both Late Archaic material at the bottom and Early Woodland material in the upper levels.[5] Sherds of a now-reconstructed vessel were found in the upper levels above straight-stemmed and side-notched projectile points (see Figure 4.1). Wilford considered the site a long-term fishing camp because of the predominance of fish in all levels. The remains of small mammals, turtles, and mussels were also found in all levels.

Havana-Related Middle Woodland, 200 BC–AD 200

Two Havana-related Middle Woodland period phases have been proposed in Minnesota, Howard Lake and Sorg. Howard Lake is a poorly understood and rarely investigated Middle Woodland phase centered on the major rivers, lakes, and wetlands of southeastern Minnesota. Its region of greatest artifact concentration appears to be the wet prairies and lakes of southern Anoka County just north of Minneapolis–St. Paul, where concentrations of large mounds and small habitation sites occur in some areas.[6] The Sorg phase is another understudied Middle Woodland complex in southeastern Minnesota. Its main center of site concentration is around Spring Lake, a Mississippi River floodplain lake south of St. Paul.[7]

The most diagnostic traits of both phases are wide-mouth jars that have thick vessel walls (6 to 12 millimeters), straight rims, slightly constricted necks, somewhat rounded shoulders, and subconoidal bottoms that resemble decorated varieties of pottery in Havana-Hopewell complexes in Illinois (Figure 4.3). As in other areas broadly north of the Illinois heartland of the Havana tradition, only selected traits of the tradition seem to be present in Minnesota and then only late in the classic portion (circa AD 100–200) of the sequence.[8] As in southwestern Wisconsin, the most common types of Havana pottery in Howard Lake and Sorg ceramic assemblages are regional varieties of Naples Stamped, a decorated Havana ware. A dentate variety of Naples Stamped with straight dentate stamps, ovoid stamps, trailed lines and bosses, and inwardly beveled lips is by far the most common variety in these samples. Smaller numbers of the cord-wrapped stick variety of Naples Stamped are also present.

Figure 4.3. A Havana-related pottery vessel from the Sorg site.
Courtesy of the Science Museum of Minnesota.

In Illinois, Havana assemblages commonly contain two distinctive lithic traits, medium- to large-sized corner-notched projectile points, like Snyders, Norton, and Manker, and a true blade technology. By-products of the blade technology include distinctive pyramidal cores and small blades that are often called ribbon flakes because of their long, thin, narrow shape. Broad-bladed Dickson knives, rectangular chipped stone "hoes," and the extensive use of exotic cherts are other common features of Havana lithic assemblages.[9]

In Minnesota, the diagnostic features of Illinois Havana lithic assemblages seem either absent, such as the blade technology and polyhedral cores, or underrepresented, such as Snyders and Manker points, in Havana-related assemblages. A 1977 archaeological survey in Anoka and Isanti Counties, the northern heartland of the phase in Minnesota, identified only two Snyders-like points in collections. Rather, most points that seem to be associated with local Havana-related assemblages resemble regional varieties of southern Dickson and Northern Plains Pelican Lake and Samantha points.

Homer Hruby in a 1977 study of the lithic assemblage from the Anderson habitation site, the type-site of the phase, concluded the following: there was technological continuity with earlier Archaic and Woodland assemblages, perhaps because of the extensive use of glacial cobbles as a source of raw materials; a wide variety of extractive technologies were used as indicated by the large number of light cutting and scraping tools with multiple working edges; the occupants of the site were probably highly mobile, for the tools were relatively small, had multiple working edges, and exhibited a large amount of flaking; and most of the material was locally available, although formal tools, such as points and scrapers, tended to be made of high-quality material like Knife River flint and Hixton silicified sandstone. In sum, Howard Lake phase lithic assemblages seem to represent a local tradition to which some Northern Plains and southern Havana traits were added.

The typical Havana burial area south of Minnesota is a group of two or three to fifteen earthen burial mounds that are conical in shape. Mounds vary widely in diameter and height, with a few very large mounds about 30 feet in height. Larger mounds in a group (those over 5 feet in height) nearly always contain diagnostic Havana-Hopewell burial items, such as copper earspools, pan pipes, and celts, perforated bear canines, platform pipes, pearl beads, and elongated, often stemmed, nonutilitarian bifaces.[10] Primary extended burial is the most common form of burial in larger mounds, though cremation and secondary bundle burials also occur and may be more common in smaller mounds. A secondary bundle burial is one in which the flesh from the skeleton was removed before burial, and the remaining bones gathered and buried together in a bundle (probably in a skin or other material that has not survived through time). Burials were usually placed in rectangular, subfloor tombs lined or covered with logs or bark.

Little is known about the internal structure and content of Howard Lake phase mounds, for few have been professionally excavated, and no Sorg phase mortuary sites are presently known, though mounds are present at some multicomponent sites with a Sorg component. Nonetheless, archaeologists generally assume—based on the size of Havana-Hopewell mounds in Illinois and Ohio—that the largest mounds in this area of the state, which are among the largest in the state, date to the Havana-related Middle Woodland period. They typically are conical in shape and range in height from about 12 to 20 feet and in base diameter from about 80 to 100 feet.[11]

The following three sites are classic expressions of the Howard Lake phase as it is currently understood.

The Anderson (21AN8) habitation site is on an extensive sand ridge at the southern end of Howard Lake near the Rice Creek outlet in the Anoka Sand Plain.[12] Repeated salvage excavations at the site have revealed the presence of Paleoindian through late prehistoric materials, making Anderson one of the most continuously used sites in the state. While decorated Havana-related ceramics are well represented at the site, Havana lithics, such as Snyders points and Dickson knives, seem absent.

The Howard Lake mound site (21AN1) is located about 4,000 feet northeast of the Anderson site on the eastern edge of Howard Lake. The site consists of one large elongated mound (125 feet long, 90 feet wide, and 19 feet high) and at least five smaller mounds.[13] An excavation of one of the smaller mounds (Mound 3) by Wilford in 1950 revealed the presence of at least nineteen overlapping bundle burials and one cremation in a large, rectangular submound pit. Red ocher was associated with six burials, and a possible clay/ocher mask with one. Although no Havana-Hopewell artifacts were associated with the pit, Howard Lake phase materials were in the mound fill.

The Indian Mounds Park site (21RA10) is on a bluff overlooking the Mississippi River in St. Paul. Sixteen of the eighteen mounds in the cluster were excavated in the second half of the nineteenth century.[14] While some of the mounds likely date to the Late Woodland period, others contained a combination of Hopewellian-like traits, including exotic material (red ocher, galena), hammered sheet copper over a possible pan-pipe, a clay death mask, a drilled bear canine, and mortuary features like stone crypts and log tombs. Mound 12, which contained the greatest number of Hopewellian-like traits, was a conical mound 51 feet in diameter and 8.5 feet high.

Late Middle Woodland, AD 200–500

The transition from Havana-related complexes to Late Woodland complexes in southeastern Minnesota and the Upper Mississippi valley in general was, apparently, a gradual process among resident Native American populations. Continuity between Middle and Late Woodland complexes is particularly evident in design treatments on ceramic vessels and in projectile point types. For example, new ceramic wares, such as Linn ware, are demonstrably regional derivatives of earlier wares that retain design treatments and motifs of earlier Havana wares. Because of this stylistic continuity, phases of the period are generally considered Middle rather than Late Woodland. Since the archaeological record of the late Middle Woodland period in southeastern Minnesota remains largely unknown, I summarize traits of the closely related Allamakee and Millville phases of northeastern Iowa and southwestern Wisconsin, respectively. I assume that traits of these phases, if not the phases themselves, extend up into southeastern Minnesota.[15]

Despite a paucity of information, several trends are apparent in site components of this period that have been studied. First, the widespread presence of Havana-related ceramics is replaced by a series of more spatially restricted derivatives.[16] This process of regionalization or progressive cultural differentiation is apparent in phases like Allamakee in northeastern Iowa and Millville in southwestern Wisconsin. Second, the cultural practices of these late Middle Woodland peoples are less elaborate than those of the Havana-related people discussed in the previous section. For instance, while the construction of earthen mounds continues, burial practices become simpler, and grave goods rare or so undiagnostic that it is difficult to assign some mounds to specific archaeological phases with confidence. Finally, significant changes occur in the form, technology, and surface modification of ceramic vessels. For example, vessels have more globular bodies and complex rim profiles, walls are thinner and temper is much finer, and exterior surfaces are cordmarked and become decorated with corded instruments.

Linn ware, the thin-walled diagnostic ceramic of the period in this region of the Upper Mississippi valley, is characterized by the retention of Havana-related dentate-stamped decoration early in the period, as in Levsen Stamped, and reduction in decoration late in the period, as in Spring Hollow Plain and Cordmarked. Levsen Stamped, which is characterized by "bands of dentate, or sometimes cord-wrapped stick, oblique impressions bounded on both sides by horizontal impressions of the same instrument," is thought to succeed Naples Dentate Stamped in this region (Figure 4.4).[17]

Classic Steuben weapon points with shallow side notches seem to be carryovers in biface technology in northeastern Iowa and southwestern Wisconsin from the Havana-related period early in the phase (circa AD 250–400), while smaller, shallow-side-notched Ansell points appear late in the sequence (Figure 4.5). True arrow points may appear in the latest portion of the period. Scrapers, drills, knives, and some ground stone axes are other tools in the stone tool assemblage, while flake tool lithic technology increases in importance through time.

Burial in the late Middle Woodland period in this region of the Upper Mississippi valley was in relatively low, circular earthen mounds. David Benn and William Green summarize the characteristics of Allamakee phase mounds as follows:

> Allamakee phase mounds . . . have a distinctive character. Hopewellian influences in McGregor mounds, such as subfloor rectangular burial chambers, rock alignments, and exotic artifacts, gradually disappeared during the Allamakee phase, to be replaced by somewhat more haphazardly constructed features of rock altars and layers, individual burial pits, broadcast bones in layers, evidence of burning soil and rocks, crematories, and inclusion of more Linn ware vessels—especially Lane Farm vessels (Benn 1979:61; Logan 1976).[18]

Figure 4.4. A Linn ware Levsen Stamped rim sherd.
Courtesy of the Minnesota Historical Society.
Printed with permission.

Figure 4.5. Steuben projectile points.
Courtesy of the Minnesota Historical Society.
Printed with permission.

During the period, burials were also placed in pits not covered by mounds, as at the Millville site, where five individuals were found in four pits.[19] The three adults were women ranging in age at death from forty to fifty-five years old. They were buried in semiflexed positions with no special grave offerings. The women were 5 foot 1 inch to 5 foot 3 inches tall at death and showed evidence of extreme tooth wear and loss of teeth from periodontal disease, and of cradleboard flattening.

No late Middle Woodland burials have been reported for southeastern Minnesota, but I assume that when identified, they will share many of these same traits, as will habitation sites.

THE INITIAL WOODLAND ARCHAEOLOGICAL RECORD IN SOUTHWESTERN MINNESOTA

The beginning of the Woodland tradition in the prairies of southwestern Minnesota is marked by the initial presence of a small amount of ceramics similar to La Moille Thick and later by the widespread appearance of Fox Lake ceramics, which include incised-over-cordmarked vessels similar in appearance to Dane Incised and Black Sand vessels in Wisconsin and Illinois to the east and southeast, respectively. Unlike those ceramic wares, however, Fox Lake complex components seem to date to the Middle Woodland (here 200 BC to AD 700) rather than Early Woodland period (circa 500 to 200 BC), although there are few secure radiocarbon dates for the phase, mainly because of stratigraphic mixing within sites. Components of the complex are also found in eastern South Dakota and north-central Iowa.[20]

For the most part, sites with Fox Lake complex components are situated along the margins of lakes, streams, and rivers in the Prairie Lake resource region. Compared to other areas of the state, the complex seems to have been part of a very stable Plains-oriented bison-hunting lifeway that began in the earlier Archaic and continued through the following Lake Benton complex to circa AD 1200/1300. Although the evidence is mainly based on site location, it is assumed as well that Fox Lake people exploited nearby lacustrine and riverine resources. Unlike in other resource regions in the state at the time, there is no evidence that Fox Lake people buried their dead in earthen mounds, either as primary or intrusive interments. Nor is there evidence that these people were regular participants in regional interaction networks, such as the Havana-Hopewell exchange network. Unusual for Minnesota Woodland complexes, Fox Lake seems to have been a fully western Plains–oriented rather than eastern Midwest–oriented archaeological complex.

The absence of clear Fox Lake associations with burial mounds remains a puzzle, for mounds were being constructed in neighboring areas at the time. For instance, charred logs from the Morrison Mound site just north of the region have been radiocarbon dated to 690 BC. The Laurel mounds in northern Minnesota date at least as early as 20 BC, the Jamestown Mound in North Dakota to AD 20, and the Sny-Magill mound site in northeastern Iowa to 550 BC. Within the Prairie Lake region, the earliest radiocarbon date for a mound is AD 875 for the Round Mound on Lake Traverse.

Except for their distinctive ceramics, the traits of Fox Lake complex assemblages have been difficult to isolate because of extensive component mixing in sites. Most sites that contain a component of the complex also often contain Archaic and later Lake Benton, Cambria, and Oneota components. The definition of Woodland complexes in the Prairie Lake region is mainly based on analyses of artifact assemblages from the Fox Lake, Pedersen, and Arthur sites. The Fox Lake site is on Weber Island at the west end of Fox Lake about a mile north of the town of Sherburne in Martin County. Pedersen is on an island in Lake Benton 90 miles northwest of Fox Lake. The Arthur site is located 25 miles southwest of Fox Lake on the east side of Lake Okoboji East in Iowa.

The composition and date of the earliest ceramic assemblages in the prairies of southwestern Minnesota remain poorly understood. Ceramics similar in appearance to La Moille Thick are thought by Scott Anfinson on typological grounds to be the earliest ceramics in the Prairie Lake region.[21] However, these examples are not common and differ in certain details from La Moille Thick, such as the presence of smooth, rather than cordmarked, rim interiors. They have well-defined vertical cordmarking on the exterior surface, thick body walls (circa 10 millimeters), and decoration limited to a single horizontal row of fingernail impressions on the rim. Thick, fingernail-impressed sherds have been found at the Fox Lake site, the Mountain Lake site, and the Kunz site.

Fox Lake complex ceramics consist of moderate- to small-sized vessels with conoidal to subconoidal bases, bold exterior cordmarking that is usually vertically oriented but may be oblique or horizontal, thick walls (6 to 12 millimeters), sand temper, and

Figure 4.6. Fox Lake phase rim sherd showing trailed line impressions.
Courtesy of the Minnesota Historical Society. Printed with permission.

slightly inverted to everted rims (Figure 4.6).[22] About two-thirds of the known vessels have some form of decoration formed in decreasing order of importance by trailing, bossing, punctuating, and dentate or cord-wrapped-stick stamping. These various decorative techniques were applied either alone or in combination. Rim interiors are occasionally decorated with a single band of short, vertically oriented tool or cord-wrapped-stick impressions immediately below the lip, and lips are occasionally notched with tool or cord-wrapped-stick impressions.

In general Fox Lake ceramics appear to document a relatively stable ceramic tradition that lasted perhaps a thousand years. Thick vessel walls, sand temper, oriented cordmarking, and conoidal vessel forms are dominant throughout the phase, while decorative techniques gradually change in preference and elaboration, though punctates, bosses, trailed lines, and cord-wrapped-stick stamping remain in use throughout the phase.

Chipped stone tools associated with the Fox Lake complex appear to be common midwestern and Plains forms of scrapers, knives, drills, flake tools, and choppers.[23] No particular type of chipped stone tool is found only in components of this phase and not in other neighboring phases or archaeological cultures.

The relative percentages by site of types of lithic tools based on inferred functions provide tentative information on site function and even seasonality. End and side scrapers, which usually account for half of all chipped stone tools, are the most numerous stone tools at every Prairie Lake region Woodland tradition habitation site except Pedersen. Arthur, Big Slough, Synsteby, Mountain Lake, and Pedersen have relatively high percentages of projectile points among all stone tools, while Fox Lake and Oakwood Lakes have less than 15 percent. About half of the stone tools at Pedersen are projectile points. Bifaces, most of which were probably used as knives, usually account for about 20 percent of the chipped stone tool sample. Specialized tools for drilling, punching, and engraving are not common in most Fox Lake components, although utilized flakes may have served these functions.

In general the chipped stone tool assemblages reflect an emphasis on animal capture and processing activities like cutting meat and scraping hides. It must be stressed again that all of the sites discussed here are multicomponent, so overall tool percentages may not accurately reflect component percentages. Most of the sites have major Initial Woodland components, however, and seem to have relatively consistent tool percentages through all excavation layers.

Ground stone tools include full-grooved mauls, grooved and ungrooved celts or axes, hammerstones, grinding stones, nutting stones, and abrading or sharpening stones. Use of ground stone tools was not extensive, for only a few examples are in assemblages from each site. For instance, two grinding stones, two celts, three hammerstones, and two sharpening stones were recovered from Fox Lake levels at the Fox Lake site, but only a single ground stone maul was in corresponding levels at Pedersen (Figure 4.7).

In general summary of a complicated situation, Fox Lake projectile points exhibit more eastern affinities early in the phase and more western affinities late in the phase, although there is much geographic variation within the region. Early Fox Lake stemmed points usually have expanding stems and resemble eastern Midwest types like Monona Stemmed, Steuben Stemmed, Durst Stemmed, and Apple Blossom Stemmed.[24] Corner-notched points are clearly associated with the Fox Lake complex, but their affinities are more western than eastern. The closest similarities may be with Pelican Lake points, but there is much variety, and well-defined corner-notched points do not appear to be a dominant Fox Lake trait. Notably lacking are Snyders and Norton points, which are associated with Middle Woodland assemblages in the heartland of the Midwest.

Side-notched points are the most widely varied point form in the complex. The most common forms resemble Plains types like Avonlea, Besant, Hanna, and Oxbow. Points resembling contemporary side-notched midwestern types like Raddatz Side Notched, Manker Notched, and Gibson are rare. Finally, while unnotched triangular points are usually attributed to later time periods in the Midwest and Plains, there is a clear association of moderate-sized, usually isosceles triangular unnotched points with Fox Lake complex components.

Lithic debris from Fox Lake complex components seems dominated by chert, with lesser amounts of quartzite, chalcedony, and silicified sediment. The chert, quartzite, and silicified sediment are available locally. Much of the chalcedony is Knife River flint, which could come from quarries in western North Dakota, though this material is present in

Figure 4.7. Fox Lake phase projectile points.

Courtesy of Scott Anfinson, University of Minnesota.

drift in the Prairie Lake region till. Few specific types of bone tools are associated with the phase with certainty because of component mixing. However, awls, worked beaver teeth, bird-bone beads, and bone pendants are thought to be items in Fox Lake assemblages.[25]

INITIAL WOODLAND LIFEWAYS IN SOUTHERN MINNESOTA

According to Binford, modifications "in the quantities and changing tempos of energy that flow through the living system in which [humans] participate" can be conditioned by

> 1. Tactical shifts in the energy-capturing activities of the actors. 2. Increased competition among the actors both within and between socially integrated systems. 3. The appearance of new tactical variants that may include either technological aids or new organizational means of extracting energy or the matter necessary to such extraction, or energy conservation. [and] 4. Exploration of and experimentation with the extraction of energy from new or previously untapped sources of energy or the matter required to extract free energy from new energy sources.[26]

All of these processes—a refocusing of subsistence efforts, increased competition among regional social groups, new technologies, and the exploitation of new or at least previously underused food resources—are evident in lifeway trends during the Initial Woodland period in southern Minnesota. Before examining those processes, it is useful to review once again the climatic thresholds that mark off Minnesota as an environment for hunter-gatherers.

Binford identifies the following climate-related thresholds that bracket Minnesota between different environmental zones to the north and south:[27]

- The terrestrial plant threshold occurs at an ET value of about 12.75° and a latitude of 42.6°, which roughly corresponds to a habitat in which the average temperature during the coldest month of the year is −4°C. In warmer settings than this, plant-dominated subsistence strategies can be expected. In cooler settings plant-dominated subsistence strategies would not be expected, for accessible plant resources become less available. In Minnesota's region the threshold is marked by a horizontal line that stretches roughly between Sioux City and Dubuque in northern Iowa, and across the southern border of Wisconsin.
- The subpolar bottleneck occurs at an ET value of 11.53°, which is along Minnesota's northern border or slightly north of it. In Minnesota's region it corresponds with the commencement of boreal forest biomes that have substantial biomass but very little species diversity. (I come back to this particular threshold in chapter 5.)

The terrestrial plant threshold (or transition zone) is where a shift in diet occurs between terrestrial animal hunters to the north and terrestrial plant-dependent groups to the south. The threshold is important in understanding disparities in the tempo of change in the appearance of new technologies and subsistence-settlement shifts in Initial Woodland Minnesota as compared to areas south of the threshold. Among hunter-gatherers, the tempo of intensification is strongly related to habitat variability, for the abundance of food, its seasonal availability, and spacing across the landscape condition the growth of human populations and the degree of packing of social units. According to Binford,

> The temporal sequencing of packing-related events across geographic space should pattern strongly with habitat variability. Other things being equal, packing-related events—as well as other density dependent phenomena—should appear later in settings that are less conducive to high rates of population growth and more quickly in geotopographic settings such as islands, where there are physical constraints on population expansion.[28]

How large were populations in southern Minnesota during the Initial Woodland period? Although I do not have specific number estimates, Binford identifies two population density–dependent thresholds that give us a ballpark idea of what these numbers might have been, at least relative to pre-packing population densities. Hunter-gatherers who hunt terrestrial animals as a major subsistence strategy in pre-packed settings typically have population density values below circa 1.59 persons per 38.6 square miles (100 square kilometers) (most commonly between 0.5 and 1.0 persons per 100 square kilometers). Since the Southeastern Minnesota resource region is roughly 6,000 square miles in total area, this means that the number of foragers in this resource region before the process of intensification began was less than 250 people.

Hunting terrestrial animals as a major subsistence strategy appears to begin to decrease in response to increased packing pressure after a population density value of circa 1.59 persons per 38.6 square miles is exceeded. In Binford's sample of 390 ethnographic cases, no groups were dependent on terrestrial animals once the packing threshold of 9.098 persons per 38.6 square miles was reached. Hunter-gatherer groups with a population density value that exceeds 9.098 persons per 38.6 square miles would, according to Binford's Terrestrial Model, live side by side in closely packed foraging units, where a foraging unit has a total area of about 87 square miles (225.3 square kilometers). In areas south of Minnesota that are equivalent in size to the Southeastern Minnesota resource region, population sizes would be more than 1,300 people. Regardless of the reality of these figures, the implication is that there were most likely strong population imbalances between southeastern Minnesota and areas to the south below the terrestrial plant threshold.

The density-dependent threshold of 1.59 persons per 38.6 square miles marks the beginning of major changes in lifeways, then, a change that I propose began at the beginning of the Late Archaic and continued to AD 1000–1250 in the state. Packing may condition social unit sizes, mobility and storage patterns, tool diversity and complexity, the degree of use of tended facilities, subsistence and settlement systems, and division of labor between women and men, among other activities and behaviors. Since societies that are subjected to density-dependent changes can go off in quite different directions, depending on the resources (terrestrial animals or plants, for example) exploited at the time that density-dependent pressures to intensify begin occurring and the characteristics of particular environments, it is likely that the trajectories of change in southeastern, southwestern, and central and northern Minnesota were quite different. I begin this discussion by concentrating on general features of this change that might have characterized the lifeways of hunter-gatherers living north of the terrestrial plant threshold in southeastern Minnesota, who began to focus more on terrestrial plants in their diet. As Binford's data demonstrate, the preferred strategy of hunter-gatherers experiencing subsistence stress is, where possible, increased dependence on terrestrial plants, which seems most likely to have been the case in southeastern Minnesota.

Density-dependent trends that often occur among hunter-gatherer groups that shift their food resource focus to terrestrial plants from terrestrial animals following the onset of packing include many of the trends already mentioned in chapter 3. Relevant here are reduced social unit mobility; an increase in the number of economically independent groups in a region; a decrease in the size of home ranges; a geographical repositioning of residential camps to locations (food patches) where reliable plant foods could be obtained; an acceleration of packing as a consequence of spatial restructuring to increase plant dependence; longer-term occupation of seasonal camps, which are now usually organized in terms of residential units; an increase in diet breadth as more and more species are exploited (the broad-spectrum revolution); organizational changes in division of labor; and major changes in technology as different tools and processing procedures become necessary as a consequence of the shift in emphasis to different food resources.[29] These trends most likely occurred differentially in tempo and intensity among family-based social units in the region, for like families today some people adjust more readily to stress than do others. The substantial changes in archaeological patterning produced by these changes should be readily apparent during field survey, which has been the case in southeastern Minnesota.[30]

As the tasks involved in the acquisition of food change with the shift to a focus on plant foods, the technology and labor strategies associated with task performance change as well. Tool types and frequencies, as well as design complexity, typically change, a primary example being the gradual addition of pottery to the tool repertoire. Corresponding to the addition of pottery and perhaps a greater reliance on domesticated plants was a decrease in both the use and complexity of weapons used for subsistence purposes as the exploitation of terrestrial animal resources decreased. In my view these and other changes during the period do not represent emergent (stage) change in this southern tier of the state, as is sometimes thought, but rather incremental steps in a pattern of gradual intensification in the use of predominantly wild resources. Furthermore, as Binford stresses, the adoption of new types of tools and food-getting strategies during situations of resource intensification is not a process of haphazard and undirected "diffusion" but an anticipated consequence of the intensification process itself.[31]

A related issue is the importance in this area of Minnesota of tended facilities like fish weirs, fish nets, game blinds, and similar devices. Binford proposes that in unpacked settings there is a positive relationship between latitude and the number and complexity of tended facilities up to a threshold of about 42.6° (the terrestrial plant threshold at ET 12.75°), above which winters are significantly colder, and the growing season shorter.[32] Above this threshold the pattern reverses, and the number and complexity of tended facilities decreases. It is likely then that tended facilities in "unpacked" southeastern Minnesota were fewer in number and less complex than in areas to the south, though there is no evidence at present in Minnesota that can be used to test this suggestion. However, as the subsistence focus in southeastern Minnesota gradually shifted to a greater dependence on wild and domesticated plant resources (and most likely aquatic resources like fish, mussels, and wetland plants), the number and complexity of tended facilities in this area of the state would have increased as well. In southwestern Minnesota tended facilities like bison traps of one kind or another may actually have declined in number from their use in the Middle Archaic prairie period as people diversified their food resource base, though this also is speculation.

An associated trend that should be and is seen is the relocation of settlements (referred to as "spatial restructuring" by Binford) in response to density-dependent pressures. In southeastern Minnesota, this involved the more settled concentration of camps near wetland resources and along rivers to take advantage of denser patches of terrestrial plant and aquatic resources.[33] Here it is useful to recall that foragers in unpacked settings in southern Minnesota concentrated their encounter subsistence activities in upland landscapes. This pattern continued through the Late Archaic period, even though the processes of resource intensification had been set in motion. This shift in settlement pattern during the Initial Woodland period can be viewed as yet another sign, then, of the presence of a process of accelerating resource intensification, rather than as a dramatic shift in lifeways between the Archaic and Woodland periods, as proposed in traditional interpretations.

Changes in dependence on storage and in division of labor should be anticipated as well. Cost-benefit tactics for maximizing the time utility of human labor under conditions of subsistence stress, especially in environments with short growing seasons, include storage, construction of traps and other devices, delays in fulfilling social food obligations, and a shift from an immediate return to a delayed return subsistence system.[34]

Binford demonstrates that there is a strong relationship between storage and latitude.[35] Among his generalizations are the following: most groups of hunter-gatherers between 35° and 90° latitude make moderate to major investments in stored foods; there is in general greater reliance on stored foods as the length of the growing season decreases; the size of social units during the most dispersed phase of the annual cycle generally increases in response to the labor demands of bulk procurement and processing of food resources that are available for only brief periods of the year (or when the time between procurement and the onset of spoilage is short); food resources selected for storage are usually obtained near or at the end of the growing season; and where dried seeds are available in bulk, they are generally preferred for storage because they spoil less easily than food like fish and bison meat. According to his charts and generalizations, as the pressure to intensify the procurement of food resources increases, there should be a growing investment in storage and the annual duration of its use in a region like Minnesota that has a relatively short growing season.

The division of labor between men and women is significantly altered, too, as packing and subsistence diversity increase. Binford says,

> as packing increases and the option of moving into a new foraging area decreases, there is an increase in male efforts to maintain the previous levels of net returns from terrestrial animals and an expansion of male exploitation of aquatic resources. Males also share more of the labor costs with females, as both sexes pursue food resources that may have previously either been obtained primarily by females or not been exploited at all. Strategies of this kind indicate that the broad-spectrum revolution may be in operation.[36]

With the restructuring of the division of labor after the packing threshold is passed, males become involved in capturing and gathering a greater diversity of food resources, and females become involved to a greater extent in the preparation of food for storage. Another consequence of this restructuring is that species, like deer, that were traditionally obtained by males supply less and less of the diet.

To what extent did these shifts in division of labor, food procurement practices, size and composition of social units, and place of settlement influence the way Minnesota's Native Americans understood the world around them (Wilber's upper-left quadrant)? Were the changes dramatic, or did they occur so gradually that there was no psychological awareness of their changing lifeways? I wonder. The two left "interior" quadrants in Wilber's four-quadrant perspective remain a great black hole in the archaeology of people without writing who lived in the distant past.

A characteristic of Minnesota's stone tool technology that has puzzled me is the consistently poor quality of projectile points though time. While points of similar type in lower-tier midwestern states seem generally well made, those in Minnesota seem generally poorly made (Figure 4.8). What is the explanation for this difference? Perhaps, as I used to tell students, the points are poorly made because in Minnesota's frigid environment flint knappers had to wear mittens. But the answer is more likely to

Figure 4.8. Stone projectile points from Minnesota *(on right)* with similar types of points from southern-tier midwestern states. Kramer points are in the upper row; Snyders points in the lower row.
Courtesy of the Wilford Archaeology Laboratory, University of Minnesota.

be found somewhere in Binford's correlations. Future research will show whether this characteristic is a common feature of upper-tier midwestern states whose early precontact foragers depended on terrestrial animal resources, or a result of some other feature of the environment, like poor-quality stone materials.

This review of possible or even probable trends in intensification and its consequences during the Initial Woodland period in southern Minnesota is speculative, though I believe it is supported by the sample of the archaeological record for the region. Of course, each generalization and prediction must be qualified by "all other things being equal," which is a more problematic qualification than it may at first seem. Food abundance can be influenced by a range of natural events, such as catastrophic floods and wildfires, by diseases among food resource populations, and by major short-term climatic events, which are difficult to identify in the paleoecological record today. These factors could have unexpectedly reduced or enhanced both human and wild resource populations.

Lacking also is fine-grained information on the structure of within- and between-habitat variability across southern Minnesota. What food resources were actually present at what levels of abundance and ease of access? Did they occur in patches, and if so, how abundant were the patches? What was their pattern of distribution? It is perhaps too obvious to stress that archaeologists have many more questions than answers when they focus on the archaeology of the Initial Woodland period in southern Minnesota. Whether entirely correct or not, Binford's ideas in *Frames of Reference* anticipate what changes should be occurring in the area during this period and provide an explanation of these changes in terms of processual dynamics. Together, they provide narratives of the past that can be tested through future research on the archaeological record of southern Minnesota.

CHAPTER 5

Northern Hunters, Fishers, and Wild Rice Harvesters

Initial Woodland Adaptations in Central and Northern Minnesota

As in southern Minnesota, Initial Woodland complexes in central and northern Minnesota are defined largely by the style and presence of the first pottery vessels in these parts of the state. These vessels, like those in the southern part of the state, are jars that appear, usually, in both larger utilitarian forms and smaller ritual/burial forms. This chapter focuses on the three most intensely investigated and reported regions in central and northern Minnesota: Mille Lacs, Headwaters Lakes, and Rainy River.

THE INITIAL WOODLAND PERIOD IN CENTRAL MINNESOTA

The Mille Lacs Region

Located in east-central Minnesota in the Deciduous Lakes resource region, the Mille Lacs region consists of the chain of Lakes Ogechie, Shakopee, and Onamia with their interconnecting waterways via the Rum River, and Mille Lacs Lake itself, which is about 42 square miles in extent (Map 5.1). A mixture of lakeshore, riverine, and upland pine and northern hardwood forest environments extends throughout the region, with white pine forests becoming more common toward the St. Croix River to the east and to the north. The prairie-forest border is located a short distance to the west, across the Mississippi River. As in other parts of this southern area of the north woods, the most important large mammals at historic contact were white-tailed deer and black bear, though elk and wolves were also present; the region was in the southern range of moose. Smaller food animals included raccoon, squirrel, muskrat, beaver, otter, and a variety of waterfowl. Walleye, northern pike, bass, and panfish were abundant in the lakes and rivers, as was wild rice within the shallower chain of lakes.

The Initial Woodland complex in the Mille Lacs region is called the Rum River phase (circa 200 BC–AD 500).[1] Because of the rich archaeological record of the region, the Mille Lacs Lake area and its Rum River outlet were an early region of archaeological

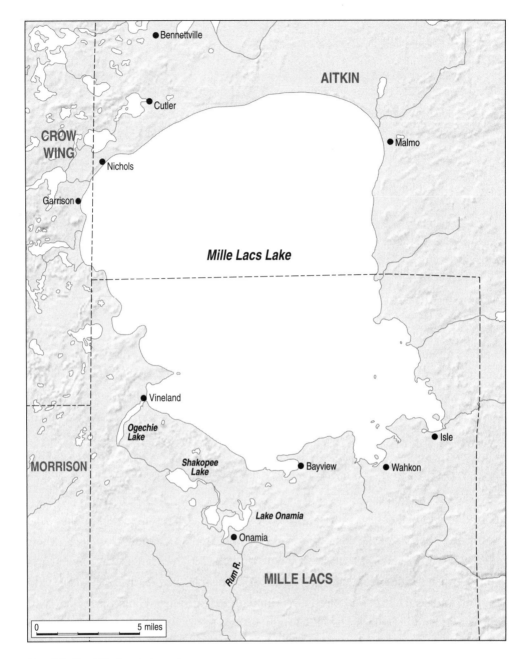

Map 5.1. The Mille Lacs Lake region.

exploration in Minnesota.[2] Identifying characteristics of the Rum River phase are the oldest burial mounds in the Mille Lacs region, Malmo pottery, and calibrated radiocarbon dates that fall within the circa 200 BC–AD 500 age range, though that age range is disputed by some archaeologists.

At present, Rum River components are moderately well known at only five sites in the region: Brower (21ML01) and Van Grinsven (21ML37), on opposite sides of the Lake Onamia basin; Malmo (21AK01), on the northeast shore of Mille Lacs Lake; Black

Brook (21ML40), a short distance south of the Lake Onamia outlet on the Rum River; and 21AK71, on the southern shore of Ripple Lake, just northwest of Mille Lacs Lake. Initial Woodland components have been identified, but not analyzed, at the nearby Cooper (21ML09/16) and Griffin (21ML18) sites, and at least three other mound groups in the region may be associated with the phase.[3]

Malmo or Malmo-like ceramics have been found outside the Mille Lacs region at the Gull Lake Dam site (21CA37) and at Langer (21CA58) in Cass County, at the Cedar Creek site (21AK58) in Aitkin County, and possibly at the Graham Lake Mound site (21OT05) in Otter Tail County.[4] The distribution of Malmo or at least Malmo-like ceramics, then, may extend from the Mille Lacs region westward across Gull Lake, which is just south of the Headwaters Lakes region, to the lakes area in Otter Tail County. This distribution includes deciduous, mixed conifer-deciduous, and prairie vegetation habitats. The Rum River phase is still assumed, however, to be centered in the mixed hardwood forests of the Mille Lacs region. At this writing, the State Historic Preservation Office (SHPO) archaeology database records the presence of Malmo or Malmo-like pottery in the following counties, with the number of sites in a county in parentheses: Aitkin (4), Benton (1), Carlton (1), Cass (5), Crow Wing (3), Douglas (1), Hennepin (2), Isanti (1), Itasca (1), Kanabec (5), Mille Lacs (7), and Otter Tail (3).

As in other pottery-containing archaeological cultures in Minnesota, the key identifying trait of a Rum River phase component is the presence of a particular kind of pottery, in this case Malmo ceramics.[5] Malmo pottery jars are thick-walled, conoidal-bottomed vessels with smooth surfaces, coarsely crushed granite (usually) temper, and rims decorated with object impressions (Figure 5.1). General similarities occur between Malmo ceramics and Havana ceramics to the south and east, and Laurel ceramics to the north. An occasional red-slipped or limestone-tempered sherd, along with a distant Havana Middle Woodland–looking cast to the decoration, hints at the Havana connection.

The composition of the lithic assemblages of the Rum River phase is equally preliminary in definition. Examined lithic samples from several Rum River phase components seem to fit the Q-pattern of lithic resource use as defined by Kent Bakken.[6] However, the pattern, which is defined as "assemblages [that] include

Figure 5.1. Malmo pottery.
Courtesy of the Minnesota Historical Society. Printed with permission.

quartz debitage ranging from 60 to 80 percent of the total, with no particular secondary material dominant," is indicative of the Woodland tradition as a whole in central and north-central Minnesota. The secondary toolstone material at the Black Brook site is an unusually diverse sample of materials exotic to the Mille Lacs region. Exotic toolstone includes obsidian, Hixton silicified sandstone, Burlington chert, Prairie du Chien chert, and Knife River flint. Several archaeologists have suggested that the presence of exotics and an abundance of quartz point to an increase in trade and external influence in the region during the period of the Rum River phase, and that the quartz itself may have come from along the Mississippi River near Little Falls, where quartz cobbles are abundant.

Other lithics in assemblages include a variety of straight-stemmed, contracting-stemmed, side-notched, and corner-notched projectile point forms, flake scrapers, perforators, anvils, and expedient tools, as well as flaked and bipolar cores.[7] Although we still do not have a firm understanding of the stone tool repertoire of the phase, it seems much more varied than contemporary Laurel stone tool assemblages in the Rainy River basin in the far north.

The earliest excavations of Rum River phase components concentrated exclusively on the exploration of the mounds at Malmo and the Anderson and Vanderbloom mounds at the Brower site along the shore of Lake Onamia.[8] For the most part, the skeletal remains were poorly preserved and fragmentary. Burials at Brower and Malmo were interred as secondary bundles in circular, dome-shaped earthen mounds in a shallow, oval central pit covered by sapling trunks or a cribwork of slender tree branches; a fire pit was usually adjacent to the burial pit (Figure 5.2). The fire burned some of the wood and bones, but it was extinguished by mound construction before the wood and bones were completely burned. The mounds are low and small in diameter in comparison to Howard Lake and Laurel mounds. Malmo mounds are rarely cumulative, which has led to the speculation that the mounds in a Malmo mortuary site represent a temporal sequence of construction over a number of years, with each mound representing a single burial episode.

The Brower site (21ML01), which is situated on an old beach ridge on the northwest side of Lake Onamia, contains a habitation area and a series of adjacent circular or conical earthen burial mounds. When Alfred Jenks excavated the Anderson Mound in 1933, it was 5 feet in height and 50 feet in diameter. The Vanderbloom Mound was 3 feet in height and 45 feet in diameter when Lloyd Wilford excavated it in 1952.[9] At least seventeen individuals were recovered from the Vanderbloom Mound, and four from the Anderson Mound. One male was thought to be thirty to forty-nine years old at death;

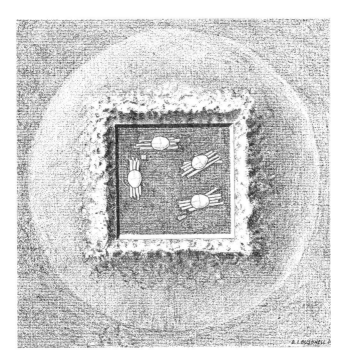

Figure 5.2. Representation of secondary bundle burials from the Malmo mounds. From Brower and Bushnell 1900.

a woman, eleven to eighteen years old; and three other individuals of unidentified sex, thirty to forty years old.[10] Dental caries were present in one individual, and severe osteoarthritis was present in a forty-year-old adult (possibly a woman). A few fractures were the only other pathologies identified in the sample of twenty-one individuals.

Wilford's detailed description of the contents of the Vanderbloom Mound provides a vivid image of the nature of one of these mounds:

On the floor of the mound had been placed sheets of birch bark. . . . On the bark, or at any rate on the original ground surface, bones of individuals were placed. . . . Logs were placed over the human bones on the mound floor, not in a haphazard fashion but in grid form, with some logs placed in a northeast–southwest orientation and others crossing them at right angles or near-right angles. . . . Some additional bones were thrown onto the log cribwork, as many fragments were found above the charred logs. The logs were then set afire and were almost completely consumed in the center and the southeast side. Before the fire had died out, dirt was thrown upon it, stopping the conflagration and preserving many partially burned logs. A considerable amount of clay was present in the dirt thrown on at that time, and it burned to a more vivid red than the sandy material of the area.[11]

During 1972 excavations at the Brower site, a secondary burial with an associated pot (probably Malmo) and a fire hearth were encountered in what was thought to be the habitation portion of the site.[12] The burial may not represent the presence of a non-mound cemetery area but rather a mound burial whose low mound had been plowed down.[13]

The Malmo site (21AK01) is along the northeast shore of Mille Lacs Lake, between the shoreline and Big Bay Creek. When surveyed in 1889, it contained 127 earthen mounds, 13 of which were excavated by a University of Minnesota crew in 1935.[14] Age estimates for fourteen of the twenty-six individuals found in the mounds are for males, one between eleven and eighteen years old at death, two between nineteen and twenty-nine, six between thirty and forty-nine, and one between fifty and sixty-four years old at death; and for females, one between nineteen and twenty-nine, and three between thirty and forty-nine years old at death. The individuals had no dental caries or abscesses and only two instances of slight degenerative joint disease.

Wilford's conclusion that mounds that contain burials characterized by an absence of associated grave goods and a secondary bundle mode of interment are Malmo phase–related has caused some confusion in Minnesota archaeology, for on the basis of those criteria, widely scattered burial mounds have been associated (or at least tentatively associated) with the Malmo phase. Among the mounds that lack Malmo ceramics but were included in the archaeological culture on the basis of burial mode alone are the Morrison Mounds (21OT02), the Graham Lake Mound Group (21OT05), and the Peterson Mound Group (21OT01), all in Otter Tail County in west-central Minnesota, and High Island (21SB01) in Sibley County.[15] The Graham Lake Mound Group, which was excavated by Wilford in 1949, contained a minimum of four individuals, a young child, two adult males, and an adult female, while the Peterson Mound Group, which was excavated by Jenks, contained a minimum of six individuals from two of the three mounds. The excavated Morrison Mounds, which contained charred logs overlaying a central burial pit and a minimum of sixteen individuals, is about 45 feet above the Otter Tail River at the outlet of Otter Tail Lake. An unusually early calibrated radiocarbon date for Mound 13 of 785 ± 261 BC is considered too early for the Malmo phase, but the age range is not inconsistent with Initial Woodland dates for the Headwaters Lakes region just east of the Morrison Mounds.

To what degree (if any) were Rum River phase people involved in the southern Hopewell Interaction Sphere?[16] A feature of the Hopewell Interaction Sphere was the movement of exotic materials throughout eastern North America for ritual and political-religious uses. In north-central North America, Hopewell Interaction Sphere influences in a region are signaled by the presence of exotic materials, such as obsidian, sheet mica, Knife River flint, and copper, and by the presence of ceramics that have some Havana-Hopewell attributes. Some of these influences are present in the Rum River phase, which suggests that these people were involved, if only peripherally, in this political-religious phenomenon.

Exotic materials or traits in the region during this period include some lime-stone-tempered Malmo sherds from the type-site (21AK1), an occasional red-slipped sherd in some sites, burned logs over burial areas, copper (at 21AK71), and the range of nonlocal stone materials at the Black Brook site, which includes obsidian, Hixton silicified sandstone, Burlington chert, Knife River flint, and Prairie du Chien chert.[17] The presence of these materials and traits supports Elden Johnson's suggestion that trade and external influence in general increased in the Mille Lacs region during the Rum River phase.[18] Likewise, the presence of Knife River flint supports Frances Clark's suggestion that this material was being traded into the Hopewell Interaction Sphere by Sonota complex peoples in western North Dakota via (at least in part) people in the Mille Lacs region.[19] David Mather suggests that the region's contribution to the flow of materials was wild rice, and Johnson suggests that it contributed copper as well.[20]

At present, the degree of participation of the Rum River phase community in the Hopewell phenomenon remains an unanswered question. Since Malmo ceramics have closer affinities with Laurel ceramics and only traces of a Havana-ceramic influence, the consensus at the moment is that the Rum River phase community remained largely outside the Hopewell Interaction Sphere.

The Headwaters Lakes Region

The Headwaters Lakes region is a complex of bogs, lakes, rivers, and pine and aspen forests in the Coniferous Lakes resource region of north-central Minnesota. Its defin-ing features are the headwaters of the Mississippi River in Itasca State Park in south-eastern Clearwater County and the series of lakes the river flows through or by in Bel-trami, Cass, Clearwater, Hubbard, and Itasca Counties. The region stretches from the headwaters of the Mississippi in the west to the Grand Rapids area in the east, and from Gull Lake in the north to the south shore of Leech Lake in the south (Map 5.2). The prairie-forest border is located a short distance to the west and southwest.

The Initial Woodland period in the Headwaters Lakes region of central Minnesota remains controversial because of claims that the earliest pottery in the region dates as early as 1300 BC, if not earlier. Christy Hohman-Caine and Grant Goltz have suggested

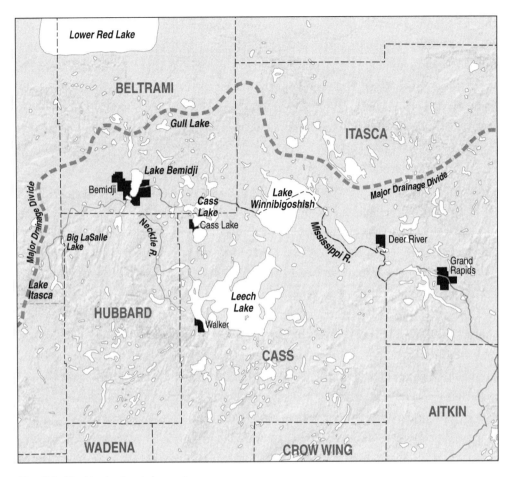

Map 5.2. The Headwaters Lakes region.

that the Initial Woodland archaeological complex of the region be called the Elk Lake complex, a taxonomic term that I adopt, too.[21] The presence of Brainerd ware ceramics, small conical burial mounds, a range of Plains-oriented stemmed and notched dart points, a focus on the exploitation of the regional "prairie/woodland ecotone," and a continuation of a "basic Archaic lifestyle" characterize the Elk Lake complex. Human burials are present in both rounded earthen mound and non-mound contexts. The complex seems to reflect a hunter-gatherer lifeway that was transitional between Late Archaic and Terminal Woodland settlement-subsistence patterns. Phases of the Elk Lake complex may be present in the Mille Lacs region and elsewhere in central Minnesota.

Brainerd ceramics are easily recognizable in Minnesota by their net-impressed and horizontally cordmarked exterior surfaces (Figure 5.3).[22] Like other (Malmo, Laurel) northern Initial Woodland wares, vessels of the ware have open orifices, vertical rims, and conoidal or subconoidal bases. Lips tend to be flat, and the vessels tempered with sand or grit. Decoration on the vessels is limited. About half of known vessels have cord-wrapped-stick impressions, incised or linear stamps, or circular or angled punctates on the exterior rim. Interior rim decoration is rare, but when present consists of cord-wrapped-stick impressions, incised or linear stamps, fingernail notches, and punctates, among other miscellaneous impressions.

Figure 5.3. A Brainerd net-impressed rim sherd. Courtesy of the Wilford Archaeology Laboratory, University of Minnesota.

The time range of the Elk Lake complex remains controversial mainly because of unexpectedly early radiocarbon dates obtained from scrapings from the residue on the inside of Brainerd sherds. Brainerd ware was once thought to be roughly contemporary with Initial Woodland Laurel in northern Minnesota or perhaps to date to the following early Terminal Woodland period in the Headwaters Lakes region. Since the early 1990s, multiple radiocarbon residue dates have pushed the first appearance of the ware in the region back as early as 1430 BC, while other dates place the recent end of its age range around AD 535 (with clusters of dates around 800 BC and less so around 400 BC).[23] This would mean that the ware survived without substantial stylistic changes for about 2,000 years. An apparent example of this phenomenon has been reported at the Roosevelt Lake site (21CA184), where Elk Lake complex dates span a very long period.[24]

Do Brainerd ceramics really date as early as 1430 BC, which would be 800 to 1,000 years earlier than the first pottery in other areas of the Midwest? In defense of that possibility, Hohman-Caine and Goltz point to the numerous radiocarbon dates obtained from food residues directly associated with Brainerd sherds in the Headwaters Lakes region.[25] However, a source of contamination may be the "reservoir effect" caused by the presence of old carbon in regional water and, perhaps, in the clays used for pot making. The presence of old carbon (and perhaps pre–Ice Age pollen and spores) causes ages to be overassessed by as much as 500 to 2,000 years.[26] This range of error has obvious implications for the precise dating of events like the first appearance of ceramics in the Headwaters Lakes region. If this possibility is correct, one would expect to find substantial differences between residue dates and dates on charcoal associated with a component, as at the Third River Borrow site (21IL76), where a pit feature containing Brainerd Horizontally Corded sherds produced a residue date of 390 BC and a calibrated charcoal date of AD 53–584.[27]

Stratigraphic evidence seems of little help at present in resolving this controversy. For example, Brainerd ware was below Blackduck ware at the Osufsen Mound (21IC02), and below both Blackduck and Sandy Lakes ware at White Oak Point village (21IC01). Clearly, then, although Brainerd ware appears to be Initial Woodland in age range, the date of its first appearance remains a research priority in Minnesota archaeology.

Lithic assemblages consist for the most part of local raw materials, in particular Swan River chert, Tongue River silica, low-grade quartz, and coarser grades of Knife River siltstone. However, small amounts of exotic lithic materials, like Burlington chert and Knife River flint, are often present at Elk Lake complex sites. Identifiable stone tools include dart points, small- to medium-sized scrapers, and square to rectangular chisels or wedges.[28] The points are similar to Northern Plains Woodland types, such as Oxbow, Pelican Lake, and Besant points, and to Hanna and Duncan points of the McKean complex. The point complex remains poorly defined, but in general the points seem similar to earlier Late Archaic and Northern Plains Woodland types. No worked antler or bone tools are identified in available reports.

At present, it is thought that Elk Lake complex burials occur in either earthen mounds or in non-mound contexts, although the nature and associations of these burials remain unclear. In their survey of burial contexts in Minnesota, Constance Arzigian and Katherine Stevenson report the presence of Brainerd Net Impressed pottery in one mound and in one non-mound burial.[29] A Brainerd Net Impressed vessel was in a subsoil pit with charred human bone fragments below Mound 2c at the Gull Lake Dam site in Cass County. A date of 235 BC was later obtained for the pit. Sherds of the ware were found as well with a single non-mound burial, possibly a bundle burial, in a pit at the Carr Lake Burial site. Besides these two associations, Brainerd sherds have been found in mound fill at a number of other sites, including Gull Lake Dam (21CA37), Slininger (21NR01), and McKinstry (21KC02). These sherds are assumed to have been incorporated into the fill from deposits scooped up from earlier occupations.

In recent years about a dozen sites have been excavated that contain substantial Brainerd components.[30] A notable example is Shingobee Island (21CA28), for two stratigraphically separated components both containing Brainerd ceramics were identified at the site.[31] The lower component, which may contain structures associated with pits and large pieces of fire-cracked rock, was identified as a late fall/early winter or winter occupation. It contained three Oxbow projectile points, a side-notched point, scrapers, chisels or wedges, small pieces of copper, and the bones of elk, bison, turtle, and possibly caribou. Two dates on charcoal from plant stems recovered from a house feature are 4090 and 4400 BP, which Hohman-Caine and Goltz, the excavators, argue may date the occupation but need confirmation. The upper component, a possible late winter/spring occupation, contained points similar to Duncan/Hanna and Pelican Lake, and the bones of deer, beaver, and otter. Over 70,000 fragments of well-preserved bone were recovered during the excavation. In general, raw stone material was mainly of local, often lower-grade material. Cores, hammerstones, utilized flakes, chopping tools, and abundant amounts of lithic (stone) debris were also present.

THE INITIAL WOODLAND ARCHAEOLOGICAL RECORD IN NORTHERN MINNESOTA

In the far northern quarter of Minnesota, the first ceramics and burial mounds are generally assumed to be associated with the Laurel culture, a northern Great Lakes archaeological complex that extends from western Quebec, northwestern Michigan, northwestern Wisconsin, and northern Ontario across northern Minnesota into southeastern and west-central Manitoba and east-central Saskatchewan, making it the most geographically extensive Initial Woodland archaeological culture in North America.[32] Within this vast area is a core area of Laurel settlement, a smaller region that straddles the southern edge of the boreal forest and the northern edge of the mixed deciduous-coniferous forests of the north woods, with the Rainy River at its center. In broader perspective, Laurel is a regional expression of an east–west continuum of Middle (Initial) Woodland complexes that extends from the Canadian prairies across the northern Great Lakes eastward into northern New England.[33] The complex dates roughly between 50 BC and AD 650/1000 in northern Minnesota and as late as the thirteenth century in areas of south-central Canada.[34]

The Rainy River Region

In Minnesota, Laurel is best known from excavations at the Grand Mound/Smith Mounds and McKinstry sites on the Rainy River, the Pike Bay Mound and Pearson sites on Lake Vermilion, and the Lake Bronson site in the prairie area of Kittson County, all (for the most part) in the northwestern corner of the state (Map 5.3).[35] Laurel components are most readily identified by the presence of a distinctive ceramic complex, Laurel ware. Other defining characteristics of the archaeological culture in Minnesota are its core location in the northern tier of counties in the state, its association with large burial mounds along the Rainy River, and the unusual treatment of the skeletons of some individuals interred in the mounds.

Laurel ceramics are characterized by the presence of relatively thick (average 6 millimeters, with a range of 3 to 8 millimeters), grit-tempered jars with conoidal bases, straight rims, slight to no neck constriction, smooth surfaces, and stamped-tool decoration on the exterior rim, neck, and occasionally upper shoulder (Figure 5.4).[36]

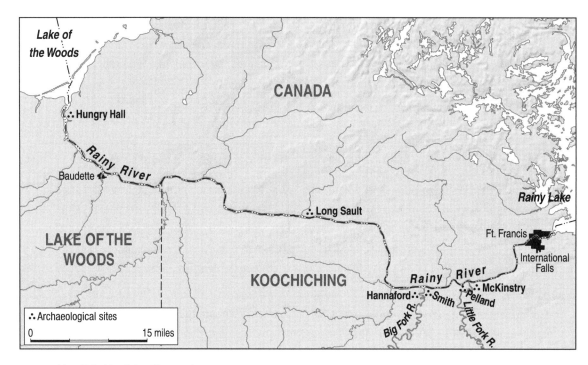

Map 5.3. The Rainy River region.

Techniques of decoration include dentate stamping, incising, push-pull bands, pseudo-scallop shell stamps, bosses, and punctates. Cord-wrapped-stick decoration, which becomes a major decorative technique in the Terminal Woodland period, is a minor technique in Laurel and is usually confined to inner rim surfaces.

A wide variety of stemmed and notched weapon point forms have been found in apparent Laurel assemblages, including large and small side-notched, large corner-notched, and small-eared forms. Other associated stone artifacts include end scrapers, knives, and utilized and retouched flake tools. A ground stone industry is apparently absent. There is also some support for the presence of trade networks for raw materials, such as Knife River flint and Jasper taconite.[37]

The Laurel bone/antler/tooth industry includes conical bone projectile points, toggle-headed and perforated antler harpoons, cut beaver incisors, awls, bird-bone tools, and ornaments of animal teeth and bone. Small copper tools, such as awls, pressure flakers, beads, and fishhooks, are present in some assemblages. Jack Steinbring suggests that these small tools are attenuated cultural descendants of the Archaic Old Copper complex. An analysis of the chemical constituents of copper at the River Point site south of Ely suggests that the source of the copper was Minong, Wisconsin.[38]

Several studies indicate that Laurel houses at least at some sites were oval-shaped structures 20 to 26 feet long by 10 to 16 feet wide, with internal hearths and storage pits, and that they were large enough to hold about ten people. Possible Laurel structures were found in Minnesota at the River Point site (21LA10) in Lake County, but the best evidence comes from the Ballynacree site (DkKp-8) in Ontario, where three structures and associated features were uncovered during excavation.[39]

Laurel burial mounds are not numerous in northern Minnesota. Where they do occur, they tend to be either large mounds, as at McKinstry and Pike Bay, or small groups, such as at the Smith site.[40] In general these circular earthen mounds occur in much smaller clusters than do contemporary mound groups to the south, although individual Laurel mounds can be much larger than their southern counterparts due to

Figure 5.4. Laurel Incised pottery vessel from the Smith site (21KC3).
Courtesy of the Wilford Archaeology Laboratory, University of Minnesota.

multiple burial episodes. In fact, the largest burial mound in Canada is on the Ontario side of the Rainy River. Many Laurel mounds grew by accretion, with the primary mode of burial being secondary bundle burial. There is evidence of extensive mound construction episodes, multiple burials, and elaborate burial artifacts. At present, there is no information on Laurel non-mound burial.

Because of an extensive human skeleton sample (a minimum of 210 individuals) that was extensively analyzed in preparation for reburial, more is known about Laurel people as physical human beings than about other Initial Woodland populations in the state. I concentrate here on the Grand Mound/Smith Mounds site (21KC3), where 206 individuals were recovered through excavation from Mounds 3 and 4.

The Smith site (21KC3) is situated at the mouth of the Big Fork River on the Minnesota side of the Rainy River. The site consists of a habitation area and five burial mounds, including the Grand Mound, the largest burial mound in Minnesota (Figure 5.5). Multiple interments of later Blackduck burials in the mounds have resulted in some mixing of samples, but an attempt was made through analysis to keep the two samples apart.[41] Torso burials, cremations, and various kinds of secondary burials were present in the Laurel levels of the mounds, with most Laurel burials being secondary bundles. Mound 4, in which 193 Laurel-related individuals were recovered, has attracted special attention because of the unusual mortuary practices present. These include long bone perforation, removal of the occipital bone, cut marks that are consistent with dismemberment, and red ocher spread over and around the burials. Part or all of the occiput, or lower back of the skull, is absent in fourteen of thirty-three skulls, 35 percent of all individuals exhibit long bone perforation (fifty-two adults and thirteen subadults), and 29 percent of all long bones have some kind of perforation. There appear to be no significant differences in occurrence of these practices between sexes.

According to Michael Torbenson and his colleagues, postmortem long bone puncturing is best represented in Laurel burial mounds, where it is especially well-represented at the Smith site.[42] Other regional examples of long bone puncturing are present across the southern margins of the Great Lakes and in the Red River valley. It is unclear to what extent long bone puncturing was carried out for the same reasons throughout this broad region, but in the western Great Lakes long bone tapping is generally thought to be associated with the release of a deceased person's spirit or soul.

Of the 193 individuals in Mound 4, 111 were adult (sixteen years old or older), and 82 were subadult. Sixty-five of the adults were male, and 41 female. Life expectancy at birth was calculated to be about twenty years, but the estimate may not be reliable, because of the fragmented nature of the sample. The health of this sample of 193 individuals was quite good. Except for some degenerative joint disease, especially at the

Figure 5.5. The Grand Mound.
Courtesy of Scott Anfinson, University of Minnesota.

knee, there was little evidence of disease or of accidents or conflict. The average stature of females was estimated to be 159.5 ± 4.4 centimeters (between 5 feet 1 inch and 5 feet 5 inches), and of males 177.1 ± 3.4 centimeters (between 5 feet 8 inches and 5 feet 11 inches).

A bio-distance study of the Laurel sample by Nancy Ossenberg concluded that the Laurel population had close biological relationships with both the southern Blackduck samples (from the Osufsen [21IC02] and Shocker [21BL01] sites) and the Manitoba phase (see chapter 8), distant relationships with northern Blackduck samples (McKinstry [21KC02] and Hungry Hall Mound 2 in Ontario), and a very weak relationship with a Hopewell sample from Illinois.[43] These conclusions led her to suggest that northern Blackduck people were an intrusive group, that there was little, if any, genetic exchange between Laurel people and the Illinois Hopewell, that southern Blackduck people were ancestors at least in part of the historic Dakota, and that Manitoba phase populations were ancestors of the historic Assiniboin (see chapter 8). While suggestive, Ossenberg's conclusions need to be supported by additional studies.

The presence of exotic materials, such as Knife River flint, obsidian, and

"Hopewell-like" ceramic attributes, in Laurel sites hints at the possibility of some form of broadscale regional interaction with other Initial (Middle) Woodland populations, perhaps facilitated by intergroup marriage and small-group visiting. However, the nature of Laurel interregional communication and contact remains unclear.

INITIAL WOODLAND LIFEWAYS
IN CENTRAL AND NORTHERN MINNESOTA

Hunter-gatherer foraging groups respond to intensification pressure, constrained mobility, and range-size reduction in their quest for food in different ways, depending on latitude, resource richness, and initial conditions (for example, whether the groups were initially dependent on terrestrial plant or animal resources). In higher-latitude settings, a shift where possible to aquatic resources is generally the most viable option among people still somewhat mobile, for "aquatic resources offer the greatest return from intensification strategies."[44] This seems especially likely in colder environments like central and northern Minnesota, where the planting of domesticated plants in gardens was less of a viable option, where the dense coniferous-hardwood forests offered less accessible food resources than the resource-richer deciduous forests of lower-tier midwestern states, and where fish-rich lakes, rivers, and streams were abundant. Where aquatic resources were absent or less abundant, Binford's data indicate that there would have been a continued dependence on hunting.[45]

If Binford's packing thresholds are used as a guide, then the density of hunter-gatherers in at least more resource-rich habitats in central and northern Minnesota had passed the packing threshold of 1.59 persons per square 100 kilometers by the beginning of the Late Archaic period.[46] Once the threshold was crossed, subsistence dependence on larger terrestrial animals became (according to the data) increasingly difficult. The result was reduced social unit mobility (for mobility could no longer be used to ensure subsistence security), a decrease in the mean size of the camp-sharing group during the most aggregated phase of the settlement-subsistence pattern, a reduction in dependence on larger terrestrial animals and a growing dependence on animals of smaller body size, the expansion of extensification strategies through the use of canoes, and an increased dependence on aquatic resources.[47]

The development of these trends is a familiar one, for intensification generally promotes subsistence diversification and selects against continued reliance on terrestrial animals as the primary food resource in order to maintain subsistence security as a social group. Said another way, subsistence diversity fosters social group stability. In Binford's unique way of expressing the trend, "in general, as the $\log_{10}$ value of population density (LDEN) increases, subsistence diversity increases (SUBDIV2)."[48]

What evidence is there for the existence of these trends in central and northern Minnesota during the Initial Woodland period? At present, the subsistence base of Rum River, Elk Lake, and Laurel social groups remains virtually unknown, at least in detail, mainly due to the small number of components excavated using fine-screen recovery techniques like flotation, the early concentration on the excavation of burial mounds, the problem of isolating components of these complexes in shallow, mixed multicomponent sites, the difficulty of recognizing nonpottery containing components of each complex (a small, ephemeral hunting station, for example), and an early focus on cultural-historical research tasks that emphasized the identification of pottery types and archaeological cultures rather than the modeling of changing lifeways. I summarize the conclusions archaeologists have reached about the subsistence base of each complex here, for the data (while still meager) are richer than for earlier periods. Their conclusions are speculations as well, but they are based on systematically examined data and provide a narrative of lifeways in the more northern regions of Minnesota that can guide research and thinking in general about lifeways at the time.

With so few Rum River phase components known, archaeologists have been reluctant to develop settlement models for the phase, other than to note that a variety of geographical settings near water were used. This objective has been stymied, too, by uncertainties regarding sites originally assigned to the Malmo culture by Wilford, who assigned sites like Morrison, Peterson, and High Island to the culture on the basis of burial mode alone.[49] An additional problem has been the tendency to label any plain, thick, grit-tempered pottery sherd in central Minnesota as Malmo.

Nonetheless, the distribution and context of the few Rum River phase components known indicate that it was primarily a lakeshore-oriented culture whose members moved seasonally from one camp to another in a seasonal round much like that of their Late Archaic predecessors. The number of known sites indicates that population size must have been still quite small, although a variety of contemporary sites that lacked ceramics may have been overlooked as components of the phase, for Rum River phase stone tools, especially projectile points, closely resemble Late Archaic forms.

A lack of well-preserved faunal assemblages from Rum River phase components in the region also hinders the development of subsistence models. At present the sample of faunal elements that could be associated with components of the phase consists of deer and bird bones and mussel shell from the Brower site, turtle shell and parts of a bear paw from the Van Grinsven site, and a tool made from the scapula of a large (perhaps nonlocal) turtle from the Black Brook site. A stone net weight was in the Brower site assemblage. A large faunal assemblage that includes bear, moose, and domestic dog was recovered from the Gull Lake Dam site, which is outside the region.[50]

Phytolith analysis of food residues from two Malmo vessels from the Malmo site demonstrates the use of wild rice and maize (corn) at the time of manufacture of these vessels.[51] Calibrated radiocarbon dates of the residues date the vessels to AD 350–605, which is within the latter half of the Rum River phase. According to David Mather, the presence of maize in a phase site is not surprising, for the plant is present in other regions of the Great Lakes at the time.[52] Pollen cores from Lake Ogechie show that wild rice was locally available too.[53] Although very useful information, neither of these analyses indicates how important wild rice or maize was in the overall diet of the period.

That question is answered by other methods of analysis. Stable isotope studies of bone samples from four individuals recovered during excavation at the Malmo site show no use of corn (the readings were −20.4 to −21.8, with an average of −21.41).[54] Stable isotope studies are based on the ability of plants to metabolize carbon through different metabolic pathways, ^3C and ^4C. The ^4C pathway is more typical of tropical grasses, such as corn, and some other grasses in North America like big bluestem, which is found on the Plains. Animals (including humans) that consume ^4C plants show less negative or lower C13 ratios. Nonetheless, the probable presence of corn phytoliths in the food crust on the inside of a Malmo pottery vessel indicates that corn was present but not a food staple.

Macrobotanical studies suggest the presence of *Chenopodium* (goosefoot) and raspberry in the Rum River phase component at the Black Brook site, and of *Chenopodium* in the Van Grinsven component.[55] Both sites are multicomponent, and these associations remain tentative. *Chenopodium* was domesticated as early as 4,000 to 4,500 years ago in states to the south, though no claim has been made that the Mille Lacs region plants are domesticates.

The subsistence base of the Elk Lake complex remains equally vague, though it is thought to be an extension of a Late Archaic hunter-gatherer prairie-forest ecotone lifeway (with the addition of pottery) in which medium- and large-size mammals were the focus of hunting and trapping, and a variety of plant foods, including starchy seeds, fruits, nuts, and wild rice, were gathered.[56] The remains of animals apparently associated with separable components of the complex have been recovered from two sites, LaSalle Creek (21HB26) and Shingobee Island (21CA28). The remains of elk, deer, and dog were found at LaSalle Creek, which was thought to be a late summer through early winter occupation.[57] As mentioned earlier, the lower, earlier Elk Lake complex component (a possible winter occupation) at Shingobee Island contained at least five elk, three bison, one possible caribou, a turtle, and large amounts of fire-cracked rock, while the upper component (a possible late winter/spring occupation) contained the remains of deer, beaver, and other animals.[58]

Plant remains associated with the Elk Lake complex are somewhat better known, mainly because of phytolith analysis. The macrobotanical remains of raspberries, strawberries, acorns, hazelnuts, and chenopods were in Roosevelt Lake Narrows (21CA184) deposits. A phytolith analysis of residue on the inside of Brainerd sherds from the same site indicates that early Brainerd vessels were used to process starchy nongrass seeds, such as chenopods and possibly amaranth, or possibly for nut-oil processing, but with some grass seeds.[59] Robert Thompson and his colleagues suggest that pottery was introduced into the center to facilitate the boiling of starchy seeds.[60]

The timing of the first use of wild rice remains a topic of debate. Some archaeologists argue that this event occurred sometime after AD 1, while others point out that wild rice may be present in the Headwaters Lakes region as early as 1000 BC.[61] Wild rice phytoliths have been reported from a number of Elk Lake complex sites, including the Ogema-Geshik site (21IC12), with a calibrated radiocarbon date of over 3,000 years, which is the oldest date for use of wild rice in Minnesota; the Palmer Pines site (21HB19); and the Cass Lake site (21CA352), with a date of 865 BC. Wild rice phytoliths were also found on Brainerd pottery residue at the Lake Carlos site (21DL02, with a date of AD 160), which is outside the region.[62]

If the appearance of pottery is an indicator of intensification, then the Headwaters Lakes region may have been a naturally rich habitat, for indicators of intensification often appear earlier in "optimal" habitats and later in less optimal, less hunter-gatherer-friendly settings. Here an optimal setting is one where fish and aquatic plants, like wild rice, were both abundant. It is possible as well that the population of the region grew disproportionately larger compared to other areas of the state because of the abundance and accessibility of these resources. In fact, there were likely many more people living in central Minnesota during the Initial Woodland period than in the southern third of the state, if the relative abundance of sites and ceramics are reliable indicators of population size.

The most widely accepted subsistence-settlement model at present for the Laurel culture is a very general one that simply suggests that Laurel populations in Minnesota had a mixed hunting and gathering economy characterized by pronounced seasonality and the exploitation of a variety of habitats, including the mixed deciduous-coniferous forest, the boreal forest, and the northwestern prairies. Matthew Thomas and David Mather conclude, however, that

> lakeside fishing villages became fairly common at this time, suggesting a greater degree of sedentism, and possibly territoriality. Laurel people were still highly mobile like the Archaic inhabitants of the region before them; however, increased artifact

densities at sites, the appearance of domestic architecture, the restrictions imposed by the use of ceramics, and the requirements of group subsistence activities, such as ricing in the fall and spring fishing, suggest that the mobility patterns of these band-level peoples may have become relatively more structured and restricted.[63]

They also suggest that Laurel populations were organized in egalitarian bands in which work was divided along gender and age lines. Whether there was more complex organization involved during mortuary rituals or perhaps in interregional ritual exchange remains to be determined.

The analyses of animal bone from regional sites provide some support for this model. For example, excavations by the Minnesota Historical Society at McKinstry (21KC02) clearly demonstrate the importance of fishing at that site complex, and Scott Anfinson and his coworkers recovered bison bones in association with Laurel ceramics at Lake Bronson.[64] More recent faunal studies at McKinstry identified the presence of sturgeon, beaver, sucker, turtle, pike, walleye, and moose in the assemblage.[65] Two tentative conclusions were reached that are of interest here: first, fall fisheries became more readily accessible to later Terminal Woodland people with the innovation or at least greater use of gill nets, and second, the number of sturgeon captured decreased from Laurel to Terminal Woodland times as the number of beaver and suckers captured increased.[66] All of these studies are hampered, however, by sample recovery and other methodological problems.

No evidence exists at present for the extensive use of native North American cultigens or other domesticated plants by Laurel populations. However, a few wild rice grains have been found at the McKinstry site, a possible wild ricing feature was identified at the Big Rice site (21SL163) north of Virginia, and the presence of maize has been demonstrated to be widespread, if more an item used in ritual and possibly alliance building than subsistence in the boreal forests north of Minnesota.[67] A study of phytoliths on four Laurel sherds from McKinstry found no evidence for the presence of maize or wild rice.[68] It is possible that the harvesting of wild rice was a socioeconomic focus at some sites, which implies that wild rice–processing features, like jigs, should be present at some sites and that there should be evidence of Laurel seasonal activity at particularly rich harvesting beds. However, the importance of wild rice to Minnesota Laurel people remains uncertain at present. Such a strategy has implications for group size, division of labor, storage, settlement, and technology.

Do these data and speculations fit the trends expected to be found during a process of resource diversification? I think the answer is at present a qualified yes. Among the trends that seem to be ongoing in all three regions are an increasing human population base (though populations are still quite small); an increasing diversification of the subsistence base as evident in the presence of an array of aquatic animal resources (fish, turtle), grains (wild rice, goosefoot), nuts, and fruits as seen in some samples; and (a hint of) increasing sedentism (in the form of the appearance of lakeside villages). It is important to note that the lifeways in all three regions are considered an extension of local Late Archaic lifeways, as should be expected if the anticipated trends are ongoing. It is also important to note that archaeologists working in these regions have not explicitly tested for the presence of these trends. As they become aware of them, the quality of information about the presence or absence of indicators of intensification in these regions should greatly improve.

In closing this chapter, I turn to an interesting but still unresolved problem. I have been puzzled for many years by the extreme difference between the size of the areas in which far northern and southern pottery types in the state are found. As mentioned earlier, Laurel ceramics are found in a very large area that extends from western Quebec westward to east-central Saskatchewan, and from northern Minnesota northward through the boreal forest. Terminal Woodland Blackduck pottery has a somewhat similar distribution (see chapter 8). By contrast, ceramic wares in central and especially southern Minnesota have much more localized distributions. What accounts for these differences in the size of distribution of ceramic wares?

Although I do not yet know the reason or reasons for these differences, I assume that they are directly related to the distribution of environmental variables and to different patterns of interaction between neighboring social units. The northern ceramics I am talking about have their greatest distribution above what Binford calls the subpolar bottleneck, which begins at about 49.5° latitude, or between 11.45° and 11.60° effective temperature (ET). Forest environments north of this threshold are largely needleleaf evergreen boreal forests that have relatively high biomass but little species diversity. With their short growing season (just a bit more than four months a year) and relative lack of abundant food resources, these forests support only minimal populations of hunter-gatherers.

Hunter-gatherers adapt to this far northern environment in a number of ways. First, compared to Minnesota hunters, they move more often and for greater distances every year in the search for food. Second, storage becomes of critical importance, which affects the size and distribution of localized labor forces. And third, at least some adopt a collector subsistence strategy in which task groups go out from residential camps in search of food. Intensification, when it occurs, generally involves a major shift to increased exploitation of aquatic resources (fish) where available or to increased dependence on hunting.[69] Because of the scarcity and unpredictability of food resources, group adaptations tend to be somewhat unstable, resulting in cycles of population growth and decline. Why were ceramic wares more widely distributed among Native Americans living in these conditions above the subpolar bottleneck than among Native Americans living in central and southern Minnesota? The problem remains a problem.

TERMINAL WOODLAND AND MISSISSIPPIAN PERIOD

CIRCA AD 500–700 TO 1650

CHAPTER 6

Terminal Woodland Effigy Mound Builders and Bison Hunters

Terminal Woodland Adaptations in Southern Minnesota

By AD 500, new trends in the manufacture of ceramic vessels and stone projectile points become apparent among Woodland cultures in southeastern Minnesota and adjacent parts of Wisconsin, Iowa, and Illinois. Changes in some aspects of social organization and religion were apparently occurring, too, for burial of elite individuals in large earthen mounds with nonutilitarian items made from exotic materials disappears. Other trends already visible in Late Archaic and Initial Woodland cultures in the region, such as increased reliance on domesticated plants and human population growth, continue and probably are more fundamental to understanding the transformation in human lifeways that was occurring.

Many but not all of these cultural innovations and elaborations reached southwestern Minnesota by at least AD 900. More dramatic changes occurred throughout the southern part of the state between AD 900 and 1100, when agricultural societies with large, often defended villages and new material equipment appear. Later forms of these "Mississippian" cultures still occupied parts of southern Minnesota when European missionaries and adventurers first paddled the Mississippi and Minnesota Rivers.

Since a wide variety of cultural practices continued to differentiate Native Americans in southeastern and southwestern Minnesota, I continue to discuss them separately, as I did in chapter 4.

THE TERMINAL (LATE) WOODLAND ARCHAEOLOGICAL RECORD IN SOUTHEASTERN MINNESOTA

The gradual transformation of Early and Middle (Initial) Woodland archaeological complexes sometime after AD 500 into new complexes in southeastern Minnesota and adjacent regions of Wisconsin, Iowa, and Illinois remains poorly understood. Part of this transformation involved innovations in weaponry (the bow and arrow) and mound form (effigies), and the disappearance of Havana-Hopewell traits, such as Havana ware, elaborate mortuary ritual associated with large earthworks, an elaborate smoking-pipe complex, long-distance acquisition of exotic materials, and (possibly) the presence of socially ranked societies.

Other aspects of this period in southeastern Minnesota, such as increasingly larger human populations, greater dependence on domesticated food plants, new ceramic vessel forms with thinner walls and finer temper, the appearance of greater numbers of localized cultures, greater population nucleation into larger settlements, greater numbers of sites, expansion of year-round settlement into small secondary valleys and adjacent uplands, and reduction in amounts of imported stone for chipped stone tools, seem best understood as interlinked products of the acceleration in pace of trends that have their roots in the earlier Late Archaic period, especially social circumscription, social group packing, and resource intensification. The overriding themes in the Late Woodland in southeastern Minnesota are, then, gradual change and continuity.

As evident as these trends are in some areas of southwestern Wisconsin, eastern Iowa, and northwestern and central Illinois, they are difficult to document in southeastern Minnesota. As James Theler and Ernie Boszhardt phrase it, "the nature of post-Hopewellian Woodland cultures along the Mississippi River north of La Crosse is virtually unknown."[1] One reason may be a real lack of sites, for large-scale surveys in this region of the state have failed to document a strong Late Woodland presence. It seems possible that the Woodland tradition in general in this area never had a population density as large as other areas of the state and as in some adjacent areas of Wisconsin, Iowa, and Illinois. Scott Anfinson suggests that this apparent lower level of use is "due to a more limited wild food base. It was the horticultural Mississippians that first realized the greater economic potential of southeastern Minnesota."[2]

Because of the sparseness of the known Late Woodland archaeological record in southeastern Minnesota, I discuss what that archaeological record and its associated lifeways might be like based on information from bordering states, where an Early-Middle-Late Woodland terminology is used (as opposed to our Initial-Terminal Woodland terminology). In particular, I borrow James Stoltman and George Christiansen's divisions of the Late Woodland period into Initial, Mature, and Final for the quad-state (Illinois, Iowa, Minnesota, and Wisconsin) driftless area, since all or parts of Dakota, Goodhue, Wabasha, Winona, Olmsted, Dodge, Houston, Fillmore, and Mower Counties in southeastern Minnesota are in the driftless area.[3]

Initial Late Woodland, AD 500–700

The Initial Late Woodland period is considered a transitional phase between late Middle Woodland and Mature Late Woodland lifeways in southwestern Wisconsin and northeastern Iowa, where the closely related archaeological remains of the period are called the Mill phase and the Lane Farm phase, respectively. These phases combine traits present in the region's earlier late Middle Woodland phases (Millville and Allamakee) and the Effigy Mound culture, a Mature Late Woodland archaeological culture.

The presence of Initial Late Woodland components in these areas is most easily recognized by the presence of Lane Farm Cord-Impressed, a pottery jar with a somewhat rounded base and constricted neck. Lane Farm Cord-Impressed jars have cord-impressed decoration on the exterior of the rim, rocker stamping over at least some of the body below the rim, relatively thin, hard walls, and fine-grit temper.[4] Both the rim exterior and shoulder were smoothed before decoration was added by pressing fabric or individual cords onto the rim and rocker stamping onto the body; the rocker stamping may have been made by swinging (rocking) a clamshell back and

Figure 6.1. Lane Farm Cord-Impressed pottery.
Courtesy of the Minnesota Historical Society. Printed with permission.

forth to form connected, curvy Vs (Figure 6.1). No Lane Farm Cord-Impressed pottery has been identified to my knowledge in Minnesota, but it should be present in the state's southeastern corner.

Other traits of the period are small corner-notched points, which may have been the first arrow points in the region, small conical mounds, and after AD 600 some elongated linear mounds. The mounds contain limited grave goods and include primary flexed burials either on the floor beneath the mound or sometimes in subfloor pits. Among the rare grave goods are part of a clay elbow pipe, cylindrical copper beads, and some projectile points, including a small corner-notched point. At present, we have limited bioarchaeological information for this time period in southeastern Minnesota.

It is not clear which weapon points fall into this period, but late Middle Woodland points, like Steuben Stemmed and Manker Corner Notched, may be present early in the period and may be the first arrow points in the region. Points such as Scallorn,

Figure 6.2. Late Woodland projectile points. *Left to right:* Scallorn (3), Klunk.
Courtesy of the Minnesota Historical Society. Printed with permission.

Klunk Side Notched, and Koster Corner Notched may be present late in the period (Figure 6.2). The Scallorn type includes small corner-notched or expanding-stem arrowheads with barbed shoulders. The forms vary greatly and can range from broad to slender, with straight to convex blade edges. Klunk Side Notched points are small points with a convex to straight base, moderate to large side notches, and slightly convex-sided blades. Koster Corner Notched is a small, thin corner-notched point with a short expanding stem that has a convex or straight base.

At present, the Initial Late Woodland period in the driftless area is known from a limited number of sites. The Mill phase is represented by components in excavated shell middens at Mill Pond and Mill Coulee, and the Lane Farm phase from a stratified context at the FTD site and five burial mounds in Allamakee County in the northeast corner of Iowa.[5]

Mature Late Woodland, AD 700–1000

The Mature Late Woodland period in the Upper Mississippi River valley south of Minneapolis–St. Paul is represented by the Effigy Mound complex, which has been most extensively studied and has its widest distribution in southern Wisconsin.[6] Smaller numbers of sites are present, however, in northern Wisconsin and adjacent areas of Iowa, Illinois, and Minnesota. Based on the distribution of the pottery ware associated with the complex elsewhere, the complex (or at least its ceramic component) extends throughout southeastern Minnesota to about the Blue Earth River.

Although Effigy Mound people also constructed earthen conical and linear mounds, the most spectacular, visible remains of the complex are the mounds they built in the shape of animals. Many of these shapes have been associated with particular animals, such as bears, deer, panthers, and turtles, although most are so generalized that definite identifications cannot be made. The most common forms are birds in flight and side profiles of four-footed animals. The mounds rarely exceed 2 or 3 feet in height but may be 500 or more feet long. Some mound groups are very large, while other groups consist of only one or a few mounds. Most groups, however, contain between about six and eighty mounds. The mounds are usually situated on ridgetops or other elevated areas bordering major lakes and rivers.

Unlike earlier Havana-related mounds in the region, the content of Effigy Mound mounds is sparse or absent altogether. This often makes the identification of the builders of the mounds difficult if not impossible, though the presence in mound fill of cultural debris from nearby camps and villages provides a *terminus post quem* date, that is, a date after which construction must have taken place. When grave goods are present, they are most often personal or utilitarian objects, such as ceramic vessels and projectile points. Burials take many forms and vary in number and placement in mounds. Primary and secondary (bundle) burials are most common, but cremations occur and may have been a relatively common mortuary practice outside mound burial programs. Apparently, burials were added to some mounds over a span of several hundred years.

Altogether, only thirteen to fifteen sites in Minnesota contain effigy mounds or possible effigy mounds.[7] These include eighteen to twenty bird effigies, three panther, one human, one possible turtle, one possible fish with fins, and four possible snake. Except for a flock of birds in flight at the Prior Lake Effigy Mound cluster in Scott County (see description below), the other effigy mounds in the state are south of Minneapolis–St. Paul in driftless area counties that border the Mississippi River (Dakota, Goodhue, Houston, Wabasha, and Winona Counties).

While effigy mounds are the most highly visible trait of the Effigy Mound culture, a diagnostic and more widespread trait of particular importance to archaeologists is Madison ware, for components in non-mound sites are identified as Effigy Mound by the presence of this ceramic ware (Figure 6.3).[8] General characteristics of vessels of this ware grouping are thin walls (4 to 6 millimeters), fine-grit tempering, cordmarking on the exterior surface of a globular

Figure 6.3. Madison Cord-Impressed rim sherd.
Courtesy of the Minnesota Historical Society. Printed with permission.

Figure 6.4. Angelo Punctated pottery. Photograph by Edward Fleming.
Courtesy of the Logan Museum of Anthropology, Beloit College.

body, a constricted neck and out-flaring rim, and decoration most often consisting of cord impressions. Most Madison ware vessels share a close similarity in design treatment in that they are decorated in geometrical patterns on the exterior rim surface with cord impressions. Madison ware has been reported in site collections in Blue Earth, Dakota, Goodhue, Fillmore, Nicollet, Sibley, Wabasha, Washington, and Winona Counties.

Another likely diagnostic trait of some later (AD 900–1100) Mature Late Woodland components is the presence of Angelo Punctated ceramics, which are jars with punctate and fine trailed line decoration, occasionally in complex patterns, over a cord-roughened surface (Figure 6.4).[9] Like Madison ware, temper is fine grit. The ceramic ware is thought to share some similarities with Great Oasis pottery, which dates between about AD 950 and 1100 (see chapter 7). Angelo Punctated pottery has been found at sites in Goodhue and Fillmore Counties, and possibly at Lee Mill Cave in Dakota County.

A characteristic of the transition from Early/Middle Woodland to Late Woodland pottery vessels throughout most of northeastern North America is significant change in vessel form and technology of manufacture. Vessels change in shape from simple conoidal or subconoidal forms to globular forms with more complex rim profiles, walls become thinner and harder, and temper becomes finer (and in Mississippian-related archaeological cultures often switches from grit to shell). These changes seem to emphasize thermal and mechanical stress resistance and may be related to basic transformations in subsistence practices. Just what these transformations may have been are discussed in the section on lifeways below.

Small stemmed, side-notched, and unnotched triangular arrow points, scrapers, knives, utilized flakes, and the by-products of the flaking process are common artifacts in Effigy Mound components in southwestern Wisconsin and northeastern Iowa. There are temporal differences in the popularity of these points, with stemmed and notched points more common before about AD 800, and simple triangular points more common after that date. Small stemmed and notched point types most likely include Scallorn, Koster Corner Notched, and Klunk Side Notched, which are present as well in the Initial Late Woodland period. The simple unnotched triangular points are Madison points, an arrow point type found widely throughout the eastern United States after about AD 800.[10]

Pounding, grinding, and nutting stones have been found in Effigy Mound culture components, too, as well as adzes, axes, and a few polished celts. Other common items of Effigy Mound material culture include bone awls, needles, punches, and beamers, and probably fishnets and fabrics. Copper knives, punches, and projectile points, bone harpoons and gaming pieces, simple fired clay elbow pipes, and galena are present less frequently. The ceremonial obsidian blades, cut mica, ear spools, effigy pipes, elaborately worked bone and shell, and other exotic artifacts of the Havana culture are conspicuously absent.

The material culture of the Effigy Mound culture exhibits several traits and developmental trends whose significance is discussed more fully below. These include the near absence of nonutilitarian items intended for elites or for mortuary use alone; the growing popularity of simple unnotched triangular projectile points; new ceramic technologies, forms, and design treatments; a clustering of ceramic design motifs into smaller regional spaces; an elaboration in complexity of ceramic design treatments and motifs through time; and the persistence of a unique and shared identity over a vast territory for at least 600 years.

The Sorg site in Dakota County and the Prior Lake Mound cluster in Scott County represent an Effigy Mound culture-related habitation and mound site, respectively.

The Sorg site (21DK01) is one of a cluster of related sites on Spring Lake along the Mississippi River in Dakota County. Elden Johnson, who excavated the site in 1953, 1954, and 1956, identified a sequence of Middle and Late Woodland deposits, with the latter deposits stratigraphically above the former.[11] Late Woodland ceramics included Madison Cord Impressed, Madison Punctated, and Madison Plain. Johnson named the regional Late Woodland complex the Nininger focus and suggested that it was related to Wisconsin's Effigy Mound complex.

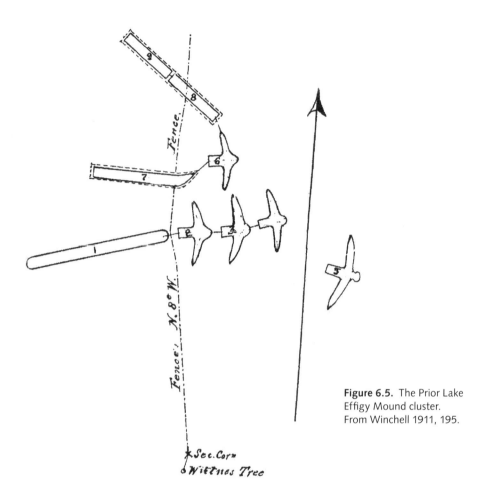

Figure 6.5. The Prior Lake Effigy Mound cluster. From Winchell 1911, 195.

The Prior Lake Effigy Mound cluster (21SC16) is in an upland setting in Scott County peripheral to the driftless area. It is the only site with effigy mounds in Minnesota that is not in a county bordering the Mississippi River. When mapped in 1883, the cluster consisted of five bird effigies and four linear mounds between 1½ and 2 feet high.[12] The bird effigies, which were aligned as if they were members of a flock, had straight bodies and crescent-shaped wings like those of a swallow in flight; the wings extended at right angles from the body, and the birds' rear ends were rectangular (Figure 6.5). The dimensions of one bird, which was investigated during a salvage operation, give some idea of the size of these effigies. The body alone was 52 feet long and 15 feet wide, while the roughly elliptical head measured 18 feet by 15 feet. One wing was 69 feet long and 12 feet wide, and the other 72 feet long and 12 feet wide. No artifacts were found within the mound. This is the only effigy mound in Minnesota that has been test excavated by an archaeologist.[13]

Final Late Woodland, AD 1000–1200

The Final Late Woodland period marks a profound change in the archaeological record of southeastern Minnesota and the Upper Mississippi valley south of Minneapolis–St. Paul. Pure Late Woodland sites become rare; stockaded sites with an admixture of Late Woodland and Middle Mississippian traits (see chapter 7), including pottery, appear in areas of southwestern Wisconsin and northeastern Iowa and perhaps in the Red Wing locality in Minnesota; the construction of effigy mounds ceases (by about AD 1050); and large areas of the driftless area are apparently abandoned. By the end of the period, mound construction of any kind and the Late Woodland tradition itself come to an end in this area of the Upper Mississippi valley. This situation is in marked contrast to cultural developments at the time in the Great Lakes area and eastward, where a common community type is a stockade village occupied by corn-growing Late Woodland people who make grit-tempered collared pottery.

In the quad-state area of the Upper Mississippi River valley (the juncture of Wisconsin, Illinois, Iowa, and Minnesota), Final Woodland ceramics belong to the Grant series. These ceramics are a regional variant of more southern Canton ware and of what David Benn and William Green refer to as the High Rim horizon.[14] Grant ware vessels are grit-tempered, cord-roughened globular jars that may have prominent castellations, collars, squared orifices, or other special rim treatment that raises the height of the rim (Figure 6.6). Compared to Madison ware, Grant ware vessels have somewhat higher, more

Figure 6.6. Grant series pottery. Fred Edwards Cord-Impressed from the Bryan village.
Courtesy of the Wilford Archaeology Laboratory, University of Minnesota.

flaring rims, a broader vessel shoulder, thicker cord impressions made by less complicated cord types, fewer combinations of decorative bands, and a more careful smoothing
of the exterior surface before decoration was applied. Decoration when present consists
most generally of single-cord impressions that form zigzags, chevrons, and other designs
over plain or cord-roughened rim surfaces. Bowls are present in some assemblages.

The particular shape of these high-rim vessels has been explained in several different ways. Benn and Green suggest that the vessels were designed for simmering large
quantities of seed foods into a gruel.[15] In this regard, they point to the vessels' globular
body, which distributes heat better and holds more seeds than a similar-sized vessel with
a conoidal or semiconoidal base and constricted neck, which retains heat better than an
openmouthed vessel, and to long-term regional trends in the refinement of vessel form
and paste technology that made vessels ever more effective boiling containers for seed
foods. It has also been suggested that the high rim of the vessels, which is far higher than
required to affix a cover, was designed to provide space for the display of elaborate chevron motifs, castellations, and various types of bracing, like collars. Perhaps the chevron
motifs were intended to depict the breast and wings of the falcon/thunderbird, as suggested for some Illinois valley Canton vessels and for some later Mississippian period vessels.[16]

Grant ware is regularly found in assemblages intermixed with Middle Mississippian pottery, as at Fred Edwards in southwestern Wisconsin and Hartley Fort in northeastern Iowa. Culturally mixed components have also been found in habitation areas at the Mero I and Bryan sites, and in burial mounds at the Mero I and Birch Lake mound cluster in the Red Wing locality of Minnesota and Wisconsin (see chapter 7). Of particular interest is the presence of Mississippian-type vessels in a panther effigy at the Mero I site.[17]

On the Minnesota side of the Red Wing local-ity, Grant ware has been tentatively identified at the Bryan site and at the King Coulee site in Wabasha County. It is also present at sites on the Wisconsin side of the locality.

Weapon points during this period include simple unnotched Madison triangular arrow points and Cahokia Side Notched cluster arrow points (Ca-hokia, Reed, Harrell, and/or Des Moines) (Figure 6.7).

Figure 6.7. Madison *(top)* and Cahokia Side Notched arrow points. Courtesy of the Minnesota Historical Society. Printed with permission.

Cahokia Side Notched cluster points resemble Late Woodland/Mississippian Triangular cluster points except for the presence of notches on the side and occasionally on the base.

THE TERMINAL WOODLAND ARCHAEOLOGICAL RECORD
IN SOUTHWESTERN MINNESOTA

The transition to Terminal Woodland artifact styles occurred somewhat later and more gradually in the Prairie Lake resource region of southwestern Minnesota. While there may be a shift to the bow and arrow and limited (if any) use of burial mounds early in the period, the subsistence-settlement pattern does not appear to change at this time, and the ceramics show only gradual shifts in decorative styles and manufacturing techniques. By AD 700, however, more dramatic changes are evident in the ceramic technology, and the use of burial mounds appears to be widespread. These changes in ceramics and mortuary practices mark the end of the Fox Lake phase and the beginning of the Lake Benton phase. The Lake Benton phase probably persisted well into the Late Prehistoric period, coexisting and probably interacting with Plains Village, Cambria, and Great Oasis neighbors until AD 1200/1300, when the resource region seems to have been abandoned except for hunting or gathering forays, or both.[18]

Although Lake Benton ceramics are the most distinguishing identifier for the presence of a Lake Benton component, these ceramics are more difficult to identify than are Fox Lake ceramics because of their similarity to other wares, especially the St. Croix–Onamia series in central Minnesota.[19] However, within the Prairie Lake resource region Lake Benton ceramics are marked by the extensive use of exterior cord-wrapped-stick impressions and by the absence of trailed lines and bosses (Figure 6.8). Though ceramic styles changed gradually from Fox Lake to Lake Benton ware, manufacturing techniques changed more rapidly. These include a shift from sand to crushed-rock temper and a more extensive use of surface smoothing. Lake Benton ceramics also exhibit many of the characteristics and trends of other early Late Woodland complexes in the upper Midwest in that they become thinner walled and more globular in shape through time.

The widespread popularity of cord-wrapped-stick decoration on Lake Benton ceramics is unusual, for this decorative technique is a characteristic of Late Woodland ceramics in the forests of central and northern Minnesota rather than of ceramic assemblages to the east, south, and west of the Prairie Lake resource region, where decoration is more commonly made using single twisted cord impressions. Single twisted cord–impressed ceramics are widespread in Late Woodland contexts in the Midwest, as represented by Madison Cord Impressed and Lane Farm Cord Impressed, and in the east-central Plains, as represented by Loseke ware. The decorative technique is also

Figure 6.8. Lake Benton phase pottery vessel.
Courtesy of the Minnesota Historical Society. Printed with permission.

associated with early Plains Village ceramics, including the Initial and Extended Middle Missouri variants in the central Dakotas, Mill Creek in northwestern Iowa, and Cambria in southwestern Minnesota. The common presence of cord-wrapped-stick impressions on Lake Benton pottery suggests that the Native Americans who made the pottery had a closer relationship (at least in this manufacturing sphere) with hunter-gatherers who lived in the forests of central Minnesota than with people who lived in the prairies around them.

Other identifying characteristics of Lake Benton phase components are their presence within the southwestern corner of the state south of the Minnesota River and west of the Blue Earth River, calibrated radiocarbon dates that fall within the AD 700–1300 period, and probable association with the first earthen burial mounds in the resource region.

As with Fox Lake phase assemblages, Lake Benton assemblages contain no non-projectile point chipped-stone tool types exclusively associated with the phase. Lake Benton has the general hunting-oriented tool kit with end and side scrapers, regular and irregular shaped knives, a few specialized drilling and engraving tools, and a wide variety of flake tools that first make their appearance in the resource region in the Middle Archaic.

Because soil churning has mixed together Fox Lake, Lake Benton, Plains Village, and Oneota assemblages or some combination of two or more of these assemblages at many sites, it is difficult to determine which projectile points found at these sites are associated with a Lake Benton component. The strongest associations appear to be with small side-notched points with straight to slightly concave bases (Figure 6.9). These points are commonly referred to as Plains Side Notched and are exemplified by the Avonlea point type. Some corner-notched points, equilateral triangular points, and perhaps side-notched points with deep concave bases may also have persisted in use after the fading away of Fox Lake ceramics.

Regardless, the presence of equilateral points in later Fox Lake components indicates that the shift from the dart to the bow and arrow in the Prairie Lake resource region occurred at that earlier time and not following the emergence of the Lake Benton phase. Lithic raw materials in Lake Benton assemblages show a continued reliance on chert, chalcedony, and quartzite from local till sources. No information on bone, antler, or other kinds of artifacts is presently available.

Figure 6.9. Lake Benton phase projectile points. From Hudak 1974, Plate 7.

A total of forty-three sites are reported to have Lake Benton components.[20] For the most part these sites are concentrated in the Prairie Lake resource region south of the Minnesota River and east of the Blue Earth River, though some components are north and east of these rivers, and in eastern South Dakota and north-central Iowa. It is thought that more Lake Benton components are present north of the Minnesota River than currently recorded because of the difficulty in some instances of distinguishing Lake Benton ware from vessels in the St. Croix–Onamia ceramic series. The implication is that because the components are outside the presumed core area of the Prairie Lake resource region, they are more likely to be identified as Onamia rather than Lake Benton (see chapter 8). No evidence of houses, substantial storage pits, or internal site patterning has been uncovered in these Lake Benton components. The few features encountered at the Johnsrud site were shallow basins (10 to 25 centimeters deep) filled with habitation refuse.

Most burial mounds in the Prairie Lake resource region seem to be temporally if not culturally associated with the Lake Benton phase, for none have radiocarbon dates of Fox Lake age, and earlier ceramics are neither associated with the original mound burials nor present in the mound fill. Of the fifty-four mounds known from thirty-seven excavated mound sites in the resource region, thirty-two mounds from twenty-two sites are probably associated with the Woodland tradition, and the remainder with Plains Village complexes.

The excavated Woodland mounds share a number of characteristics.[21] Most are circular in outline, while a few are slightly elongated to linear in shape. No effigy mounds are present. Assumed Lake Benton mounds typically have moderate to large basal diameters (30 to 80 feet, with an average of 50 feet) and relatively low heights (1 to 10 feet, with an average of 4 feet). They occur alone or in small groups, with the average group containing four mounds, the largest group twenty-six mounds, and the next largest group fifteen mounds. The largest mound group (21NL1) is at the eastern margin of the Prairie Lake resource region. All but four of the mound groups are located on lakes, and only a few are associated with habitation sites. The dominant burial mode is the presence of multiple secondary burials in a shallow pit. The number of individuals buried in a pit ranges from one to twelve skeletons, with an average of six individuals. Both sexes are usually present, and all age groups can be represented. Evidence of cremation or charring is rare. Grave goods are not common, but when present, are usually shell ornaments, such as beads and pendants. Red ochre, hearths, and cobble concentrations are occasionally present. Many of the mounds contain intrusive burials of later prehistoric and even historic age.

The following three sites exemplify the problems and potential of working at Lake Benton phase sites.

Pedersen (21LN02), the type-site of the phase, is a deeply stratified, multiple component site on an island in Lake Benton in Lincoln County.[22] Although a final report on site excavations has not been prepared, levels 2 through 4 of the 1973 excavation contain the strongest Lake Benton affiliation. Anfinson has used the relatively large artifact assemblage in these levels to give a rough idea of what a Lake Benton assemblage looks like, to show how Lake Benton and earlier Fox Lake assemblages differ, and to demonstrate continuity between the two archaeological cultures.[23]

The Round Mound (21TR01) is one of the few Terminal Woodland mortuary sites in the Prairie Lake resource region to have undergone some bioarchaeological analysis.[24] The Round Mound is one of three mounds in a mortuary site about 1½ miles from Lake Traverse in Traverse County. The mound contained fifty-two human burials, nine bison burials, and a stone cairn placed among the human burials. Of the fifty-two human burials, thirty-five were identified as adults, seven as adolescents, four as children, three as young children, and three as infants. Eleven of the burials were primary interments, and thirty-one were secondary bundle burials. The remaining burials were too fragmentary to identify burial mode. Lloyd Wilford thought the primary burials were intrusive Cambria burials (see chapter 7), and the bundle burials Kathio phase–related (see chapter 8) based on mode of burial. However, as indicated earlier, his assignment of burials to archaeological complexes solely on the basis of burial mode remains controversial and is best regarded today as only one possible interpretation. No diagnostic artifacts were found in the mound.

Johnsrud Area B (21DL76) is one of the few undisturbed, single component Lake Benton sites where the flotation of site sediment has been carried out.[25] The site is near the shore of Lake Oscar in Douglas County. The remains of small and large mammals, fish, and wild and domestic (maize) plant parts were recovered. The site seems to have experienced a single expedient and brief use, with raw materials obtained locally. An analysis of wood remains identified a preponderance of oak of the red oak group, but also silver maple, basswood, and American elm. The mixture of tree species suggests a somewhat different forest community in the area than the current maple-basswood forest.

TERMINAL WOODLAND LIFEWAYS
IN SOUTHERN MINNESOTA

Although a highly dynamic period of economic, demographic, and socioreligious change, the Terminal (Late) Woodland in southeastern Minnesota has received slight attention as a subject of study in itself by Minnesota archaeologists. As a consequence, my interpretations of lifeway changes during this period are tentative. Nonetheless, the changes that seem to have taken place remain consistent with what would be expected according to Binford's thought-provoking ideas in *Constructing Frames of Reference*.

Present evidence suggests that the long-established hunter-gatherer lifeway in southeastern Minnesota seems to have continued to about AD 800, after which significant changes occurred in technology, population distribution, and social structure. In her review of Initial Woodland lifeways in the driftless area, Lynn Alex concludes, for example, that the content of early components "show a continuation of local resource exploitation similar to that seen at earlier Millville phase sites."[26] Why did these changes occur, and what in particular changed?

Wisconsin archaeologists James Theler and Constance (Connie) Arzigian provide scenarios for lifeways before AD 800 and after AD 800 for southern areas of the driftless area above the 42.6° latitude terrestrial plant threshold.[27] This cycle has a fall-winter-early spring segment and a late spring-summer segment.

In the fall, small family bands moved into the more protected areas of the driftless area, where they concentrated on the harvesting and processing of white-tailed deer between the months of August and September. Small mammals, elk, and black bear were taken in smaller numbers, and an occasional bison was slain in prairie habitats. Both wild and domesticated plants and probably dried mussels processed during the summer were carried along to the fall-winter-early spring camps for consumption. Among the wide variety of plant foods found in archaeological sites representing this segment of the annual cycle are nuts (hickory, butternut, and walnut), chenopod seeds, maize, sunflower seeds, wild rice, great bulrush seeds, hackberry seeds, wild bean, and ground cherry seeds. Most known sites are residential camps in rockshelters in the dissected uplands of the driftless area. Other site types associated with this segment of the subsistence-settlement cycle are open-air, short-term task-specific extractive camps and more intensely occupied base camps.

The late spring-summer segment of the cycle revolved around the procurement of aquatic resources and plant foods in more open riverine settings of the Mississippi and its major tributaries. Fish and freshwater mussels were the most important animal foods, although mammals were captured, too, including white-tailed deer. It was during this segment that mussels and many plant foods were gathered and processed for winter consumption. Most known site components associated with this segment of the seasonal cycle are residential camps located in the floodplain of the Mississippi River adjacent to abundant aquatic resources. These sites typically lack the hide/leather-working tool assemblage so common in fall-winter-early spring camps.

Did Late Woodland communities in southeastern Minnesota follow this proposed pre–AD 800 Effigy Mound settlement-subsistence pattern? The simple answer is that we do not know at the present time. Possible examples of fall residential camps in rockshelters in Minnesota are Tudahl (21FL3) and Nohre (21FL13), while the Hyland Park site on a peninsula in Hyland Lake near Prior Lake and a site on Grey Cloud Island in Cottage Grove may be examples of open-air, short-term extractive camps. Both of these small sites contained a hearth or two, small amounts of pottery, the remains of several deer, and chipped stone artifacts appropriate for the capture and processing of these animals.

At least in the Prairie du Chien area of Wisconsin, a shift away from the seasonal cycle described above is apparent by about AD 800. Although components in the Mill Pond site show that mussel-processing stations unassociated with residential areas existed long before this date, an increase in the number of such stations and the amount of shell they contain point to an intensification of mussel harvesting between AD 800 and 1000. Theler suggests that this shift is related to increased population packing and scheduling conflicts induced by increased dietary dependence on maize, and the collapse of two critical resources, deer and firewood, among other factors.[28] Since maize matures in the fall, the seasonal movement to interior upland locations would have been delayed. To hedge against a poor maize harvest, a delayed or possibly poor deer harvest, or both, Effigy Mound groups in the area seem to have harvested large amounts of shellfish, which they dried for winter consumption.

The presence of maize cultivation in Effigy Mound sites is not surprising, for it appears in a few Middle Woodland sites in Illinois and is present in the form of phytolith assemblages on Initial Woodland Malmo sherds in central Minnesota and Laurel sherds to the north in Canada. In southeastern Minnesota twelve-row maize has been found with Madison Cord Impressed pottery and a possible oval wigwam-like structure at the Nelson site (21BE24) in Blue Earth County.[29] However, the use of maize seems still limited to small-scale gardening, for no substantial subsurface storage pits similar to those found in abundance at later Oneota village sites are present. Effigy Mound peoples were still hunter-gatherer-fisher folk, then, who were adding some cultigens to their diet. Other domesticates include squash at the King Coulee site in Wabasha County at AD 780, and sunflowers and knotweed from Effigy Mound sites in southwestern Wisconsin.[30]

Most archaeologists agree that after about AD 800 Native Americans with an Effigy Mound Late Woodland culture in the driftless area and immediate environs lived in family-based bands that followed a yearly round within territories they considered their own. Bill Hurley suggests that these territories probably covered about 40 to 50 square miles and that there were four or so of these territorial groups in the driftless area.[31] Mound form and distribution have also been used as a source of information about Effigy Mound social organization.

Besides being organized in territorial bands, Effigy Mound societies are also thought to have lived an egalitarian lifestyle. There is growing evidence, however, that regional differences in local group size and social complexity were developing in conjunction with an increasingly differential reliance on cultivated plant foods. Theler and Boszhardt suggest that population increases led to a more sedentary, circumscribed way of life, increasing dependence on maize horticulture, disruption of the earlier pattern of seasonal dispersal of family bands, larger aggregations of people organized in a nuclear pattern of household residence and cooperation, tribal social organization, and stronger intraregional and interregional economic ties, since it was no longer efficient, necessary, or even possible for each household to be a self-sufficient unit.[32] According to their interpretation, the eventual collapse of two crucial resources (deer and firewood) caused the interior of the driftless area to be abandoned at about AD 1050–1100. Their interpretation raises questions about the reasons for change in lifeways in the Late Woodland period in the driftless area.

Let's consider two scenarios that try to account for this change. According to the emergent-state hypothesis, as expressed by James Stoltman and George Christiansen, the admixture of ceramic traits in the Mero I Final Late Woodland component in the Red Wing locality represents "an episode in the evolutionary trajectory leading to mature Oneota culture that came to dominate the upper Mississippi Valley region after AD 1200."[33] They describe this trajectory in the final paragraph of their summary of the Late Woodland stage in the driftless area of the Upper Mississippi valley:

Under the emergent-state hypothesis, we visualize the following scenario. During the late tenth century AD, Effigy Mound culture was in its mature stages throughout most of southern Wisconsin. Practicing a cultivating ecosystem type of subsistence (Stoltman and Baerreis 1983), Effigy Mound peoples led a highly mobile lifestyle that involved periodic congregation at mound groups where burial rites and mound construction served to affirm corporate social bonds while simultaneously demarcating and sanctifying territorial boundaries. Between AD 1000 and AD 1050, profound cultural influences, ultimately derived from the great American Bottom center of Cahokia, began to permeate the upper Mississippi Valley (Stoltman 1991). These influences almost certainly were multidimensional, having social, economic, religious, and possibly even political overtones. Within this context, enhanced by the success with which maize could be grown in volume and stored for long periods, it can be imagined that the Effigy Mound peoples abandoned much of their traditional domain within the heart of the Driftless Area to congregate at such key locations as the Red Wing locality, where the valued goods, services, and information emanating from the Cahokia world could be readily accessed. Mound construction was not immediately abandoned, as is documented by the enormous concentrations of mounds in the Red Wing locality—T. H. Lewis reported over 2,000 there (Gibbon and Dobbs 1991:281). Eventually, however, mound building waned and was seemingly no longer practiced in the region after circa AD 1200. Perhaps the adoption of an increasingly sedentary lifestyle and, along with it, new forms of communal ceremonies (like planting and harvesting rites) provided a new social milieu within which the old practice of periodic congregation at dispersed Effigy Mound sites no longer was viable. It was in this overall setting, we postulate, that the indigenous Late Woodland peoples of the Driftless Area and its environs "evolved" into Oneota culture, which we see at Diamond Bluff as "a work in progress."

An alternative cultural interaction hypothesis suggests a more multifaceted, if also ultimately linear, scenario.[34] According to this perspective, the cultural innovations that were transforming the heartland of the Mississippi valley between AD 800 and 1000 also strongly influenced Woodland peoples in the Upper Mississippi valley and elsewhere.[35] These innovations led by AD 1050 to the emergence of a chiefdom level of cultural complexity at the site of Cahokia in the American Bottom near St. Louis, and to the appearance of Oneota communities in eastern Wisconsin and of Plains Village communities along the Minnesota and Missouri Rivers (see chapter 7), among the shift of many other communities to a more settled, maize-growing lifeway. Importantly, the turmoil that Theler and Boszhardt believe was caused by purely internal developments, such as population packing and loss of critical resources, was caused as much, if not more so, I believe, by tensions sent throughout the upper Midwest by cultural developments at Cahokia and elsewhere in the American Bottom and in areas to the south.[36] I rely here on Morton Fried's notion that the emergence of a tribal level of social organization is a response in large part to the interaction between less complex and more complex (and perhaps aggressive) social groups.[37]

It is within this context, I believe, that some late Effigy Mound peoples were drawn to the Red Wing locality by circa AD 1050, perhaps by a contingent of Middle Mississippians, where they formed an intertwined assemblage of peoples. Chapter 7 describes the Silvernale phase, which developed from these (or other) origins. Both the construction of effigy mounds and of Woodland ceramic vessels soon ceased as new worldviews and sociopolitical alliances emerged.

These developments in southeastern Minnesota, although perhaps buried in detail, seem consistent with the scenario that Binford predicts. I return to these cultural changes in this cultural resource region in chapter 7.

The subsistence pattern of the Lake Benton phase appears similar to that of the Fox Lake phase, with the possible addition of maize (thought to be traded in), although the quality of existing data for Lake Benton components is poor.[38] The Arthur and Big Slough sites both contain major Lake Benton components, but the stratigraphy at both is confused. Assuming that most of the faunal remains from Arthur are associated with the Late Woodland components (since most of the ceramics are), then the basic Lake Benton subsistence pattern features a variety of mammals (dominated by bison and muskrat) and fish. The same assumption can be made for the Big Slough site, where a similar faunal inventory exists, although stratigraphic trends suggest a slight increase in bison and a decrease in fish and birds through time.

It seems then that Lake Benton hunters and gatherers apparently relied, like their Fox Lake predecessors, on a variety of large and small mammals and on fish, with bison probably the most important species in the varied inventory. Investigations of faunal remains from two single-component Lake Benton sites at Lake Oscar generally support this interpretation.

In spite of the widespread use of domesticated plants in contemporary Plains Village and Midwestern Late Woodland complexes, there is no evidence that Lake Benton people practiced horticulture, although they may have obtained maize through trade. They probably made extensive use, too, of local native plants, an assumption supported by the recovery of hazelnut and winter grape (as well as maize) through flotation at the Johnsrud Area B (21DL76) site on Lake Oscar.[39]

The Lake Benton settlement pattern seems similar to that of Fox Lake as well, for most Lake Benton components are at sites with a Fox Lake component. These sites are thus located on islands, peninsulas, or isthmuses at lakes, presumably for protection from fire and hostile neighbors, but also perhaps to harvest trees spared from fire.[40]

Unlike during the Fox Lake period, the Prairie Lake resource region was now being occupied or at least utilized by multiple cultures, including Cambria, Great Oasis, and possibly other Plains Village groups (see chapter 7). It seems that some of these contemporary people, such as those associated with the Cambria complex, lived in sizable villages and cultivated domesticated plants, while Lake Benton populations continued to be relatively mobile hunter-gatherers who lived in short-term habitation sites. Both of these cultural groups disappear from the archaeological record after about AD 1200. After this date the resource region was mainly used by Oneota procurement groups whose villages were along the Blue Earth River in south-central Minnesota and in northwest Iowa (see chapter 7).

Unlike the southeastern part of the state, the Prairie Lake resource region in the southwestern corner appears to have experienced a lower level of resource intensification, though indicators of increased intensification are present, such as the presence of burial mounds and a greater use of plant foods like maize. Rather than experiencing the in-place cultural transformation of hunter-gatherers in the southeastern part of the state, the hunter-gatherers responsible for the Fox Lake and Lake Benton archaeological cultures seem to have eventually abandoned the area and the bison-centered lifeway they had practiced for at least a thousand years in the prairies of southwestern Minnesota.

CHAPTER 7

First Tribes in Southern Minnesota

Mississippian and Plains Village Adaptations

The long Woodland dominance in southern Minnesota came to an end between AD 900 and 1100 with the sudden appearance of Native American societies with new material cultures, subsistence-settlement patterns, social organizations, and ideologies. These societies were more dependent on maize than earlier local Woodland societies, and lived in larger, more permanent settlements that were often fortified. Their sites are easily recognized by their distinctive pottery, which was usually decorated on the shoulder rather than the rim and often had smoothed rather than cordmarked exterior surfaces, shell temper rather than grit temper, and handles rather than collars or castellations.

In the 1930s and 1940s, these new complexes were grouped into subdivisions of the Mississippian cultural tradition because many of their material and adaptive traits were considered more like those of complex cultures in the central Mississippi River valley than like those of local Woodland cultures. Because of their geographical location, the more hierarchically organized, fully sedentary farming societies in the central Mississippi River valley were called Middle Mississippian, while the simpler societies on their northern fringe were called Upper Mississippian, if they were woodland or prairie adapted, and Plains Village Mississippian, if they were plains adapted. It was generally assumed at one time—and some archaeologists still make this assumption—that these fringe societies were either migrants from the south or heirs of Woodland populations whose own cultures were radically modified through contact with Middle Mississippian societies. Today, archaeologists realize that the processes leading to the appearance of these new societies were more complex—and interesting—than these simple scenarios suggest. As a consequence, the terms *Upper* and *Plains Village Mississippian* with their connotations of southern dependence are falling from general usage. I continue to use the term *Mississippian* here, however, because it is widely used, its use makes comparisons with other areas easier, and some term is still necessary to mark the transformations that did occur.

THE ARCHAEOLOGICAL RECORD OF THE SILVERNALE, GREAT OASIS, CAMBRIA, AND BIG STONE COMPLEXES

The Silvernale Phase

Middle Mississippian traits are concentrated in two areas of Minnesota. One area is along the trench of the Minnesota River from Mankato to the Red River of the North. The other is near Red Wing at the confluence of the Cannon and Mississippi Rivers. The Red Wing area has long been known as one of the richest archaeological regions in Minnesota. By the early 1900s, T. H. Lewis, J. V. Brower, and other amateur archaeologists had recorded and mapped more than 2,000 mounds in the area and had documented the presence of several village sites.

Modern archaeological investigations began in the late 1940s with Moreau Maxwell's excavations for Beloit College at the Mero site across the river in Wisconsin and Wilford's excavations at the Bryan and Silvernale sites, three of the large village sites mapped earlier. Wilford recognized that the clearest expression of Middle Mississippian traits in the state occurred within this complex of sites, which he referred to as the Silvernale focus, one whose ceramics resembled those in Middle Mississippian sites in Illinois and southern Wisconsin.[1] The nature of the Silvernale phase, as it is now called, and its relationship to the strong Oneota presence in the area and to the immense site of Cahokia in Illinois, which was the center of a complex chiefdom, have been disputed among archaeologists for many years.

Key identifying characteristics of Silvernale phase components include the presence of large, fortified villages usually surrounded by numerous conical earthen burial mounds, the extensive use of Grand Meadow chert and Hixton silicified sandstone in the chipped stone tool assemblage (the sources of these raw materials are in southeastern Minnesota and western Wisconsin, respectively), the presence of locally made and perhaps imported shell-tempered pottery jars with Middle Mississippian rolled rims, angular shoulders, and Ramey scroll designs (Figure 7.1), evidence of a maize-based horticultural subsistence base (corn kernels, bison scapula hoes, and numerous large subsurface storage pits), and a Plains-related bone-antler-tooth industry.

Other characteristics of the phase itself include the presence of an earthen platform mound, copper and marine shell objects with Southeastern Ceremonial complex motifs, such as a "short-nosed god" maskette, small amounts of exotic pottery (e.g., Cambria phase–related), the importance of fishing and deer hunting in the diet, radiocarbon dates that cluster between AD 1050 and 1200, and a geographical location (except for a rare sherd or two) confined to the Red Wing area of Minnesota and Wisconsin.[2]

If concentrating only on the Middle Mississippian elements in the ceramic assemblage, it might be tempting to label Silvernale a Middle Mississippian complex. But other artifacts in the assemblage have an Upper Mississippian cast to them. For example, the chipped stone assemblage with its relatively large numbers of scrapers resembles Cambria and Oneota village site assemblages more closely than assemblages from more southern Middle Mississippian habitation sites. The stone materials used also seem local to the Upper Mississippi River valley (e.g., a fine gray chert, oolitic chert, jasper, quartzite, agate). In addition, Middle Mississippian stone discoidals, hoes, spades, and knives are absent. It is probably for these reasons that Wilford assigned the phase to the Upper rather than to the Middle Mississippian aspect.

Figure 7.1. A Silvernale phase pottery vessel. Courtesy of the Minnesota Historical Society. Printed with permission.

Clark Dobbs in numerous publications has suggested that the dense concentration of Mississippian-related and Oneota village sites and earthworks at the confluence of the Cannon and Trimbelle Rivers with the Mississippi in Goodhue County, Minnesota, and Pierce County, Wisconsin, represents a discrete region of settlement, which he has named the Red Wing locality (Map 7.1). The 58-square-mile locality, which is about 500 miles upriver from Cahokia and the American Bottom, contains more than 2,000 mounds and earthworks, eight major villages, and dozens of smaller secondary sites. According to Dobbs, "The Locality is the most northern center of Mississippian interaction in eastern North America and is (arguably) the largest cluster of Mississippian-related sites in the northern Mississippi Valley."[3]

Dobbs has also defined five types of Mississippian sites for the Red Wing locality: large villages, including Bryan, Silvernale, Mero, and Adams; smaller villages, including Energy Park, Double, Bartron, and probably Belle Creek; small outlying sites that may represent farmsteads or minor communities; small special function sites that contain few formal tools but relatively large numbers of cores and flakes; and small special function

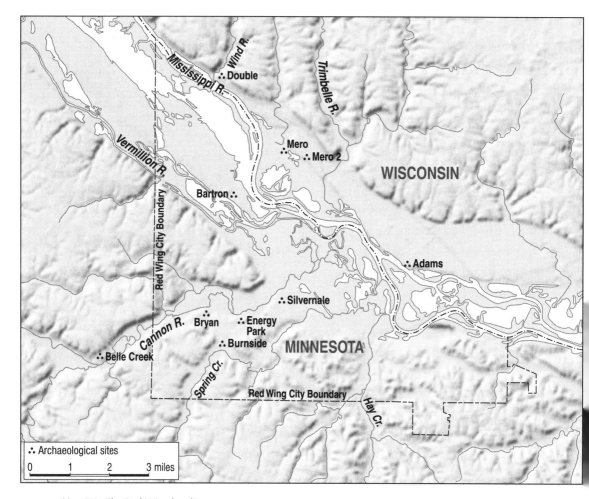

Map 7.1. The Red Wing locality.

sites characterized by the absence of pottery and formal tools, the presence of a moderate to very low artifact density, and a high proportion of retouched or utilized flakes.

The most extensively excavated and examined Silvernale phase site is Bryan, which is a 20-acre village on a terrace overlooking the Cannon River. Portions of a palisade, numerous storage/refuse pits, and four types of buildings have been discovered at the site. The four types of building are a semisubterranean, rectangular (7.5 by 6.7 feet) posthole structure with a floor about 1.6 feet below the upper surface of the C-horizon of the soil profile; a semisubterranean, circular structure 8.6 feet in diameter with a floor about 2.3 feet below the surface of the sod; a square pattern of post molds; and a circle of post molds. Several roughly square semisubterranean houses have also been excavated at the Mero site on the Wisconsin side of the locality.

Five different types of mound groups have been defined for the locality. These are mound groups containing more than fifty mounds that are principally or exclusively conical and/or linear in form; groups of ten to fifty that contain linear, conical, and effigy mounds; groups of fewer than ten conical mounds; specialized groups containing mounds and/or other features like rock cairns; and sites containing earthen embankments and/or fortifications. The relationship of these mounds to the Silvernale phase remains somewhat moot, although Middle Mississippian ceramics are present in the mounds that have been excavated. In 1885, a flat-topped rectangular platform mound on a terrace between Silvernale and Bryan was also mapped. At the time, the mound was 4 feet high and 48 by 60 feet at the base; the flat top platform was 24 by 39 feet on its sides. Flat-topped, rectangular platform mounds are a characteristic trait of Middle Mississippian village sites.

A number of individuals were also buried in belowground "storage" pits at the Bryan site. Thurston and O'Connell's bioarchaeological study of a nearly complete female older than forty years in one of these burial pits found that she had severe osteoarthritis affecting nearly every joint including the vertebral column, and extensive dental pathology.[4] She had lost at least thirteen teeth before death, and the remaining teeth in her mouth were affected by severe carious lesions, most likely the result of a high-starch (corn) diet.

The Great Oasis Phase

If the Mississippi River up to the Twin Cities is a four-lane interstate freeway, other rivers within the state are two-lane highways and rural gravel roads. While the Red Wing locality is at the head of the interstate, Cambria sites are largely scattered along a busy two-lane highway (the Minnesota River). By contrast, Great Oasis sites can only be reached by gravel roads, for they are around isolated lakes in the Prairie Lake resource region. Nonetheless, like the Silvernale phase, both complexes are exemplars of the tribalization process, which is discussed in the lifeways section of this chapter. Both Cambria and Great Oasis people lived at least part of the year in semipermanent villages and engaged in corn horticulture, though whether Great Oasis people actually planted corn in Minnesota (rather than brought it in from Iowa, Nebraska, or the Dakotas) remains a debated topic. Taxonomically, Cambria and Great Oasis are complexes within the Initial Variant of the Plains Village tradition along with the more distant Mill Creek (Iowa) and Over (South Dakota) cultures.

Lloyd Wilford first identified Great Oasis as a focus on the basis of his excavations at the Great Oasis type-site in Murray County.[5] It is now considered one of the earliest (AD 950–1100) and most widespread Plains Village cultures in north-central North America.

Besides its limited presence in southwestern Minnesota, where it is represented by only one village site (Great Oasis) and several campsites, components of the complex are present in southeastern South Dakota and along the Missouri River as far north as the big bend below Pierre, northeastern Nebraska, southeastern North Dakota, and, especially, central and northwestern Iowa.[6]

In Minnesota the presence of Great Oasis ceramics is the most easily recognizable sign that a component of the complex is at a site. Great Oasis ceramic vessels are globular-shaped jars with rounded shoulders

Figure 7.2. Great Oasis phase High Rim rim sherd.
Courtesy of the Minnesota Historical Society. Printed with permission.

and bottoms, fine grit to grog temper, a constricted neck and outflaring, often high rim, a flat lip, and relatively thin walls. Exterior vessel surfaces are smoothed or smooth-over-cordmarked, with decoration on most vessels on the rim exterior and lip (Figure 7.2). Vessel decoration often consists of complex trailed line motifs. Sites may contain deep storage and refuse pits, scattered corn kernels, and an array of bone, chipped stone, and ground stone artifacts, including scrapers, knives, small notched and unnotched arrow points, hammerstones, arrowshaft abraders, and bone fleshers. In Minnesota, components are typically in traditional Woodland positions on lakes.

Great Oasis villages characteristically contain numerous deep storage/trash pits and, at least outside Minnesota, evidence for the presence of substantial buildings. The remains of four semisubterranean rectangular lodges 20 to 40 feet long were encountered during excavations at the West Broken Kettle site, an Iowa site along a terrace overlooking a creek. A central fire pit and deep cache pits reaching a depth of 3 feet were inside the houses, which were lined by single or double rows of posts. Lodges were also encountered at the Maxwell site in Iowa and the Heath site in South Dakota.

Better known are smaller, probably summer settlements in Iowa and southeastern South Dakota. Although there is no evidence for the presence of substantial lodges at these hamlets and artifact density is lower than at winter villages, there is still a wide range of artifact types and activity areas. Pits filled with horticultural remains indicate that they are most likely the remains of small warm-weather farming communities.

Great Oasis burials have been found in cemeteries, as intrusions in Woodland mounds, and in storage pits in habitation sites. Dozens of burials, many in flexed positions, were encountered at the West Des Moines Burial site in Iowa, one of the more thoroughly investigated Great Oasis cemeteries.[7] Grave goods include whole Great Oasis ceramic vessels, a range of lithic artifacts, small mammal teeth, dozens of *Anculosa* shell beads, local freshwater artifacts, and eight "crosses" made of clamshell. Similar remains were found at the even larger DeCamp cemetery, also in Iowa.

The Cambria Phase

Most of the mounds and larger habitation sites now associated with the Cambria phase were mapped by T. H. Lewis and other pioneer surveyors in the late nineteenth century and are reported in Winchell's 1911 *The Aborigines of Minnesota*. All large Cambria village sites, with one exception, and most mounds associated with the phase are along the trench of the Minnesota River west of the big bend in the river at Mankato. Numerous prairie-lake and riverine sites in the uplands south of the river, however, also contain at least a few Cambria sherds. A few sherds have been found, too, north of the river at sites in Otter Tail County in west-central Minnesota and at sites in the Red Wing locality. For the most part, however, Cambria sites are concentrated in the Prairie Lake region of southwestern Minnesota. Today, Cambria is considered a phase in an eastern division of the Initial Variant of the Middle Missouri tradition. It is generally dated between AD 1000 and 1200.

Cambria components are most easily recognized by the presence of distinctive pottery sherds from globular jars with grit temper, constricted necks, pronounced shoulders, and smooth surfaces. A small cluster of sites about 15 miles upriver from Mankato contain rustic versions of Middle Mississippian Powell Plain and Ramey Incised pottery, as well as pottery vessels that are similar to more western Initial Middle Missouri tradition ceramic types (Figure 7.3). All other known Cambria components contain only those Cambria pottery types that resemble Initial Middle Missouri types. With one known exception, all large and secondary villages are situated within the valley of the Minnesota River, while small special activity sites with a few Cambria sherds are scattered throughout the Prairie Lake region. Cambria components also contain a wide range of stone and bone tools that are similar to those found in other villages of the eastern division of the Initial variant of the Middle Missouri tradition.[8]

Cambria phase sites have been grouped into four categories by Elden Johnson: large village sites on terraces within the Minnesota River valley, secondary villages near the large sites, small upland prairie-lake and riverine sites, and burial sites.[9] Two large villages sites—Cambria and Gillingham, with Gillingham smaller than Cambria—and three to five secondary villages—Owen D. Jones, Price, and perhaps Gautefald, Harbo Hill, and Saienga—have been identified. All of these sites are within the trench of the Minnesota River, except Gautefald, which is about 7.5 miles to the southwest at the

Figure 7.3. Cambria phase shell-tempered Ramey Incised pottery vessel.
Courtesy of the Minnesota Historical Society. Printed with permission.

juncture of Spring Creek and the Yellow Medicine River. Habitation debris at Cambria, the best known of the large village sites, covers about 3.5 acres of an intermediate terrace of the trench of the Minnesota River. The site is generally considered in a defensive position, and Johnson has suggested that it and Gillingham were probably palisaded.[10]

Many earthen burial mounds have been associated with the Cambria phase. These associations remain tentative for the most part, however, for some have not been excavated and the contents of others are not sufficiently diagnostic to establish a definite link with the phase. Small circular burial mounds are associated with each of the Minnesota valley village sites. The Lewis mound group is the only other Cambria phase site presently known besides Cambria and Price to contain Middle Mississippian–like ceramics with rolled rims. The mound group is located on a high Minnesota River terrace 2 miles southeast of the Cambria site. Unlike the flexed primary interments in other Cambria phase mounds, the burials at Lewis were in a primary extended position, which is another trait more closely associated with Mississippian rather than Woodland burial practices.

Another Middle Mississippian trait possibly associated with the Cambria phase is the flat-topped earthen mound. T. H. Lewis mapped at least four flat-topped pyramidal mounds within the trench of the Minnesota valley and on a bluff overlooking Lake Traverse.[11] An example is the Odessa site, which is situated on a 65-foot-high terrace on the northeast side of the Minnesota River. When mapped, the diamond-shaped pyramidal structure measured 54 by 42 feet at the base, and 20 by 28 feet at its flat top; the mound's elevation does not seem to have been recorded. An associated long embankment was 722 feet long, 20 feet wide, and 1.5 to 2 feet in height.

The Big Stone Phase

The Big Stone phase (circa AD 1200–1300) is the taxonomic name of a cluster of sites centered around Big Stone Lake and Lake Traverse, which are located along the border between Minnesota and South Dakota near the head of the Minnesota River.[12] Characteristics of the phase include Woodland and Cambria phase–like pottery, fortified villages, and large percentages (42 to 57 percent) of west-central North Dakota Knife River flint in lithic (stone tool) assemblages. For the most part, sites are situated on high terraces and bluff-tops, perhaps for defensive purposes, for at least ten of the sites are fortified with combinations of embankments, palisades, and ditches (Map 7.2).

Archaeologists consider Big Stone a phase of the Initial Middle Missouri tradition within the Northeastern Plains Village complex. Dennis Toom in his 2004 review of the Northeastern Plains Village complex suggests that the population base of the phase was composed of former Cambria phase residents who, after the abandonment of the Big Stone–Lake Traverse area in about AD 1300, became part of the Scattered Village complex of the Middle Missouri River valley. Some part of the Big Stone phase population may have migrated still farther north into southern Manitoba. Was the Big Stone phase descended from the Cambria phase and ancestral to the Scattered Village complex? If so, what accounts for this northwestward movement of Native Americans sometime after AD 1200? An explanation favored by some archaeologists is the rapid growth and expansion of aggressive Oneota populations in the thirteenth century.[13]

THE ARCHAEOLOGICAL RECORD OF THE ONEOTA TRADITION

Oneota sites are widely distributed throughout the deciduous forests and prairies of southern Minnesota.[14] Regional variations of Oneota pottery, called the Ogechie series, are also found at sites in the northeastern prairie region and in the north woods. Radiocarbon determinations and the presence of historic trade goods in some sites indicate that this archaeological tradition appeared about AD 1225–1250 in Minnesota, and probably earlier in eastern Wisconsin, and persisted into the early historic period in some areas. This section concentrates on southern Minnesota, where two Oneota phases have been recognized: the Blue Earth phase, whose age range in Minnesota is unsettled but may be from AD 1225/1250 to 1500; and the protohistoric/early historic Orr phase (AD 1625–1700).

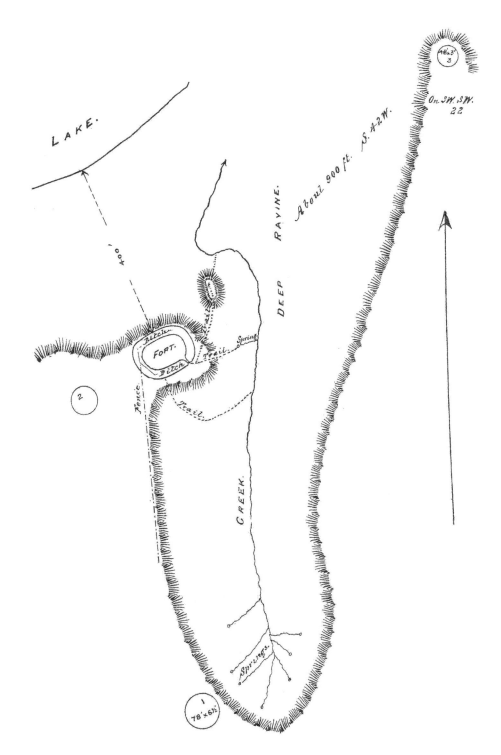

Map 7.2. The Big Stone Shady Dell fortified site. From Winchell 1911, 303.

The Blue Earth Phase

Blue Earth village sites are present in the Red Wing locality (Bartron), along the St. Croix River north of Stillwater (Sheffield), in several localities along the Blue Earth River (Center Creek and Willow Creek), and along the upper Minnesota River (Fort Ridgely).[15] Small amounts of prehistoric Oneota pottery are also present in the upper levels of many sites from the St. Croix and Mississippi River valleys in the east to the South Dakota border in the west. I consider this material part of the Blue Earth phase, too, which also has a strong presence in northwestern Iowa.

As with other ceramic-containing archaeological complexes in Minnesota, the presence of distinctive ceramics is the trait most frequently used to identify a Blue Earth Oneota component at a site. Vessels are shell-tempered, round-bottomed, globular jars with rounded lips and generally high straight to slightly out-curving rims that are slightly everted (Figure 7.4). Vessel capacities in a sample of jars from the Center Creek locality along the Blue Earth River range from 0.5 to 5 gallons. Short, double strap handles and loop handles are common. Vessel surfaces are smooth, except for occasional patches of smoothed-over cordmarking. Nearly all vessels are decorated on the shoulder.

Other, less common items used to identify Oneota components include the occasional presence of catlinite disc pipes, paired sandstone abraders, freshwater mussel–shell fish lures or decoys, bison and elk scapula hoes, and copper beads and ornaments

Figure 7.4. An Oneota Blue Earth phase pottery vessel. From Winchell 1911, 743.

(e.g., stylized serpents, maces, and raptorial birds). Chipped stone tools at village sites consist of simple unnotched triangular projectile (Madison) points, end and side scrapers, knives, drills, wedges, gravers, choppers, blade tools, and expedient flake tools.

Blue Earth settlements are typically open (unpalisaded) village farming communities that contain the remains of corn, beans, and squash and numerous circular subsurface storage pits. Evidence that hunting and gathering were important subsistence pursuits is present in these settlements and at special activity camps. In Minnesota, Blue Earth components are present south of the Minnesota River, except for a few sites in the St. Croix Valley.

Clark Dobbs and Orrin Shane identified two Oneota settlement localities, Center Creek and Willow Creek, along the Blue Earth River, each of which has about fifty Blue Earth phase sites.[16] For the Center Creek locality, which is at the confluence of Center Creek and the Blue Earth River, Dobbs has identified six settlement types.[17] The types are small hide-processing stations (small sites with low artifact densities and relatively large numbers of scrapers), habitation areas where hide processing was important (sites of variable size and artifact density with relatively large amounts of pottery and scrapers), lithic workshops (moderate-sized sites 2.5 to 7.5 acres in extent with high proportions of nonutilized flakes, projectile points, and end scrapers and low proportions of other lithic tools), butchering stations (moderate to large sites with low proportions of pottery, projectile points, and scrapers and high proportions of utilized flakes), butchering/lithic workshops, and large horticultural villages (very large sites with dense artifact scatters and high proportions of ceramics, projectile points, and knives).

An interesting aspect of the settlement pattern of these two localities is the near absence of Blue Earth sites east of the Blue Earth River (except for cemeteries). The river may have served as a boundary between social groups, or settlement west of the river may have provided easier access to bison on the prairies to the west or to closely related social groups in northwestern Iowa. Dobbs and Shane have suggested that the Center Creek and Willow Creek localities may represent tandem villages, a pattern found among the Otoe and Ioway, historic groups generally considered descendants of the Oneota in this region of the Upper Mississippi River basin.[18]

Blue Earth phase cemeteries encountered during gravel removal operations are present in a number of areas along the Blue Earth River. The burials were apparently extended primary interments. A cemetery on the east side of the river in the Center Creek locality, 21FA84, may have contained as many as one hundred burials, and another cemetery probably once existed on the same side of the river about 3.7 miles north of 21FA84. Partial secondary burials are found in small numbers in major villages, too. No mound burials are known to be associated with this locality.

The Orr Phase

In North America, the word *protohistoric* refers to those initial contact situations in which indigenous peoples do not yet have direct face-to-face relationships with Euro-Americans but nonetheless have contact through intermediaries. An example is the movement of trade goods or disease through intermediaries, such as the Ottawa in the upper Great Lakes, to a distant people, such as the Eastern Dakota. The term *early historic* as used here refers to early face-to-face contacts between indigenous peoples and Euro-Americans during which no or few major changes occur in the lifeway of the indigenous peoples. An example appropriate to Minnesota is Father Hennepin's residence at Mille Lacs for part of a year in 1680. Hennepin's stay at Mille Lacs provides the earliest written descriptions of life among the Mdewakanton Dakota and establishes a connection between the contemporary archaeological record and a particular people, but did not (as far as we know) change the lifeway of the Mdewakanton.

In Minnesota, evidence of protohistoric or early historic contact, or perhaps contact in both periods, is most apparent in two localities, the Mille Lacs region in the center of the state and the Riceford Creek locality along the Root River in the state's southeastern corner. I concentrate here on the protohistoric/early historic period in the Riceford Creek locality.

Oneota-related Orr phase sites are confined to the Root and Upper Iowa Rivers and a few of their secluded interior tributaries in extreme southeastern Minnesota and northeastern Iowa, where they date been 1625 and about 1700.[19] James B. Griffin, Mildred Mott Wedel, Lloyd Wilford, and others have long identified the phase as the probable remains of the protohistoric/early historic villages of the Ioway Indians and perhaps their close Siouan-speaking relatives, the Otoe.[20]

Since Orr phase material culture is similar to the material culture of the latest Oneota sites across the Mississippi River in the La Crosse locality, except for the presence of small amounts of Euro-Americans trade items, it is assumed that the Ioway moved across the river in the early to mid-seventeenth century, for no European trade goods are associated with the La Crosse Oneota sites. Radiocarbon dates affirm this assumption.[21] French documents establish the presence of the Ioway in the Root and Upper Iowa drainage systems at the time of face-to-face contact in the late 1670s.[22] According to contemporary accounts, they were hunting bison in the prairie lake country of southern Minnesota and north-central Iowa, and were rich in catlinite and bison hides. The trader, Michel Accault, who was attracted by their wealth in bison hides, was apparently the first European to visit them between 1677 and 1680.

Orr phase components are most easily recognized by the presence of Allamakee Trailed pottery, a distinctive late Oneota ceramic type, and the presence of historic trade materials. Like other Oneota pottery, Allamakee Trailed jars are shell tempered, globular in shape, and decorated on the shoulder with trailed lines. The type differs from earlier Oneota pottery in having a combination of frequently notched lips, wide trailed lines, and paired, opposing strap handles usually attached to the rim below the lip. Other identifying characteristics are the presence of simple triangular Madison type projectile points, numerous end scrapers, ground stone artifacts, projecting stem catlinite pipes with a disc bowl, numerous basin-shaped storage/refuse pits in habitation sites, and the concentration of habitation and burial sites in the Root and Upper Iowa drainage basins. Glass trade beads, iron knives, brass ornaments, and other historic trade goods have been found in association with indigenous items, in particular Allamakee Trailed pottery, at such sites as Farley Village (21HU2), Hogback (21HU1), and Wilsey (21HU4) in Minnesota, and O'Regan (13AM21), Flynn (13AM43), Malone (13AM60), Woolstrom (13AM61), and Lane Enclosure (13AM200) in Iowa.

Orr phase sites, which are mostly cemeteries and burial mounds, are present along the Root River and its Riceford Creek tributary in Houston and Fillmore Counties in Minnesota, and along the Upper Iowa River and some of its secluded tributaries, such as Bear Creek, in Allamakee and Winneshiek Counties in Iowa. Sites in Minnesota include Hogback (21HU1), Farley Village (21HU2), Wilsey (21HU4), Yucatan Fort (21HU26), Tudahl (21FL3), Riehl Mound (21FL8), and Rushford (21FL9).[23] The secluded nature of Orr sites in both Minnesota and Iowa suggests to some archaeologists that they were intentionally placed in secluded positions away from the main artery of the Mississippi River for defensive purposes, either from enemies or disease, or perhaps a combination of both.

The Hogback site (21HU1), which is the largest of the cemeteries that Wilford excavated, is about 2 miles from the town of Yucatan on a bluff overlooking the west bank of Riceford Creek. Wilford's excavation of the Hogback cemetery in 1947 and 1953 recovered a minimum of fifty-five individuals.[24] Age ranges at death for males were one between eighteen and twenty, two between twenty-one and thirty-five, one between thirty-six and fifty-five, and three "old adult." Ranges for women were one between thirteen and seventeen, four between twenty-one and thirty-five, two between thirty-six and fifty-five, and one "old adult." Ranges for the twenty-five individuals of indeterminate sex were nine between birth and two, twelve between three and twelve, and four between thirteen and seventeen. These age ranges at death are similar to those reported for earlier Woodland populations.

According to Wilford, burial sites in the Root River valley

fall into 2 categories—burial mounds, and what may be called cemeteries. Mounds are not plentiful. The known mounds are all on top of the high bluffs overlooking the river. The cemeteries are in the valley, on spurs or ridges projecting from the base of the bluff onto the valley floor. Slab rock is used in both types of sites. In mound burials the bodies are placed in graves, and often covered with rock to the top of the pit. A low mound of earth is placed over the pit or pits, and a veneer of slabs laid on the mound. Cemetery burials often have slabs on edge beside the body, or laid flat on the body, or both. Burials are characteristically on the back, fully extended, and are often accompanied by grave goods, particularly ornaments and small mortuary vessels.[25]

Wilford found Orr phase mortuary vessels in association with several burials in Houston and Fillmore Counties. These vessels differ in size and decorative detail from Allamakee Trailed utilitarian jars, as is apparent in his description of the pottery:

> Some vessels are as small as a teacup and the largest is only 21 cm. long and 14 cm. high. The elliptical shape is the more common, and such vessels usually have a handle at each end. Round vessels may have 4 handles. Handles are of the narrow strap variety, and meet the neck below the rim more often than at the rim, which is the reverse of Blue Earth. The decoration of the upper bodies is less ornate than Blue Earth. Trailed lines are not as wide and deep; the chevron is not common; and some decorations are confined to simple vertical or oblique lines running down from the base of the neck. Punctates are often used as area fillers, rather than as line fringes. Such areas are often found below the handles. Festoons may be used from handle to handle on the vessels with 4 handles.[26]

The vessels were often placed at the shoulder of the body.

The reason for the abandonment of the La Crosse locality by the Oneota in the early seventeenth century has been a focus of debate. Increasing warfare, the pull of bison herds to the west, and climate change have all been suggested as the stimulus for this move. For example, increasingly unpredictable and severe weather after AD 1300 during the onset of the Little Ice Age may have made corn horticulture a less attractive subsistence focus throughout the Prairie Peninsula, though this interpretation and each of the other suggested causes of the move have been challenged. Recent and fairly convincing analyses suggest that the primary stimulus for the move was epidemic disease acquired through the Great Lakes trade route.[27] Repeated episodes of disease led to the depopulation of the La Crosse locality and the movement of the smaller, more vulnerable group of survivors into refuges on the west side of the Mississippi River. A sense of vulnerability may also have been the reason the Ioway moved west in the late seventeenth century, where they apparently joined (or reunited with) their close relatives, the Otoe, in northwestern Iowa.[28]

MISSISSIPPIAN, PLAINS VILLAGE, AND ONEOTA LIFEWAYS

What took place at the beginning of the Mississippian period in southern Minnesota? How can the sudden appearance of what appear to be completely new archaeological cultures be explained? Did new ethnic groups enter the state, or did resident groups rapidly adopt new sociocultural systems—or did some combination of these two processes take place? In my view, the sudden appearance of new sociocultural systems in southern Minnesota at this time represents the onset of the fourth phase in my reconstruction of the developmental trajectory of Binford's Terrestrial Model. This phase, which began with emergent evolutionary change, saw the appearance and spread of tribal lifeways throughout this area of the state.

Emergent change is something quite distinct from the gradual accretional modifications that are the outcome of the processes of resource intensification (as took place during phase three in the four-phase scenario). In Binford's words, in rapidly emergent kinds of change "new niches will appear to arise out of nowhere, since the new organization that they entail may include little that would permit us to see continuity with the parent system" and "there need not be any continuity between the system within which an emergent change occurs, although the persons who occupy the old and new niches could be the same." The result is "change [in] the way the world works in rather dramatic ways."[29]

If a niche is defined as the existence of a particular kind of "relationship between human populations and the plants and animals around them," then an emergent change involves the appearance of a new kind of relationship.[30] In the emergence of a tribal-level social organization, this usually involves a switch to a reliance on domesticated food sources or an abundant wild food resource. Once the niche emerges, members of ethnically and linguistically diverse groups will often move rapidly into the new niche, where they adopt new technologies and patterns of social interaction. Where the switch involves a new dependence on domesticated plants, the move usually involves the aggregation of people into sedentary villages in areas infrequently used or unoccupied earlier by hunter-gatherers. In many cases, there appears to be a complete break in a region in the archaeological record.

I find three other aspects of this transformation helpful in thinking about the change that occurred in southern Minnesota.[31] First, the size of more sedentary ethnic units is typically larger, and the size of the area they control smaller than among tactically mobile foragers. Second, the transformation can occur either internally within a single ethnic group or as an integrating process that brings together people from different ethnic groups. And third, the intake of animal protein typically decreases among horticultural people as the overall dependence on domesticated plant foods increases.

This shift in reliance on different kinds of food resources should be apparent in the archaeological record.

The archaeological record of the Silvernale and Cambria phases is consistent with this picture of emergence. There is substantial evidence of a switch to a diet based heavily on maize consumption. In addition to the recovery of carbonized maize fragments from sites in the Red Wing locality and from the Cambria site, stable carbon and nitrogen values for individuals from the Bryan site and Orr phase sites support this conclusion. In a 1994 study by Dan Pratt, ^{13}C values for four individuals from the Bryan site ranged from −12.6 to −13.9, and ^{15}N values from 8.4 to 10.0. These values indicate a significant consumption of maize and a low intake of animal protein or a high intake of legumes.

Carbon and nitrogen isotopic values for individuals from three Orr phase sites are similar to those from Bryan.[32] Three adults from the Rushford Mounds (21FL09) have ^{13}C values of −18.0, −13.7, and −13.4, and ^{15}N values of 8.6, 9.7, and 9.6. The ^{13}C values of nine individuals from the Hogback site (21HU01) range from −12.5 to −14.4, and the ^{15}N values from 6.0 to 11.1. Finally, the ^{13}C values for six individuals from the Wilsey site (21HU04) range from −12.5 to −14.6, and ^{15}N values from 10.2 to 12.0. These values are interesting, for Mississippian groups in southern Minnesota are usually portrayed as having a balanced diet in which meat from bison and deer was an important component. These values suggest a greater dependence on maize than previously thought.

Was the appearance of horticultural groups in southern Minnesota by about AD 1050 the result of emergent evolution, as suggested here? If so, were the people who filled this new niche migrants from outside the state or regional Woodland people, or perhaps some combination of both possibilities? At present, archaeologists do not agree on the answers to these questions. I have consistently supported the position that all of the Mississippian groups in southern Minnesota (Silvernale, Cambria, Great Oasis, and Oneota) were for the most part descendants of regional Woodland people, as were the Mississippian people at Cahokia in their area.[33] One reason for my position is the lack of archaeological phases outside the state (except for the Wisconsin side of the Red Wing locality) that are identical to or nearly identical to the Silvernale and Cambria phases. Another is the persistence in these phases of a burial mound tradition. A third reason is the early presence in the Red Wing locality of what appears to be an Effigy Mound presence intermingled with elements of a Mississippian material culture and lifeway. And a fourth reason is Morton Fried's notion that tribal groups for the most part emerge through interaction with more structurally complex (and perhaps aggressive) social groups rather than through internal development alone.[34]

But the issue remains unsettled for at least two reasons. First, the results of biodistance studies of the relationship between human skeletal populations in the Upper Mississippi valley region are suggestive but inconclusive. A 1974 study by Elizabeth Glenn concluded that the one individual studied from the Bryan site had close affinities to a sample of Mississippian individuals from the Aztalan site in Wisconsin, that there was a clear division between eastern Wisconsin and western Oneota groups, and that there was some support for a relationship between Minnesota Oneota and Cambria populations, though there was overall biological heterogeneity in the total sample.[35] An earlier biodistance study by Martin Peterson also reported a biological relationship between Minnesota Oneota and Cambria populations.[36] And second, there is a sharp discontinuity in Minnesota between Woodland and Silvernale-Cambria phase ceramic traditions. Unlike emergent tribal groups in the lower Great Lakes area and eastward that retain a Woodland-based ceramic tradition, the ceramic traditions of emergent groups in Minnesota, while unique, show numerous "Mississippian" connections but few signs of a Woodland heritage, with the probable exception of Great Oasis. It is possible, then, that migrant groups or some mixture of migrant and local groups could have formed the population base of southern Minnesota's emergent cultures.

Two other debated issues are the relationship of southern Minnesota's emergent village farming groups with Cahokia and the Mississippian world, and the eventual fate of these groups. I have proposed that the Red Wing locality was a node in a Cahokia-centered exchange network through which material goods and new worldviews flowed, and Elden Johnson has made a somewhat similar suggestion for the Cambria phase.[37] In an argument rich in detail, Robert (Ernie) Boszhardt suggests that the rapid expansion of Middle Mississippian people and influences through the Upper Mississippi River valley was prompted and accompanied by contagious diseases, which were themselves formative in the creation of Middle Mississippian–related lifeways in the region.[38]

Among still other proposals, Thomas Emerson and Timothy Pauketat suggest that the mechanism for cultural interaction between Middle Mississippian elite and nonlocal hinterland groups may have been ritual events that included feasting and gifts of pottery.[39] The pottery given as gifts was Ramey Incised and its companion Powell Plain, for the emergence of these village centers coincides with the widespread appearance of these pottery types, or imitations of them, in the Upper Mississippi River valley. According to this view, Ramey Incised pottery served as a metaphor of the Mississippian cosmos, and the feasts themselves involved a sharing of Middle Mississippian ideologies, material items, and worldview. At the same time, material symbols of Late Woodland socioreligious beliefs, like effigy mounds, disappear. Though fascinating and a continuing center of scholarly debate, the issue of the relationship between emergent groups in southern Minnesota and Middle Mississippian groups to the south remains unresolved.

The second issue is the fate of these groups, for both the Silvernale and Cambria phases seem to terminate by about AD 1200. Boszhardt argues persuasively that at least some of the Oneota who inhabited the Red Wing locality by about AD 1225/1250 moved southward to the La Crosse area of Wisconsin by AD 1300, and Eric Hollinger suggests that the growth and aggressive expansion of the Oneota in the thirteenth century pushed the Cambria phase population northwestward in a series of moves.[40] More generally, it appears that Oneota groups become widespread throughout southern Minnesota by about AD 1250 or soon thereafter, an expansion that I attribute in part to the waning of Middle Mississippian influences in this area at that time.

Was climate change at least in part responsible for the direction that culture change took in the Upper Mississippi River valley region between AD 800 and the historic period? As Binford reminds us, "Insofar as climatic changes restructure the character and form of habitats, it is to be expected that adaptive responses track such changes."[41] James B. Griffin once argued that Oneota cultures devolved from Middle Mississippian ones in the Upper Mississippi River region in response to a general deterioration in climate, and John Penman attributed the southward movement of the Oneota from the Red Wing locality to La Crosse to the onset of the colder Neo-Boreal climatic episode.[42]

As Map 7.3 shows in a simple manner, there was a significant cooling period in Minnesota after about AD 1200 to 1250. In the 1960s, David A. Baerreis and Reid Bryson in their study of climatic episodes in the upper Midwest pointed out the correlation between the northward expansion of Mississippian culture and the "Medieval" warm period between about AD 800 and AD 1200.[43] They also noted the correlation between the expansion of what they considered less agriculturally committed Oneota communities and the cooler Pacific and Neo-Boreal ("Little Ice Age") climatic episodes. Since the 1960s, researchers have tended to downplay the role of climate in north-central North America as a primary causative factor in culture change.[44] At present, this issue remains unresolved and underinvestigated in this region of North America, though I believe it remains an issue in play, for single-factor explanations of major cultural changes in the Upper Mississippi River region seem too simple to me. Rather, warfare, epidemic disease, population growth, climatic deterioration, the movement of eastern tribes westward, the encroaching presence of Euro-American fur traders, and undoubtedly other factors more likely played intertwined roles in the emergence, spread, and dissolution of tribal lifeways in southern Minnesota in the late prehistoric period.

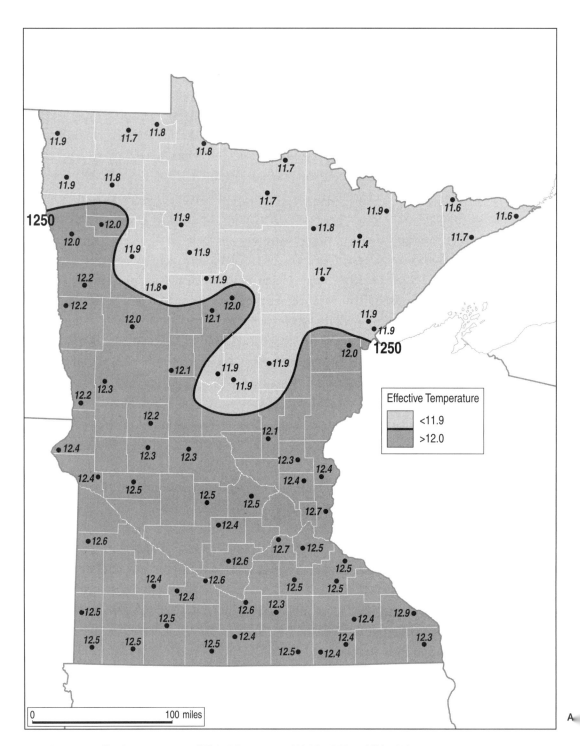

Map 7.3. Effective temperature (ET) in Minnesota at (A) AD 1250 and (B) 1650, showing the impact on temperature of the Little Ice Age. The thick black lines separate ET values below 11.9 north of the line from values higher than 12.0 south of the line.

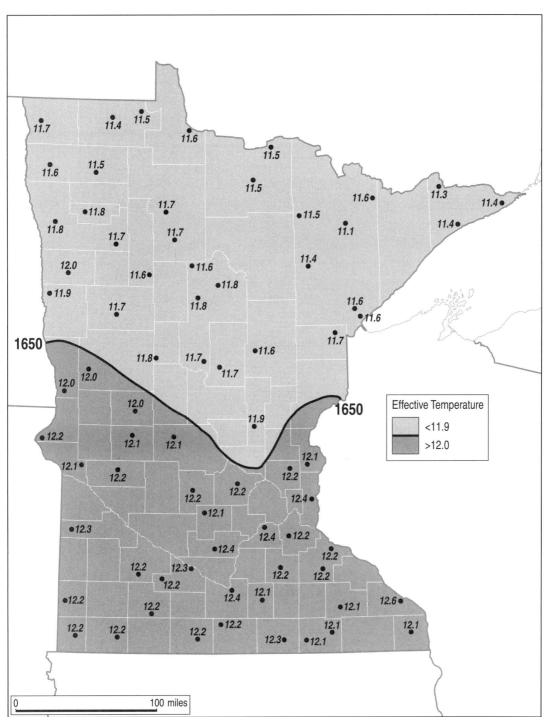

B

CHAPTER 8

First Tribes in Central and Northern Minnesota

Terminal Woodland Adaptations

The Terminal Woodland period (AD 500–1750) in Minnesota's central and northern forests and prairies was, as in southern Minnesota, a time of momentous change. New ceramic forms and styles appear and are replaced by completely different forms and styles; the size of Native American populations substantially increases; palisaded sedentary villages appear in some areas; and the harvesting of wild rice becomes a widespread and intensive seasonal subsistence activity. In this chapter, rather than discussing the central and northern sections of the state separately, as in chapter 5, I adopt an area-wide period framework. This framework more adequately reflects the three sequential periods of change that occurred in central and northern Minnesota.

THE EARLY TERMINAL WOODLAND ARCHAEOLOGICAL RECORD

Since the Laurel culture persists relatively unchanged in northern Minnesota through this period, I concentrate in this section on central Minnesota and the St. Croix complex. The St. Croix complex, which is a transitional Initial Woodland/Terminal Woodland taxonomic unit, stretches from the northwestern corner of Wisconsin across eastern and central Minnesota into the Red River valley and on into adjacent areas of the Dakotas.[1]

The early Terminal Woodland period in the forests and prairies of central Minnesota exhibits many parallels with early Terminal (Late) Woodland developments in the southeastern deciduous forests and prairies of the state. There was a transitional phase that lasted about 300 years (AD 500–800); Native American population sizes increase; the size and number of habitation sites increase; a trend toward increasing sedentism is apparent; burial mounds become more abundant and widespread; small unnotched and notched triangular arrow points replace notched and stemmed dart forms; ceramic vessels become thinner and more globular; and dependency on a single plant food, in this case wild rice, begins to increase. It is during this period, too, that the initial phase of the Arvilla burial complex spreads across central Minnesota to the Red River valley.

At present, the most diagnostic traits of St. Croix complex components are Onamia series ceramics and linear mounds, both of which are associated with the more spatially extensive Arvilla burial complex. Onamia series ceramics are subconoidal to semi-subconoidal, grit-tempered, cordmarked vessels having a pronounced shoulder and a vertical rim that is decorated with a dentate stamp or, occasionally, a cord-wrapped-stick (Figure 8.1). Vessels range from small bowls to large jars and have noticeably thinner walls than earlier Malmo vessels, averaging about 6 millimeters in thickness. For the Mille Lacs region, Elden Johnson includes both St. Croix and Onamia ceramics, which together form the Onamia series, in an Isle phase.[2] Since Onamia ceramics continue into the following Vineland phase, and may emerge sometime after

Figure 8.1. The Fort Poualak bowl: a St. Croix complex pottery vessel. Photograph from the Lake Onamia–Trunk Highway 169 data recovery project. Mather 2000b, Figure 42. Printed with permission.

St. Croix pottery first appears, only St. Croix ceramics are diagnostic of the Isle phase.

Because of the early concentration on mound excavation and the characteristic mixture of components in shallow sites, patterns of use of lithic technology specific to the St. Croix complex remain speculative. For the Mille Lacs region, Kent Bakken's Q-pattern, which is present and indicates a heavy reliance on quartz, applies to the Woodland tradition as a whole in the region.[3] Johnson lists small side-notched points as a trait of the Isle phase, and similar-appearing side-notched points are apparently associated with St. Croix ceramics in the Snake River valley and in Arvilla complex mounds.[4] It seems likely that St. Croix complex projectile points are either finely made

Figure 8.2. A Prairie Side Notched projectile point. Courtesy of the Science Museum of Minnesota.

unnotched isosceles triangular points (Madison points) or small side-notched points similar to Prairie Side Notched (Figure 8.2).

St. Croix ceramics have been found as primary interments in mounds at five sites: Altern in the Yellow River area of northwestern Wisconsin, Cooper in the Mille Lacs region, Stumne just south of Lake Pokegama on the Snake River in eastern Minnesota, Berscheid on Little Birch Lake in central Minnesota, and De Spiegler on the South Dakota side of the Red River.[5] The mounds are linear or ovoid to conical in shape. The Stumne Mound group contains thirteen linear and two conical mounds. The linear mounds are 100 to 460 feet long, 1.5 to 4 feet high, and on average 18 feet wide. The mounds are arranged in parallel lines (Figure 8.3), a pattern also present in the Altern and Fort Poualak/Hay Lake mound groups. The Fort Poualak/Hay Lake cluster contains seventy-three linear, ovoid, and circular mounds. The longest linear mound at the site apparently once stretched 725 feet. These linear mounds are about 2.5 feet high and 8 to 12 feet wide.

A bioarchaeological study of the human skeletal material recovered from the Berscheid site, which is on a long sand ridge that runs along the shore of Little Birch Lake, concluded that there were as many as eighteen individuals among the human skeletal remains recovered: six males, six females, and six individuals of indeterminate sex.[6] Their age distribution was four between the ages of seventeen and twenty-five at death, three between twenty-five and thirty-five, two forty-five years or older at death, and nine classified only as adult. Signs of dental disease and skeletal pathology were minimal, with only one individual showing a presence of degenerative arthritis. Another individual showed signs of sharp-force trauma on the skull.

Figure 8.3. The Stumne mound group.
Courtesy of the Minnesota Historical Society. Printed with permission.

Johnson has identified a consistent and recurring pattern of burial traits that span this transitional period—and that is more spatially extensive than the St. Croix complex—that he calls the Arvilla burial complex.[7] The traits include linear and circular mounds, deep subsoil burial pits, flexed and disarticulated primary and bundle secondary burials, frequent use of red and yellow ocher, associated utilitarian and ornamental grave goods dominated by bone and shell artifacts, Prairie Side Notched and Broad side-notched projectile points, blade side scrapers of Knife River flint, and small mortuary vessels of St. Croix Stamped or Blackduck ware.

Other common items associated with the complex include chipped stone side scrapers, deer antler hafts for beaver incisors (several of which still contain the inset tooth), bone awls and pins, and antler tip flaking tools, as well as shell beads, pendants, and gorgets, eagle talons, bear claws and canines, bird beaks, wolf or dog canines, and bone and turtle carapace pendants. The shell ornaments are made from *Natica* and *Dentalium* shells and the columella of the *Busycon perversum* conch, all of which are marine shells, and from local mussel shell.

The Arvilla burial complex has been found at sites from the St. Croix River valley across central Minnesota to the Red River valley and northward along the Red River through the Pembina plain to the Winnipeg area. The dating of the burial program remains a debated question; however, it appears to have swept westward across the state during the early Terminal Woodland period.

THE MIDDLE TERMINAL WOODLAND ARCHAEOLOGICAL RECORD

Sometime between AD 600 and 800, the transition to a Terminal Woodland adaptive pattern was probably complete in central and northern Minnesota. Cultural complexes after this period to between AD 1100 and 1300 share a similar appearing material culture and a subsistence base that may have depended heavily on the harvesting of wild rice. This sequence of complexes is called the Blackduck-Kathio-Clam River continuum here, for it is composed of three spatially adjacent complexes whose clusters of ceramic attributes seem to grade into one another in a cline-like manner, a reflection, I believe, of the shared band-level social organization at the time.[8]

The complexes are the Clam River phase in the north woods of northwestern Wisconsin and adjacent areas of Minnesota; the closely related Kathio phase, located along the southern boundary of the north woods in east-central and central Minnesota and in the west-central lakes district that stretches across the deciduous forest zone into the prairie province; and the Blackduck phase, which is situated in the forests and prairie fringe to the north and northwest of Kathio, with site concentrations in the Headwaters Lakes and Rainy River regions.[9] Differences between these phases, although not pronounced, are primarily defined in terms of decorative motifs on pottery vessels, spatial location, and, perhaps, subsistence emphases that are still not well defined.

As in other Woodland complexes in Minnesota, the presence of Blackduck-Kathio-Clam River components at a site is most easily recognized by the presence of the continuum's distinctive ceramics. Blackduck, Kathio, and Clam River ceramics are characteristically grit-tempered and cordmarked jars with a globular shape, constricted neck, short outward-flaring and perhaps thickened rim, and flat lip (Figure 8.4).[10] Decoration is usually confined to the upper area of the interior rim, lip, and the upper rim and neck portion of the exterior vessel surface. Decorative techniques include cord-wrapped-stick stamping, "comb" stamping, punctuations of various kinds, and vertical brushing on the exterior rim surface. The continuum's ceramics are the most baroque appearing of the state's prehistoric ceramic series and the most commonly encountered ceramics in the north woods of central and northern Minnesota. The presence of unilaterally barbed bone harpoons may be a diagnostic artifact in the Rainy River region.

Other defining characteristics of the continuum's components in Minnesota are

Figure 8.4. A Blackduck pottery vessel from the Smith site.
Courtesy of the Wilford Archaeology Laboratory, University of Minnesota.

the presence (often) of one to a few modest conical burial mounds adjacent to habitation sites, their diversity in site type compared to earlier archaeological complexes in the region, and their frequency, for the continuum's components are the most commonly encountered component of any precontact complex in the state's north woods.

Since most pottery associated with the continuum has been recovered from multicomponent habitation sites, the association of other classes of artifact with specific complexes is a problem. In a master's thesis on the issue, G. Edward Evans suggested that oval and lunate chipped stone knives; side scrapers; trapezoidal, oval, and thumbnail end scrapers; tubular-shaped drills; steatite and clay pipes; bone awls and needles; unilateral barbed harpoons made of mammal bone; antler flakers; bone spatulas; cut beaver incisors; bear canine ornaments; and native copper fishhooks, gorges, and beads are associated with Blackduck pottery in northern Minnesota.[11] It seems likely that this assemblage characterizes all three complexes in the continuum with some slight differences between regions. Elden Johnson has excavated portions of rectangular pit houses at the Winter site along the Snake River in an apparent Clam River context.[12]

The age ranges of the Kathio, Clam River, and Blackduck complexes remain unresolved and somewhat controversial at present.[13] Kathio is thought to date from AD 900 to 1300 on the basis of a few radiocarbon dates and the position of ceramic wares within the Mille Lacs region sequence. The Clam River complex is thought to date as early but may persist into the late prehistoric period in northwestern Wisconsin. A radiocarbon date of AD 1560 for a Kathio–Clam River vessel from the Triangle Island site in Kanabec County, Minnesota, suggests that the ceramic series may have persisted after AD 1300 in the southeastern corner of the north woods in the state, too. Blackduck phase sites are generally considered common by AD 800, and some date as early as AD 600 in both the Headwaters Lakes and Rainy River regions. The complex is thought to end in both regions somewhere between AD 1000 and 1200.

Mortuary sites of the Blackduck-Kathio-Clam River continuum are characterized by groups of modest-sized conical mounds.[14] There is an apparent difference between the Kathio and Blackduck phases, however, in the mode of burial within these mounds. Kathio people were apparently buried as secondary bundles without grave goods; the bundles were laid on the surface of the ground, and very low conical mounds that are almost never cumulative were erected over them. In contrast, early phase Blackduck burials are usually partially flexed primary burials in what has been interpreted as a sitting or semi-sitting position. Many of the mounds appear to have been built on the edge of habitation sites. In the Rainy River region, Blackduck burials frequently occur, too, as intrusions into or additions onto Laurel mounds. Grave goods accompany some but not all Blackduck burials.

Blackduck burials in the Rainy River region, especially from McKinstry Mound 2, have been a focus of interest and investigation for many years.[15] McKinstry (21KC02) is a 20-acre multicomponent habitation and mortuary site at the confluence of the Little Fork and Rainy Rivers. The mortuary complex included two burial mounds, Mound 1 and Mound 2, the latter of which was completely excavated by Wilford in 1932. He found that six episodes of intrusive Blackduck burials consisting of multiple individuals had been dug into or around an original large Laurel mound that had been constructed over a single individual. Large fires set on top of the mound during the three oldest episodes cremated the skeletons to varying degrees and left extensive layers of burned clay.[16]

Of the 114 individuals removed from Mound 2, bioarchaeological analyses determined that 61 were subadults (under sixteen years old at the time of death) and 53 were adults. Twenty-nine of the adults were identified as male, 17 as female, and 7 remained unidentified to sex. This underrepresentation of women is also found in other midwestern Woodland sites. Life expectancy at birth was estimated to be

16.8 years, and average stature for males 5 feet 5 inches, and for females 5 feet 2 inches.[17] In general the population was healthy with no evidence of bone fractures. Degenerative joint disease was present on nineteen vertebrae from 5 individuals, slight to moderate periostitis was evident in long bones from 4 individuals, and 16.5 percent of all canine teeth exhibited enamel hypolasia, which was somewhat greater than on Laurel skeletons from Smith Mound 4 (12.0 percent).

Mortuary practices associated with Blackduck burials in the Rainy River region include long bone and cranial tapping (perforation), red ocher treatment, the placing of clay masks on crania or beside burials, multiple primary burials, and indirect cremation. At McKinstry Mound 2, twenty individuals (thirteen adult male, six adult female, and an adolescent) exhibited perforation of the cranium (bone tapping), while 62 percent of all adults and 37 percent of all subadults were covered in part by red ocher, with no apparent sex preference. In Minnesota, tapping has been found in Laurel, Blackduck, and other sites.[18] Masks of clay were applied directly onto defleshed skulls or placed on artificial "heads" formed of bundles of cattail leaves bound with twined cordage.[19] Nineteen individuals in the sample were associated with masks or with clay pressed into the eye orbits, forming eye plugs. Clay masking is present at other sites in the region and in Wisconsin at the Cyrus Thomas site (47DN01) along the Red Cedar River.

A study of the cranial morphology of Woodland peoples in central and northern Minnesota by Nancy Ossenberg concluded the following: northern and southern Blackduck populations do not cluster closely; Laurel sites are more closely related to southern Blackduck, but not the northern Blackduck, sample; southern Blackduck is at least in part ancestral to the historic Dakota; and Arvilla is ancestral to the Cheyenne.[20] What is interesting here is the idea that the distribution of Blackduck pottery spans more than one ethnic group, a suggestion made earlier by Edward Evans in his study of the Blackduck phase.[21]

Finally, if numbers of sites can be taken as a rough indicator of regional population size, then Blackduck and Kathio populations were substantially larger than earlier regional populations. An extensive survey of the shoreline of Lake Winnibigoshish, for example, recorded the presence of seventeen sites with Blackduck components and only seven with earlier Brainerd components.[22] An equally rough count of rim sherds recorded 575 Blackduck rims and only 16 Brainerd rims. Roughly similar results were obtained in a shoreline survey of the Gull Lake-Leech Lake-Pine River-Lake Pokegama reservoir region.[23] In that survey, thirty-four sites contained a Blackduck component, twelve a Brainerd, four a Malmo, and three a Laurel. While these are only rough data, for the relationship between surface and subsurface content always remains problematic, they do support a more substantial early phase Blackduck presence.

THE LATE TERMINAL WOODLAND ARCHAEOLOGICAL RECORD

The late Terminal Woodland period in Minnesota's central and northern forests and prairies extended from about AD 1250 to the beginning of the historic period in the mid-seventeenth century. Perhaps the single most important event in this period is the abrupt appearance and gradual spread throughout the north woods of central Minnesota of a new archaeological complex called the Psinomani complex. But other significant events occurred in this part of the state as well, including the contraction northward of Blackduck culture and its transformation into the Rainy River composite, the spread of Oneota and Plains Village ceramic traits across central Minnesota, and the adoption, perhaps for the first time, of a fully Terminal Woodland lifeway.

The Psinomani Complex

Psinomani components are most easily recognized by the presence of Sandy Lake pottery.[24] Unlike earlier pottery in the region, the temper of Sandy Lake jars is usually shell or a mixture of shell and grit. Exterior vessel surfaces are cordmarked, smooth, or stamped with grooved paddles and are rarely decorated (Figure 8.5). Ogechie ware, a northern Oneota ceramic, is present in small amounts in many Psinomani components

Figure 8.5. A Sandy Lake pottery vessel from the Cooper site.
Courtesy of the Wilford Archaeology Laboratory, University of Minnesota.

(Figure 8.6).[25] Simple and complex paddle stamping on the surfaces of some Sandy Lake vessels, which is a widespread trait across central and northern Minnesota, is considered a Plains-derived ceramic attribute. Except for ceramics and perhaps the composition of the associated small, unnotched triangular projectile points, which may be predominantly of quartz, the material culture of the Psinomani complex is very similar to that of Kathio and Blackduck.

Site types range from large semisedentary villages, to wild rice harvesting and fishing stations, to a variety of local hunting and gathering sites.[26] However, settlements now occur in tight, spatially separated clusters compared to the earlier dispersed Blackduck-Kathio-Clam River continuum settlement pattern. Sandy Lake ceramics are also present in large summer bison-hunting sites in the adjacent prairies, at least some of which are palisaded villages. These latter sites are assumed to be part of the annual settlement-subsistence round of the complex. In the Mille Lacs region, the Cooper and Wilford village sites represent the first site type, at least during the Bradbury phase. Cooper, for example, is palisaded, contains substantial lodge-style houses, and has what may be wild rice storage bins attached to the palisade (Map 8.1).[27] The faunal and floral assemblages also conform to this site type in that they are varied and indicate year-round occupation.

Figure 8.6. An Ogechie pottery vessel found along the Rum River near Milaca. From Brower and Bushnell 1900, 60.

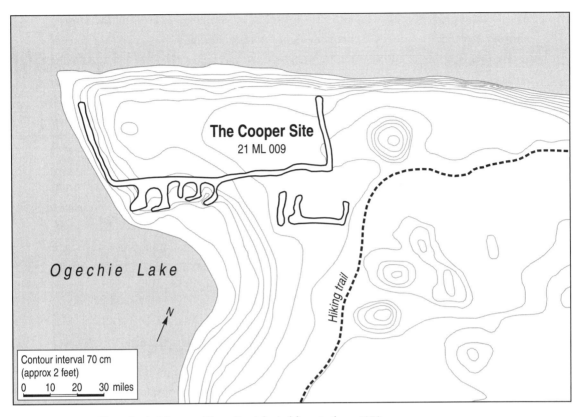

Map 8.1. The palisaded Cooper village site. Adapted from Lothson 1972.

Prairie bison-hunting camps are probably represented by the Shea site and possibly by the Mooney site.[28] The Shea site, which is about 500 feet from and above the Maple River, covers about 40 acres and was surrounded at one time by a dry moat and possibly a palisade. The main subsistence activity was bison hunting, although a few other animals were hunted and trapped. The discovery of thirty-two fragments of maize kernels suggests the presence of some gardening too.

Estimates of the date of emergence of the culture of which the Psinomani archaeological complex is a manifestation vary widely, ranging from AD 1300–1400 in the Mille Lacs Lake region to about AD 1100 in the Headwaters Lakes region.[29] Eventually establishing the time and place of origin of the complex is critical, for they mark the appearance and spread of a new lifeway in central and northern Minnesota. My date of AD 1250 is just a guesstimate, then, based on my understanding of the sociocultural dynamics of the time and the dating of the emergence of the Oneota tradition to the south and the terminal date of Blackduck ceramics in the Headwaters Lakes region.

In spite of the (assumed) relatively large populations of the late Terminal

Woodland period, surprisingly little information is available concerning Psinomani complex mortuary practices. Existing evidence documents the presence of three burial tracks: primary flexed interment with an associated mortuary vessel in a shallow sub-surface burial pit underneath a small circular conical mound, intrusive mound interment, and nonmound interment. The first burial track has been reported at the Cooper Mound site on the east shore of Lake Ogechie and at the Norway Lake site just north of Pine River in Cass County.[30] Both primary extended and secondary bundle burials were found in two low circular conical mounds at the Cooper Mound site, and a primary flexed interment in a single mound at Norway Lake. The Norway Lake individual was an adult female between the age of twenty-one and thirty-five at death. An osteological analysis concluded that she was between 5 feet 2 inches and 5 feet 6 inches tall, had slight osteoarthritis lipping on the cervical vertebra, and had not excessively worn teeth.[31] Two intrusive burials in the Osufsen Mound (21IC02) are thought to be associated with the Psinomani complex too.

The Rainy River Composite

While dramatic changes were occurring across central Minnesota by AD 1250, if not earlier, material culture change was taking place, too, in the Terminal Woodland period in the Rainy River drainage system and northward throughout northwestern Ontario and southern Manitoba. Growing familiarity with these changes led in 1990 to a new taxonomy for the region that more clearly highlights these changes.[32] The taxonomy collapses most of what had been called "Late Blackduck" ceramics into what is now called the Rainy River composite. The Rainy River composite includes a group of temporally and somewhat spatially distinct complexes that include Duck Bay (AD 1100–1350), Bird Lake (AD 1100–1350), and Winnipeg River (AD 1350 to the late 1600s). According to Brian Lenius and Dave Olinyk, the architects of the new taxonomy, these complexes share common traits and "may have shared similar social, political, and religious activities within the context of building and utilizing Late Woodland mounds along the Rainy River," activities that may have joined them together into "a single cultural entity."[33]

In Lenius and Olinyk's rereading of the late culture history of far northern Minnesota and areas to the north, the Rainy River composite formed through a coalescence of Blackduck and Laurel cultures at about AD 1000. Blackduck and Laurel are thought to have coexisted in the area from at least AD 700 to 1000, after which they cease to exist as distinct ceramic traditions. The Rainy River composite emerges during a hundred-year transitional period (AD 1000–1100) called the Rainy River coalescent, after which a Duck Bay and Bird Lake cultural peak appears (AD 1100–1350). This peak is followed by a territorial contraction associated with the Winnipeg River composite (AD 1350–late 1600s). The historic descendants of the Rainy River composite are thought to be Algonkian-speaking people, such as the Ojibwa.

At present, the Rainy River composite is primarily defined by the presence and distribution of the composite's diagnostic complex of ceramic attributes, which are described in some detail in Lenius and Olinyk's 1990 article. Composite ceramic assemblages contain both utilitarian and small ceremonial vessels, the latter receiving the most attention because of their often intact recovery in burial mounds. In general early composite jars (AD 1000–1350) combine Blackduck and Laurel ceramic traits (Figures 8.7 and 8.8). From Blackduck, these include oblique and horizontal cord-wrapped-stick design elements, a globular vessel form, and cordmarked or textile-impressed bodies. Laurel traits include stamped design elements, plain or smoothed surface finishes, and decoration located on the exterior rim surface. Later composite vessels (AD 1350–late 1600s) seem to be largely undecorated, fabric-impressed, simple-necked jars.

Nonceramic utilitarian artifacts seem to be similar to those found in earlier Blackduck and Laurel components. These include small side-notched and unnotched triangular arrow points; stone knives, scrapers, and drills; and bone awls, needles, flakers, and harpoons, among other artifact types.

Rainy River composite ceramics are present as far south as the Headwaters Lakes region in central Minnesota, as far east as Lake Superior, as far north as northwestern Ontario, and in Manitoba as far north as the Pas. However, each of the complexes within the composite has a much more limited core area within this broad region. The primary area of occupation of the Bird Lake composite is southeastern Manitoba along the Winnipeg River and some of its tributaries, like the Bird River. Its area of secondary occupation is Lake of the Woods and the Rainy River area, where Duck Bay ceramics have been found at the Smith Village and McKinstry Mound 2 in Minnesota. The Bird Lake tertiary area of intermittent use includes the prairie area of southwestern Manitoba, the Interlake area in central Manitoba, and the Headwaters Lakes region in central Minnesota, where Bird Lake ceramics were found at the Shocker site.

The primary area of occupation of the Duck Bay composite was the Lake Winnipegosis area of west-central Manitoba. Its secondary area was along a corridor route from the Lake Winnipegosis area to the Rainy River area, where Duck Bay Stamp ceremonial vessels have been found at the Grand Mound at the Smith site and at McKinstry Mound 2 on the Minnesota side of the river. The Duck Bay tertiary region of use extends north and west of Lake Winnipegosis from the Manitoba Interlake area to The Pas. This distribution suggests that at least some Duck Bay people traveled about 875 miles from their core area to the Rainy River mound sites on a regular basis.

Figure 8.7. A Bird Lake–like vessel from the McKinstry site.

Courtesy of the Wilford Archaeology Laboratory, University of Minnesota.

Figure 8.8. A Duck Bay–like vessel from the McKinstry site.

Courtesy of the Wilford Archaeology Laboratory, University of Minnesota.

The area of distribution of Winnipeg River complex ceramics is more restricted, suggesting that the Rainy River composite collapsed into the central area of the composite around Winnipeg River and Lake of the Woods after AD 1350. The complex's secondary area of use seems to have been the nearby Rainy River area, where ceramics of the complex have been found at the Nett Lake (21KC1) and Smith (21KC3) sites on the Minnesota side of the river. The area of distribution of Rainy River coalescent sites is less well defined but certainly includes (but is not limited to) the Rainy River and Winnipeg River areas.

Lenius and Olinyk suggest that Plains-related groups replaced the Duck Bay complex, while Sandy Lake pottery-producing groups largely replaced the composite in far northern Minnesota.[34] The composite apparently continued in its reduced core north of Minnesota until about AD 1650.

THE BRADBURY PHASE

In the Mille Lacs region, the phase that spans the protohistoric/early historic period is called the Bradbury phase (AD 1680–1750). In Johnson's taxonomy, the phase begins with the (possibly) forced presence at Mille Lacs of Father Louis Hennepin and two other French explorers in 1680 and ends with the final abandonment of Mille Lacs by the Dakota in 1750.[35] French artifacts were uncovered during excavation in Mound 1 and in other burials at the Cooper site and at the Wilford site.[36] As David Mather concludes,

> These finds linked the Mille Lacs archaeological record with the writings of Father Hennepin and other French explorers, confirming the ascription of the Late Prehistoric Mille Lacs villages to the Mdewakanton Dakota. (Johnson 1985; Birk and Johnson 1992)[37]

Traits of the Bradbury phase are the presence of Ogechie and Sandy Lake ceramics, large house floors in villages, the Q-pattern of stone raw material use, conical mounds, and French trade goods. Since all of these traits, except for French trade goods, are present in the preceding Shakopee phase, the identification of components of one or the other phase can be difficult, especially in mixed, multicomponent sites.

An additional distinguishing trait besides the presence of French trade goods may be trends in the attributes of Sandy Lake ceramics. Johnson thought that Bradbury-phase Sandy Lake ceramics were exclusively shell tempered and shared more attributes with Oneota (Ogechie) ceramics than earlier.[38] The trend in temper from grit to shell is supported by several radiocarbon dates. Grit-tempered Sandy Lake pots from the Crosier site (21ML33) have been radiocarbon dated to AD 1409, while Sandy Lake pots from the

Figure 8.9. Historic artifacts from the Cooper site.
Courtesy of the Wilford Archaeology Laboratory, University of Minnesota.

Basswood Shores site (21DL90) have a mean date of AD 1752.[39] If other investigations support this trend, the presence of exclusively shell-tempered Sandy Lake pots in a component would distinguish components of the two phases.

French trade goods include honey-colored gunflints and Jesuit rings, both of which were present at the Cooper and Wilford sites. Other early trade objects in the region include axes, trade knives, and brass tinkling cones. Some of these artifacts were found with Ogechie and Sandy Lake ceramics in Cooper Mound 1 and in other burials in the Cooper habitation site (Figure 8.9).[40] It is assumed that these are trade items rather than indicators of French residence in the region. Nonetheless, their presence and the writings of Father Hennepin and other late seventeenth-century explorers confirm that Bradbury phase habitation sites are surviving remnants of the villages of the Mdewakanton Dakota.

Bradbury phase components have been identified at the Cooper (21ML 9/16), Petaga Point (21ML11), Wilford (21ML12), and Crosier (21ML33) sites, all of which are near the shore of lakes along the Rum River outlet to Mille Lacs Lake. Rectangular houses with depressed floors have been encountered during excavation at the Petaga Point and Cooper sites. Johnson described a house floor he excavated at Petaga Point in 1967 as follows:

The house floor as it was exposed is shown in the diagrammatic sketch [reproduced here as Figure 8.10]. The house is rectangular in plan, measures approximately 6 × 11 meters with an additional 2 meter entrance passage, and has a floor depressed approximately 50 cm below the original surface. Post molds are peripheral along the four walls and the main fire pit is offset and located toward the entrance. No interior post molds indicating a roof support pattern were found, and the house is oriented on a northwest-southeast axis. The structure had been burned and masses of charcoal and partially burned wood lay over the floor.[41]

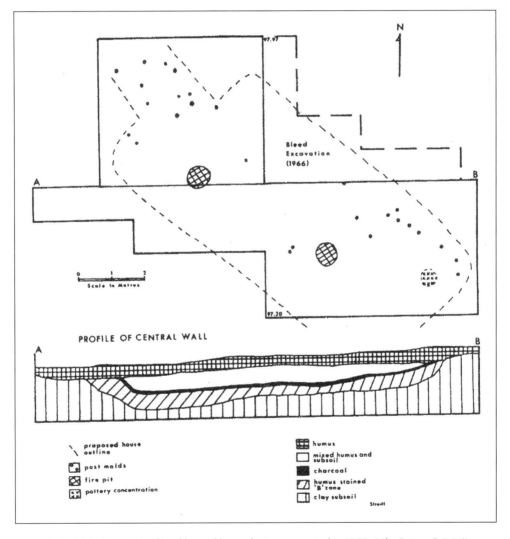

Figure 8.10. Plainview and profile of burned house feature excavated in 1967 at the Petaga Point site. Reproduced from E. Johnson 1971. Courtesy of the Wilford Archaeology Laboratory, University of Minnesota.

As many as seven other structures were located from surface features. As Johnson adds, the structures were "clustered together but in no formal spatial arrangement. There is no indication of any defensive fortification at the site."

Radiocarbon dates run on burn layer (charcoal) samples from the house excavated by Johnson at Petaga Point in 1967 and from another recently excavated burnt house at the same site place the construction of the houses between AD 1650 and 1700.[42] These lodges seem similar in structure and appearance to the bark houses that the Eastern Dakota (descendent relatives of Bradbury phase populations) built along the Minnesota valley in the late eighteenth and early nineteenth centuries.

TERMINAL WOODLAND LIFEWAYS
IN CENTRAL AND NORTHERN MINNESOTA

What cultural processes were at play in the north woods of Minnesota during the late prehistoric period? How can we account for the sharp discontinuity between the Blackduck-Kathio-Clam River and Psinomani archaeological records? From my perspective, the discontinuity represents—like the discontinuity between Terminal (Late) Woodland and Mississippian archaeological cultures in southern Minnesota—the emergence of a tribal lifeway. The emergent nature of this shift is apparent in the abruptness of its occurrence, the replacement of subsistence-oriented mobility (foraging) by food-getting strategies that do not include residential mobility to any great extent (collecting), the appearance of a new niche that emphasized the intensive harvesting of wild rice and a greater reliance on stored food, and the appearance of new traditions of material culture, as seen most clearly in the replacement of one ceramic tradition by another.

It must be stressed that at present these and other trends I focus on in this chapter are suggested but not demonstrated by the archaeological record.[43] They are consistent, however, with trends in Binford's "frames of reference" approach and with Johnson's understanding of subsistence and settlement practices in central Minnesota during the Terminal Woodland period as summarized below:

> a dependence upon large mammals of forest, ecotone, and prairie; a dependence upon the wild plant foods of local upland and aquatic habitats; and a significant utilization of fish, waterfowl, and molluscan fauna available locally. The subsistence pattern that emerges suggests a reasonably continuous intensive extraction of food resources from the locality, and the intermittent seasonal incursion into the forest-prairie mosaic zone and into the more westerly grasslands to procure bison, elk, and deer.[44]

There is at present evidence within this central Minnesota area, too, for the presence of extensive wild rice harvesting and specialized fishing camps, as well as the occasional use of maize, squash, and tobacco.[45] Subsistence and settlement trends in early Early and Middle Terminal Woodland sites, while again open to debate, support the existence of trends toward further food resource intensification and population growth.[46]

In my reading of the facts, as elusive and debatable as they are, the appearance of the Psinomani complex marks the emergence of an Intensive Wild Rice Harvester tribal lifeway in central and northern Minnesota. In the remainder of the chapter I explore how this transformation likely affected settlement patterns and the size of local groups, the organization of labor forces and the prevalence of tended facilities, and degree of social complexity, as well as the reasons for these shifts. Admittedly, the review is inadequate, for the social history of the period is dynamic and complex, and only a limited number of topics can be addressed here. Still, the review is a step in the direction of a more anthropologically informed understanding of what took place in Minnesota's north woods during the late prehistoric period.

In precontact Minnesota, the transformation of band-based societies into tribal societies involved the shift from a forager way of life to a collector way of life. A collector way of life is distinguished from a forager way of life by the concentration of populations in "a central settlement that is maintained and used over a multiyear period."[47] Rather than family foraging groups moving from one food patch to another, task groups that are usually composed of males range outward from a residential location and bring back essential resources, though family groups move seasonally to special food procurement locations, as during fish runs, wild rice harvests, and bison hunts. In general, the number of people occupying a residential site (here a village) is larger than for mobile peoples, household size is larger, and more people are included in an ethnic group, though there is a reduction in the size of the area controlled by the ethnic group. There is also a reduction in dependence on terrestrial animals and increased exploitation of an aquatic biome (wild rice harvesting, the use of gill nets in fishing) where the use of domesticated terrestrial plants and animals is not (or is less of) an option.[48] Together, these changes amount to a substantial shift in effective environment.

Related trends are the convergence of ethnically (and perhaps linguistically) diverse groups into the new niche (here the tribal lifeway based on intensive wild rice harvesting), the aggregation of people from peripheral regions to more favorable food resource locations, and "the emergence of a new organizational collectivity that displays a great deal of internal homogeneity in material culture and behavior."[49] All of these trends seem to be characteristic of the Psinomani lifeway, for people seem to have aggregated into clusters of relatively sedentary villages near favored aquatic resource locations, an increase in dependence on wild rice harvesting seemingly occurred (using number of rice fragments and jigs in a site component as an indicator), and a general homogeneity of material culture appears and spreads outward over most of central and northern Minnesota (note the *seems* and *seeminglys* here).

The adoption of a residentially based collector lifeway "results in a very different organization of male and female labor than [occurs] among foragers who are residentially mobile."[50] This shift is a response in large part to the increased labor input required in acquiring bulk food resources and preparing them for storage in situations where the onset of spoilage is a problem (think here of wild rice harvesting, fish spawns, and buffalo hunts). Because of the problem of spoilage, plant foods (wild rice, maize) will become the stored resource of preference, even if animal resources (fish, buffalo) are more abundant. According to the ethnographic record, "males are usually involved in procurement and the females in processing" in situations like those described above.[51]

A common means of "recruiting productive females to participate in a relatively stable, family-based labor unit" in circumstances like this is polygyny, a marriage practice in which a man may have more than one wife.[52] This practice has implications for the age at first marriage for both females and males, mean household size, the number of families in a village, and the tendency toward communal houses. There are at least three reasons to believe that this practice and the reorganization of labor described above were features of Native American life in the Mille Lacs region at least during the early historic period. First, during his stay in the Mille Lacs region in 1680, Father Hennepin mentions the practice of polygyny among the Mdewakanton Dakota.[53] Second, large lodge-like structures are present in a number of late prehistoric/early historic Mille Lacs region sites, as mentioned earlier in the chapter. And third, there is abundant evidence of the bulk processing of foods by Mille Lacs–centered Native Americans in both the archaeological record (the abundance of wild rice grains and ricing pits) and the early historic record (wild ricing, fish spawns, and buffalo hunts), even though the cultural associations of the precontact evidence remain unclear.

Other common features of residentially based collector lifeways among tribal people are the increasing prevalence of tended facilities, such as large fish dams, weirs, and seine nets, the institutionalized stewardship or ownership of food-yielding venues (like beds of wild rice or a favored fishing spot), and, where possible, an expansion of the number of places in which food resources occur. In the Mille Lacs region, the latter process may have included the sowing of wild rice to produce new or better beds and the burning of vegetation to produce better browse for game animals. Changes in social complexity commonly occur, too, among emerged groups in the appearance of integrative mechanisms like secret societies, age grade systems, and moieties, among other means of intergroup networking.[54] Evidence of all of these trends and features should be found in the archaeological record of the Psinomani complex.

Why did this emergent change in lifeways occur in the north woods of Minnesota? In what ways was this change different from the emergence of village farming communities in southern Minnesota? Following Morton Fried's notion that a tribe is a mode of social organization forced into existence when band-level groups interact with hostile or at least competitive groups having larger-scale social organization, I suggested in chapter 7 that the emergence of village farming tribal communities in southern Minnesota was triggered by interactions between Terminal (Late) Woodland people living in that area and more complex Mississippian societies living to the south of them. I have previously suggested that the abrupt emergence of tribal-level groups in central Minnesota was a direct response to interaction with southern Minnesota Oneota groups beginning in about AD 1225/1250.[55] The presence of Oneota-like Ogechie ceramics in Psinomani assemblages and a similar rearrangement of social organization among band-based Ojibwa groups that had moved into central Minnesota in the historic period in response to hostilities with Eastern Dakota groups in southern Minnesota were cited in support of this view, among other lines of evidence.[56]

In the last part of chapter 7 I raised questions about the role that climatic change may have played in southern Minnesota during the late prehistoric period. How did the increasingly cold temperatures and snowy winters of the Little Ice Age (the Neo-Boreal climatic episode) affect the Psinomani tribal lifeway after AD 1550? The environment of these Native American peoples was certainly changing, as evident in the expansion at the time of the Big Woods in southern Minnesota. Was the prolonged presence of these colder and snowier conditions a contributing cause (among many) to the western and southern movement of the Lakota and Dakota peoples out of Minnesota's north woods? At this time, these questions remain underinvestigated in Minnesota archaeology.

Long-Term Pattern in the Past

The search for cross-cultural patterns in human organization is a central and distinguished aim of an anthropological approach to social theory.

—Severin Fowles, "From Social Type to Social Process: Placing 'Tribe' in a Historical Framework"

In this final chapter I summarize the long-term historical trajectories identified in chapters 2 through 8. I then place these long-term historical trajectories in the context of the history of human societies throughout the world and argue that the identification of historical trajectories like these should be of interest to all of us. The chapter is intentionally brief, for I am attempting to make, but not belabor, three points beyond the content of earlier chapters. First, the identification of long-term pattern in lifeways provides a narrative that makes the prehistory of a state like Minnesota easier to understand. Besides giving a narrative framework to readers, this emphasis is of primary importance in archaeological research today, because the details of lifeways at various scales can be more informatively filled in once this background is better understood. Second, the pattern of lifeway change in any region of the world is more fully illuminated by seeing that pattern within the context of pattern in human lifeways in world history. Third, if present-day crises such as poverty and environmental degradation are not unanticipated but rather predictable outcomes of the unfolding of trends in human lifeways through time, then the study of long-term trends in the history of human societies becomes a more urgent concern than it is today.

LONG-TERM PATTERN IN PREHISTORIC MINNESOTA LIFEWAYS: A SUMMARY

In chapters 2 through 8 I identify two major kinds of pattern in Minnesota prehistory: pattern in the environment, and pattern in change in lifeways through time. Before I began writing this book, I was unaware of the presence of either pattern, though I had been actively engaged in Minnesota archaeology for thirty years. This section provides a brief summary of these two patterns, beginning with pattern in the environment.

For at least the past 5,000 years, Minnesota has been bordered by two latitudinal transitions in biotic community that are a result of a gradual reduction in solar radiation as one moves northward on the globe. The lower boundary (at about 42.6° latitude in northern Iowa) once separated terrestrial plant harvesters in warmer, moister, more southern environments from terrestrial game hunters in Minnesota, who in turn were separated in the north (at about 49.5° latitude in northwestern Ontario) from hunter-gatherers in boreal forests poor in terrestrial game animals. Within the boundaries of these two latitudinal transitions are Minnesota's "10,000" lakes (a heritage of the Wisconsin glaciation), three plant biomes that trisect the state (open deciduous forest, northern mixed-hardwood forest, and prairie parkland), and a cool temperate climate, with cold, snowy winters and warm, humid summers. Earlier, following the retreat of the last continental glacier, the region experienced extreme climatic and vegetational dislocations, including an eastward expansion of prairie parkland. The pattern in lifeway development, described below, was in large part an adaptation to pattern in this environment and its change through time.

In chapters 2 through 8, Lewis Binford's "frames of reference" approach was used to interpret Minnesota's precontact archaeological record. The result was the identification of nine types of human adaptation that I arranged in a four-phase sequence. The nine types and their place in the sequence are: (1) Pioneer Foragers; (2) Coniferous Forest Game Hunters, Deciduous Forest Game Hunters, and Early Pedestrian Bison Hunters; (3) Proto-Wild Rice Harvesters, Proto-Horticulturalists, and Late Pedestrian Bison Hunters; and (4) Horticulturalists and Intensive Wild Rice Harvesters.

The sequence evolved from the presence of free-wandering family bands who moved from one food patch to another in pursuit of large- and medium-sized terrestrial game animals in Phase 1, to the presence of family hunting bands that now lived within socially circumscribed food resource territories in which demographic packing was not yet a problem in Phase 2, to the presence of still mobile family hunting bands experiencing resource intensification pressures in smaller demographically packed territories in Phase 3, to the sudden emergence of more settled, larger tribal-level societies dependent on either maize horticulture or intensive wild rice harvesting in Phase 4. As reconstructed in this book, the pioneer foraging phase lasted 700 years, the phase of circumscribed but wide-ranging foraging 7,500 years, the phase of band-level resource intensification 4,000 years, and the phase of tribal societies 650 years (to historic contact).

This proposed sequence of adaptive change and the duration of its phases provide a framework, if only tentative, for making sense of the state's precontact archaeological record. The word *tentative* should be stressed, for Minnesota's archaeological record remains underinvestigated from a lifeways perspective.[1] My reconstruction of Minnesota's Holocene environment should be labeled tentative, as well. Through the efforts of the University of Minnesota's Herbert E. Wright Jr. and his students and colleagues, Minnesota's Holocene environment is as well known as that of any other state or province in North America. I have used only a small portion of that information in my use of Binford's "frames of reference" approach, an approach that is heavily grounded in attributes of regional environments.

IDENTIFYING LONG-TERM PATTERN IN HUMAN LIFEWAYS THROUGHOUT THE WORLD

The study of changing lifeways in a place like prehistoric Minnesota is illuminated and enriched, I believe, by comparing those lifeways with the many other types of lifeways that people have adopted. Among the questions that might be asked in this avenue of inquiry are, What was the governing process in the formation and change of lifeways in prehistoric Minnesota? How did this process differ from those that govern other types of lifeways or the same kind of lifeway in other environments? Just where in the flowing stream of human lifeways do those in Minnesota fit? In turn, the identification of long-term historical trajectories in the lifeways of precontact Minnesotans helps fill out this global picture.

As the fossil record of human biological evolution and DNA studies show, all peoples in the world today are members of a shared humanity that arose in Africa about 160,000 years ago and spread from there around the world. We are the biological and cultural heirs of these earlier people. During the history of this stream of humanity, human lifeways shifted at least among some groups of people from that of a mobile hunter-gatherer to that of a citizen in a large-scale nation-state today. Each of these types of lifeways had its own characteristics and governing process. To begin to make these comparisons—and I only begin a comparison here—I use ideas in John Bodley's book *Cultural Anthropology: Tribes, States, and the Global System.*[2]

In his study of the development of human lifeways through time, Bodley identifies three cultural worlds in which people have lived: the tribal world, the imperial world, and the commercial world. Each of these cultural systems has a different growth trajectory, governing process, distribution of power, and household living standard, among other characteristics. Each also occurs at a different scale of magnitude in terms of size of societies and economy. In this section I describe the core characteristics of these three worlds and note that precontact Native American societies in Minnesota were part of the tribal world, though influences (and perhaps people) from the imperial world infringed on their lifeways in the late prehistoric period.

Following the appearance of anatomically modern human beings in Africa about 200,000 years ago, small bands of mobile hunter-gatherers spread slowly by migration throughout the world, where they formed small societies adapted to regional environmental conditions.[3] The first foraging bands entered Australia by 50,000 years ago, and the Americas by 15,000 years ago. Bodley calls this early phase of cultural development by modern-appearing people the tribal world.[4] Tribal societies are small-scale, kinship-based groups consisting of economically self-sufficient households that organize production and distribution. They are able to maintain a sustainable relationship with the natural resources in their regional ecosystems and experience a minimum of social inequality. Let's look more closely at these characteristics, for I use these characteristics or their counterparts for comparison in my later reviews of the imperial and commercial worlds.

By *small-scale* anthropologists mean societies that seldom exceed 500 to 2,000 people, depending on level of social complexity. A society as used here refers to "an interacting, intermarrying population sharing a common culture."[5] Population densities were low, and the world was uncrowded—it is estimated that in 6000 BC, when the first more complex societies appear, there were no more than 100 million people in the world. In a similar tribal world calculation, I estimate that there were no more than 15,000 to 20,000 people in Minnesota in the late prehistoric period. The largest social units were independent kinship-based bands and villages in which the household was the dominant and central social institution. Everyone in the social universe was treated as either family or "enemy."

Societies in the tribal world had a limited technology and were organized in economically self-sufficient households based initially on mobile foraging and later on sedentary village life, in what I distinguish in this book as band-level and tribal-level societies, respectively. Since everyone's basic needs were generally satisfied, members of the community shared the goods extracted from natural resources, wealth was not accumulated, and a minimum of social inequality existed, for there were few opportunities for the concentration of much social power. Personal imperia remained small and based on kinship and marriage relations (an individual's personal imperia is "an individual's personal power network, including everyone that one might command or call on for assistance, as well as the institutional structures that one might direct").[6] As a consequence there was no need for government, and societies were for the most part stable. It was in this world that the major domestic technologies like ceramics, textiles, farming, and herding were invented and widely adopted during the intensification process.

In the tribal world the only major process is the humanization process, which Bodley defines as "the production, maintenance, and reproduction of human beings and culture."[7] People enjoyed a maximum of freedom, were in general good health, were able to make their first priority the maintenance and health of their household, had little incentive to increase production, and were able to maintain a sustainable relationship with their natural environment. This was the only mode of human existence from at least 160,000 years ago to 8000 years ago.

Examples of village-centered tribal world societies include the Eastern Dakota and later the Ojibwa in Minnesota, the neighboring Winnebago (Ho Chunk) in Wisconsin, and the majority of other Native American societies in North America at historic contact. Well-known historic period band-level foraging groups include the Shoshone in the North American Great Basin and the aborigines in Australia.

Unlike the tribal world, the imperial world is characterized "by centrally organized societies with thousands or millions of members and energy-intensive production directed by political rulers."[8] In imperial world societies wealth and social power are concentrated in a small network of a few hundred people intent on increasing production in ways that improve the well-being of their own households at the expense of an exploited majority, who subsidize the growth process through taxes, tribute, and work-related obligations. As societies grew larger in the imperial world—by AD 1200 global population had expanded to 360 million people—the increasingly complex daily activities needed to keep such large-scale societies running resulted in the emergence of specialists of many kinds, bureaucratic institutions, and armies.

The imperial world is the world of social stratification, state political organization, and Great Tradition civilizations. Imperial world societies range from chiefdoms, to small agrarian kingdoms, to large political empires. Beginning in about 6000 BC, they emerged throughout the world wherever energy-intensive production systems could be established and populations enlarged. The largest of the ancient agrarian civilizations numbered in the tens of millions of subjects. Cahokia was a complex prehistoric chiefdom. Well-known historic period chiefdoms include the small Polynesian chiefdom of Tikopia and the complex chiefdom in Hawaii, which eventually became a kingdom. Familiar ancient empires include those in Mesopotamia, Peru (the Inca), and Mexico (the Aztec). Great Tradition civilizations include the Chinese village-state in East Asia, and Hinduism and Islam in South Asia.

The primary process in the imperial world is politicalization, which Bodley defines as "the production and maintenance of centralized political power by co-opting the humanization process."[9] The result was the end of social equality as experienced in the tribal world. Given the steep pyramidal social structure of societies in the imperial world, the interests and life chances of the majority of society were subordinate to the welfare of a few elite households and the institutions of government that supported that hierarchy.

For these same reasons, imperial world societies tend to be unstable and vulnerable to collapse from internal conflict and external invasion. Within these societies, scale thresholds limit the number of people who can enjoy the privileges of the elite, ever-expanding institutional functions and costs add to the financial burden of the population, and the increasing growth of the personal imperia of the elite require larger and larger subsidies from ordinary people. Practices of imperial world societies that result in growing external animosity are the extraction of tribute from neighboring societies and the conquest of those societies in efforts to enlarge a chiefdom, kingdom, or empire. The result is the frequent overthrow of these great cultural systems, some decomposing into smaller political units and others being taken over by new, often foreign elites.[10] At times, a major cultural discontinuity occurs when empires and Great Tradition societies totally disappear; as examples, the Maya, Inca, and ancient Rome and Greece come immediately to mind. Another hallmark of imperial world societies is the depletion of valuable nonrenewable resources and often the creation of seriously degraded ecosystems, especially during periods of impending collapse.

Social power in the commercial world resides not among political elites but among economic or business elites, who beginning in Europe about AD 1400 used impersonal market exchanges, commercial enterprises, contracts, and money to amass wealth and to construct the commercial world itself. Their motivation in large part was "to escape the growth and power limits of the politically organized imperial world."[11] The successful strategy they adopted, which included the reduction of government control over business activities and the use of political power to protect business enterprises, resulted in the expansion of business enterprises and markets around the globe. At the same time, the business elite used and continue to use "their economic power to gain political and ideological power."[12] Today, the commercial world dominates the globe.

The primary process in the commercial world is commercialization, which Bodley defines as "the production and maintenance of private profit-making business enterprise as a means of accumulating capital, by co-opting the humanization and politicalization processes."[13] Culture changes linked to the commercialization process include increased economic activity, wide-ranging technological developments that include the ability to produce and distribute goods faster and at a larger scale, the use of fossil fuels as a cheap energy source, greatly increased natural resource consumption rates, and a dramatic improvement in living standards for some people. Accompanying these changes soon after their inception was a rapid expansion of the size of some societies by hundreds of millions of people. Shortly after 1800, global population exceeded 1 billion for the first time. World population rose rapidly to 2 billion by 1927, and

4 billion by 1974. At present, 1 billion additional more people are added to the world's population every twelve years.

In spite of the dramatic improvement in living standards for some people, particularly in the West, many more people throughout the world find it difficult to make a living, for power over individual lives in many areas tends to be controlled by merchants, landlords, and financial institutions. Life's necessities are no longer considered an individual's right as a member of society, as in the tribal world, but as commodities, where commodities are defined as "basic goods that are produced for their exchange value in a market economy to generate profit to be accumulated as capital."[14] The result has been widespread impoverishment (as anyone who reads a newspaper is aware), enormous social upheaval, and the subordination of "the interests of both governments and ordinary households to the interests of economic elites and the institutions they dominated."[15]

I have strayed far from Minnesota in this section, but for a purpose. A comparison of lifeways in precontact Minnesota with Bodley's three cultural worlds enriches, I believe, our understanding of the processes at work—and those not present—in precontact Minnesota. Minnesota's precontact societies were firmly within the tribal world, with the probable infringement of an imperial world chiefdom during the late prehistoric period. A task for archaeologists working in Minnesota is a continuing comparison of tribal world societies from around the world to those in the state to better understand the processes of adaptation involved and the tempo of change observed in the archaeological record.

TOWARD AN UNDERSTANDING OF
LONG-TERM PATTERN IN HUMAN LIFEWAYS

As important as descriptions of societies and processes in each of Bodley's three worlds are, description itself does not tell us why the transformation from one world to another took place. Why did the transformations occur? What was the effect of these transformations on the lived life of the average person? How will answers to these kinds of questions affect our understanding of the lived lives of precontact Minnesotans—and, I might add, our understanding of the importance of the archaeological record?

Many readers may be surprised to learn that some anthropologists, including myself, consider the rampant poverty and environmental degradation that characterize areas of the world today a consequence of long-term historical trajectories in human history. This concern is reflected in my response to students who ask me, "In our post-9/11 world, isn't the study of the archaeology of the Upper Mississippi River region a trivial pursuit? Aren't there more urgent tasks that need addressing, like the melting of the icecaps and the breakdown of our financial institutions?" My reply is that from my perspective the identification and understanding of long-term pattern in human development are two of these tasks, for the pattern continues to unfold and will do so into the future—and many of the world's problems seem to be a consequence of that unfolding pattern. What do I mean by that reply?

In books like Thomas Friedman's *Hot, Flat, and Crowded*, there is an acute awareness of present crisis but no apparent awareness that this present crisis has a history. Listen to the concern in Friedman's voice in the following:

> The argument I am making is very simple: America has a problem and the world has a problem. America's problem is that it has lost its way in recent years—partly because of 9/11 and partly because of some bad habits, lazy thinking, and financial recklessness that we have let build up. . . . The world also has a problem. . . . It is getting hot, flat, and crowded. And as we try to grow everyone's standard of living in such a world, we are rapidly depleting our natural resources, intensifying the extinction of plants and animals, deepening energy poverty, strengthening petro-dictatorship, and accelerating climate change—all at unprecedented rates.[16]

What is missing in otherwise informative books like Friedman's is an understanding of the possible or even probable roots of this crisis. What are those roots, and what are the driving forces that underlie them? Why have these forces resulted in increasing world poverty and widespread environmental degradation around the world?

Bodley's answer to these questions, which is presented as an hypothesis (the power-elite hypothesis), is that the great transformations of post–Ice Age human history are not the result of community agreement but were caused by power seekers—self-aggrandizing individuals—intent on increasing their immediate personal power at the expense of the majority, who subsidized the process.[17] As societies grew in scale, social power became ever more concentrated in the hands of a small number of individuals, who used their growing social power to continually promote their self-interests. These new developments in human lifeways are considered an extreme outcome of human beings' inborn predisposition to behave in self-interested ways.

In the tribal world opportunities for self-aggrandizing individuals to concentrate social power were few, for in an uncrowded world people could move away from a power seeker (they could, as the saying goes, "vote with their feet"). Rising population levels and increasing social circumscription after the Ice Age gave a few individuals the opportunity to take advantage of crisis situations to enhance their personal imperia.

They did this at first by creating often great religions that transcended family and clan loyalties, and later by promoting a worldview that naturalized the commercial world and the inequality it produced. Words like *progress,* the *primitive, savage,* and *civilized* are a heritage of this latter process.[18] Consequences of elite-directed changes in human lifeways include tremendous growth in the number of people living on the globe and increased economic activity, both with undesirable ecosystem modifications, for, as Bodley says, "elites can attain more power only by having more people to control and more economic resources to exploit, and this necessarily requires growth."[19]

Are the great cultural transformations in human lifeways in the post–Ice Age period an inevitable, entirely predictable process, or the outcome of short-term, self-interested acts that may not benefit the survival of human beings in the long run? Is the pathway of human social evolution deterministic, or do we have some control over its direction? These are obviously critical large-scale questions today, for the long-term survival of human beings may depend on their answers. Is Bodley's interpretation of the underlying reasons for these cultural transformations in human history reasonably accurate? I don't know myself, but if his interpretation is accurate, then a shared understanding of the cultural processes that produce growth and deliberate power inequality will become, in his words, "an essential survival skill."[20] Said another way, "If poverty and environmental deterioration are under cultural, and therefore human, control, they could be significantly reduced, or even eliminated, by intentional culture design and change."[21] Can we take the risk of not trying to understand with urgency these large-scale transformations and the processes that underlie them?

Again, I have wandered far from Minnesota archaeology, but again for a purpose. From the perspective presented here, the identification and understanding of long-term change in human lifeways in all parts of the globe become a project that all archaeologists and historians and all concerned individuals should engage in. Though Minnesota was at the periphery of great changes in social complexity, an understanding of the social processes at work in the state before historic contact remains no less important, for their understanding will reveal how and why people live the way they do in particular historic circumstances. It is essential, then, that we value the archaeological record of the state and work diligently to protect it. It is an irreplaceable part of world heritage whose close examination seems increasingly to matter.

Introduction

1. McKern (1939). For McKern, traits are characteristics of cultures that may have material manifestations in the archaeological record (Gibbon 2007). The concept of culture is introduced in the second section of this chapter. According to McKern's normative view of culture, culture consists at least in part of shared, consistent ways of doing things, which he calls traits. Thus, the identification of a consistent pattern of burial in the archaeological record, such as secondary burial in a pit below a burial mound, is the identification of a trait of a culture. Since this approach does not address the problem of getting at the meaning or function of a trait in a past culture, it is considered a descriptive rather than an interpretative approach.

2. Wilford (1941, 1955). Also see Wilford (1960).

3. Willey and Phillips (1958).

4. Syms (1977); Lehmer (1971).

5. Syms (1977), 70.

6. Willey and Phillips (1958), 48–52.

7. Ibid., 50.

8. Owen (1965). Also see Brightman (2002), Moore (1994), and Fowles (2002, 19–20) for the heterogeneous and flexible nature of bands and tribes.

9. I regard these tables as an update of Wilford's (1955, 1960) final taxonomic charts. For the most part, the taxonomic names used in the charts follow those used by Dobbs and Anfinson (1990) in their historic context document for Minnesota. The different taxonomic designations for Minnesota's archaeological cultures are mentioned as they are reviewed.

10. For introductions to transformation processes and their role in the creation of the archaeological record, see Schiffer (1996) and Goldberg, Nash, and Petraglia (1993).

11. Wilber (2000), 63–75.

12. Archaeologists generally adopt one of four research programs in carrying out a project: a trait-based descriptive approach anchored in Wilber's upper-right quadrant, a systems-based approach (as in this book) centered in the lower-right quadrant, an agent-centered approach concerned with left-quadrant issues, and a four-quadrant integral approach that some archaeologists refer to as the "thick" approach. These are complementary approaches best suited to some tasks rather than others. More on this below.

13. Bodley (2005), 25–28.

14. Ibid., 524.

15. Ibid., 25. Bodley's (2005, 22–23) two more-complex cultural worlds are the imperial world in which "rulers made maintaining and reproducing the institutions of government the dominant purpose of society," and the commercial world, which "was constructed by economic elites who sought to escape the growth and power limits of the politically organized imperial world." The cultural processes and functional organization of each of these three cultural worlds were distinctly different.

16. For the difference between static and process definitions of tribal societies, see Fowles (2002). The same argument applies to band-based societies. In the 1960s and 1970s influential ethnographic-like (ideal-type) descriptions of bands and tribes were presented by Elman Service (1979) and Marshall Sahlins (1968, 2004). By their nature, the descriptions lack reference to developmental trends through time and thus have proven less useful to archaeologists intent on studying long-term patterns of change in band-based and tribal societies. In addition, because of their ideal-type nature, they fail to accommodate all of the variety found globally in band-based and tribal societies. Many of the traits listed in Figures I.5–I.7 have exceptions, and others need a fuller description. For example, "equalitarian" does not mean that these societies "in fact lack forms of ranking, hereditary leadership, and privileged control of such things as ritual knowledge and land" (Fowles 2002, 16).

17. As stressed in note 12, different research programs have different potentials and limitations. For example, agent-centered approaches are of more central importance in the study of intra- and intergenerational change than they are in the study of long-term historical trajectories (Fowles 2002, 26). Since some readers of this book will be interested in aspects of Minnesota archaeology that differ from those I pursue here, I include extensive references to the literature to facilitate the pursuit of their interests. Be aware, though, that much of the literature about Minnesota archaeology occurs in difficult to locate, unpublished cultural resource management reports and academic theses.

18. Fried (1975).

19. Binford (2001).

20. Ibid., 163.

21. Ibid., 56. A principle of Binford's (2001, 364) frames of reference approach is that "variance in hunter-gatherer subsistence practices is strongly related to the habitat within which such groups live." Said another way, "The Rosetta Stone in understanding system state differences among contemporary hunter-gatherers is the structure of variability in climatic conditions and how climatic variables affect other environmental conditions characteristics of the era for which there are climatic records" (ibid., 197).

22. The reference here to daughter communities should not be taken to mean that "parent" communities were linguistically, culturally, and biologically homogeneous and did not change in composition through time. See note 8.

23. Population packing as used here simply means that the number of people living in an area increased to such a size that adequate food resources were difficult to obtain using traditional subsistence (food-gathering) practices. For hunter-gatherer societies whose subsistence focus is the hunting of large game animals, a shift to second-order foods means that an increasing percentage of their food energy comes from other food sources, like fish and plants. As the number of people in an area continues to grow, there is an intensified concentration (referred to by Binford as "resource intensification") on second-order and other food sources, such as the use of domesticated plant foods that could be grown in small gardens or obtained through trade.

24. Bryson and DeWall (2007).

25. Bodley (2005).

1. Environments of Minnesota

1. The standard, most accessible guide to the surface geology of Minnesota remains Ojakangas and Matsch (1982). Also see H. E. Wright (1972b).

2. For an easy to read but comprehensive guide to the streams and rivers of Minnesota, see Waters (1977).

3. For overviews of animal and plant life in the state, see Aaseng et al. (1993), Tester (1995), and Benchley et al. (1997, 21–38). An early version of this section appears in chapter 3 in Hudak et al. (2002).

4. Pielou (1988); Lynch and Lang (2001).

5. Beyers (1989); Daniel and Sullivan (1981).

6. Yahner (1995).

7. Many books describe the tallgrass prairie landscape that once covered southwestern Minnesota. The following references are a sampling of this literature: Costello (1980), Madson (1995), and Gruchow (2009). Also see Patterson (1997) and van der Valk (1989).

8. The system of resource regions used here was developed by Scott Anfinson (1990) for both compliance and research purposes. The descriptions in this book of the resource regions are paraphrases from Anfinson, who had intended to be coauthor of the book before he was appointed State Archaeologist.

9. For an excellent overview, see Teller and Clayton (1983).

10. For the formation and character of the Big Bog, see Wright, Coffin, and Aaseng (1992).

11. For a study of the ecosystem of the core of this area, see Heinselman (1996).

12. For a readable description of the Lake Superior shoreline in this area of the state, see Waters (1987).

13. The classic account is Grimm (1983). Also see Grimm (1984).

14. Bryson (1998).

15. Eyre (1968).

16. Binford (2001, 267). The formula for calculating effective temperature is $[(18 \times MWM) - (10 \times MCM)]/(MWM - MCM + 8)$, where MWM is the mean temperature in degrees centigrade for the warmest month of the year and MCM is the mean temperature in degrees centigrade for the coldest month of the year. ET is a relative number determined from the formula. It does not refer to a specific temperature.

2. First People

1. For overviews of the early peopling of the Americas, see Bonnichsen et al. (2006), Dillehay (2001), Meltzer (2010), and B. Peterson (2011).

2. The Wisconsin glaciation took place in a complex series of ice lobe advances and retreats (H. E. Wright 1971, 1972a; Dyke and Prest 1986). Minnesota's "10,000 lakes" are a legacy of these late glacial events (Ojakangas and Matsch 1982; Pielou 1991).

3. Because of the dynamic nature of the glacial environment, the history of Glacial Lake Agassiz is extremely complex (see Teller and Clayton 1983). According to Teller (1987, 53–54), "After retreating several hundred kilometers north of its 14 ka [thousand years ago] maximum in Iowa, a series of at least eight rapid readvances (surges) and retreats of the Red River-Des Moines Lobe occurred. . . . During this period, each successive glacial advance fell short of its predecessor, and each intervening glacial retreat appears to have receded slightly farther north. Several times before 12 ka the glacial margin wasted north of the divide between Hudson Bay and Mississippi watersheds at the southern end of the Red River Lowland. . . . At times, lakes developed in the southern (upslope) end of the lowland for a few hundred years before being overridden by a new

surge of ice. Finally, about 11.7 ka, ice wasted north across the divide into the Red River Valley for the last time, establishing Lake Agassiz."

4. For a summary of the origin and evolution of the Great Lakes, see Larson and Schaetzl (2001). For a geoarchaeological perspective, see Phillips (1993) and Hill (2007).

5. There is an ever-growing literature on the sequence of Late Glacial and Holocene changes in vegetation in Minnesota and their relation to climate, the presence of the Laurentide Ice Sheet and Glacial Lake Agassiz, fire, and other factors. Although single dates are generally given events like the end of the last ice age and the beginning and end of the Prairie (Middle Holocene) period in order to simplify discussion, events like these were actually time-transgressive processes that lasted hundreds and even thousands of years. For example, the abrupt decline of the spruce forest that marks the end of the Late Glacial period was time-transgressive from southwestern to northeastern Minnesota for 2,000 years, and the expansion of prairie that marks the Prairie period "was time-transgressive in the same direction over 2600 years" (Wright et al. 2004, 611). I have chosen dates for the major divisions of the Holocene typical of central Minnesota; readers will encounter other sets of dates in other literature, both by archaeologists and paleoclimatologists. Some writers who do not consistently indicate whether they are using radiocarbon or calendar dates further confuse the discussion. For a sampling of the literature, see Baker et al. (2002), Camill et al. (2003), Clark et al. (2001), Shuman et al. (2002), H. E. Wright (1976a), and Wright et al. (2004). A task for Minnesota archaeologists is the establishment of firm dates for these changes in the state's five main resource regions.

6. For overviews of overkill versus climate change arguments, see Meltzer and Mead (1985), Grayson (1991), and Fiedel (2002, 423–24).

7. For an accessible description of these point types, see Justice (1987, 17–30). While western Clovis points are apparently fairly homogeneous in appearance and method of manufacture, variation exists in Clovis-like fluted points across the continent (David Anderson and Faught 2000; Haynes 2002; Morrow and Morrow 1999). If we were to follow Howard's (1990) formal description of a true Clovis point, only a point found just west of Pine City in east-central Minnesota would at present fit that category. Fluted point distributions by Anfinson's nine expanded resource regions at this writing are: 1. Southwest Riverine (1, 1 percent), 2. Prairie Lake (22, 30 percent), 3. Southeastern (7, 10 percent), 4. Deciduous Lakes (27, 37 percent), 5. Coniferous Lakes (7, 10 percent), 6. Red River Valley (1, 1 percent), 7. Big Bog (6, 8 percent), 8. Border Lakes (1, 1 percent), 9. Lake Superior (1, 1 percent). For the Jim Regan Folsom site, see Mulholland and Mulholland (2002). Undoubtedly, many of the unassigned points and some of the "Clovis" points will eventually be identified as Gainey points. Minnesota's fluted point sample is in need of a thorough reexamination.

8. Schroeder (2007).

9. Haynes (2002).

10. For descriptions of these point types, see Justice (1987, 30–35, 46–51). For a comprehensive survey of Late Paleoindian projectile points in Minnesota, see Florin (1996).

11. This information and the location of Paleoindian points by type in Minnesota were provided by Scott Anfinson.

12. Steinbring (1974, 67). Also see Harrison et al. (1995), Mulholland et al. (1997a), and Hill (2007).

13. For descriptions of these point types and Dalton, Hi-Lo, and Quad points, see Justice (1987, 35–46, 54–60, 63–66, 71–72). A point count of Early Eastern Archaic points (or for that matter of any other type of Archaic point) has not been carried out in Minnesota. It is important to be aware that Minnesota archaeologists tend to consider the earliest Archaic materials in their region Early Archaic. According to this definition, there may be an Early Archaic in southern Minnesota, characterized by Dalton, St. Charles, Thebes, and other projectile point types or variants, which

date between 10,500 and 7500 BC (which I call Early Eastern Archaic here), while in the prairie zone that emerged later in the western and northern parts of the state, the Early Archaic (called the Early Plains Archaic) is considered more or less contemporaneous with the early part of the Middle Holocene dry period (7500–3000 BC). In this usage, Minnesota's early Archaic is space- and time-transgressive. Dating spans for the three periods of the Archaic vary widely among archaeologists, too, perhaps because of the time-transgressive nature of culture change and change in regional environments. For Alex (2000) in Iowa, the Early Archaic dates between 8500–5500 BC, the Middle Archaic, between 5500–3000 BC, and the Late Archaic, between 3000–800 BC. For Theler and Boszhardt (2003), who are writing about the Upper Mississippi River valley in the La Crosse area of Wisconsin and southward, the dates for the three periods are Early Archaic (8200–3800 BC), Middle Archaic (3800–1800 BC), and Late Archaic (1800–700 BC). For general overviews of the Early Eastern Archaic, see Gibbon (1998a, 253–55) and Fagan (2005, 370–98).

14. Irwin and Wormington (1970).
15. Salzer (1974, 43); Malik and Bakken (1999); Steinbring (1974, 65); Harrison et al. (1995); Boszhardt (2006).
16. Allan (1993).
17. Malik and Bakken (1999).
18. Jenks (1937).
19. O'Connell and Myster (1996).
20. Shane (1991).
21. Powell and Steele (1994). This conclusion seems in conflict with Myster's (2001) later study.
22. While the intersubjective understandings (culture) and thoughts of individuals are nearly always important ingredients in the written history of historic hunter-gatherer groups (think of Geronimo), they are not considered basic causative processes in Binford's Terrestrial Model, which, as emphasized in the introduction, is a Wilber lower-right processual model. To be sure, Native Americans in precontact Minnesota were actively engaged in coping with their changing world, as we are today.
23. For reviews of Early Paleoindian lifeways, see Theler and Boszhardt (2003, 53–63), Haynes (2002), and Neusius and Gross (2007, 97–143).
24. For an overview of possible pre-Clovis archaeological materials in the Americas, see Neusius and Gross (2007, 108–12).
25. Babbitt (1884).
26. Winchell (1878, 1903); Upham (1902, 1916).
27. Joan Carother's conclusions were presented in a geoarchaeology class at the University of Minnesota in 1975.

3. Prairie Everywhere

1. For an extensive review of the Archaic in the Eastern Woodlands, see Emerson, McElrath, and Fortier (2009).
2. We often think of the Middle Holocene Prairie period as that 5,000-year-long period in which prairie covered nearly all of a very dry Minnesota. Actually, it took some 2,600 years for prairie to reach its maximum extent in the state (Wright et al. 2004, 611) and another 3,600 years to recede to its approximate modern location. During this long period, some regions of the state were very dry, and others were not—and these climatic conditions and vegetation distributions were not constant. Thus, for archaeologists, reconstructing the climate and habitat of particular regions of Minnesota at any particular time during this period is not a straightforward task. See H. E. Wright (1976b) and Forester, DeLorme, and Bradbury (1987).

3. H. E. Wright (1976b, 594).

4. Grimm (1984).

5. Wright, Coffin, and Aaseng (1992).

6. Although I date the end of the Middle Holocene dry period at 2500 BC, it was preceded by a 1,000-year-long transition period. I end the Middle Archaic period in the middle of that transition. For overviews of the Middle Archaic in the Eastern Woodlands and Plains, see Brown and Vierra (1983), Fagan (2005, 12–131), Sassaman and Anderson (1996), and Gibbon (1998a, 256–58). Because of extensive aggradation of landform-sediment assemblages during the Early and Middle Holocene in response to changes in climate, vegetation, and the structure of fluvial streams, intact Early and Middle Archaic deposits are rarely found on modern ground surfaces in floodplains or on alluvial fans or colluvial slopes. Instead they are deeply buried within deposits in these landforms or have been redeposited. Consequently, archaeologists working within these periods must rely on landscape models of site location formulated by archaeogeologists and geoarchaeologists. This is a defining characteristic of Paleoindian and Early-Middle Archaic studies in Minnesota. For very useful overviews, see Bettis and Hajic (1995) and Artz (1995).

7. For descriptions of these point types, see Justice (1987).

8. Odell (1998, 35–36).

9. Duane Anderson and Semken (1980). The identification of the weapon points in this horizon has varied from Hell Gap–like and Agate Basin–like to "degenerate" Late Paleoindian lanceolate forms. At least one of the bison may be a now-extinct larger form. Similar now-extinct forms *(Bison bison occidentalis)* were present at the Simonson site (13CK61) in Iowa and the Itasca Bison Kill site (21CE1) in Minnesota, both of which may date to circa 6200 BC. These dates indicate that this now-extinct form of bison survived for some time on the eastern Plains (Alex 2000, 66).

10. Anfinson (1987, 90–94).

11. Ibid., 94–99. Anfinson dates the Itasca phase to between 5500 BC and 3000 BC.

12. Shay (1971) provides an extensive description of the Itasca Bison Kill site.

13. Alex (2000, 66).

14. Two radiocarbon dates (circa 7900–7500 BC) suggest a Late Paleoindian age for the Itasca Bison Kill, but two others suggest an Archaic association (6200–6000 BC). Anfinson (1987) argues that Itasca is an Early Plains Archaic site rather than a Late Paleoindian site because (1) extensive prairie and thus bison herds did not appear in the Itasca area until after 7500 BC; (2) the majority of the side-notched points closely resemble the Archaic points from numerous other northeastern Plains sites; (3) the nature of the site in the bog suggests a single-episode bison kill, so we are not dealing with multiple components (which would explain the two different sets of dates); and (4) while two radiocarbon dates suggest a Late Paleoindian age, two others are firmly Early Plains Archaic in age; in addition, the dates are from bone and are not AMS (accelerator) dates, suggesting caution in using them, as many bone dates come in early if the right amino acids are not present. Dates for the Rustad site also average 6100 BC, which Anfinson considers a good age for the Itasca site.

15. Steinbring (1974, 72).

16. For descriptions of these point types, see Justice (1987).

17. Arzigian and Stevenson (2003, 75–79).

18. Jenks (1936).

19. O'Connell and Myster (1996).

20. Myster (2001, 208).

21. Ibid., 209–10.

22. Although I am unsure at present why many Late Archaic point forms appear as early as 3700 BC, it is possible that their appearance is related to increasingly moister conditions after 4900 BC. By circa 1200 BC, Minnesota's landscape probably appeared as it did at historic contact. The

Late Archaic period as I define it broadly coincides with the cooler, moister Sub-Boreal climatic episode (Bryson 1998; Bryson and Hare 1974). Rising water levels at the time in the upper Great Lakes resulted in the Nipissing and Algoma stages, which are the earliest of a sequence of late high-water transgressions that flooded adjacent shoreline. For regional reviews of the Late Archaic, see Robertson, Lovis, and Halsey (1999); Alex (2000); Theler and Boszhardt (2003); and Stoltman (1997).

23. For descriptions of these point types, see Justice (1987).
24. Anfinson (1997).
25. Michlovic (1986).
26. Steinbring (1974, 73); Bleed (1969).
27. Stoltman (1986, 227).
28. Wittry (1957). For Old Copper in Minnesota, see Gibbon (1998b).
29. Arzigian and Stevenson (2003, 75–79); Myster and O'Connell (1997, 278).
30. O'Connell and Myster (1996).
31. Jenks and Wilford (1938).
32. Fiske and Hume (1963).
33. Binford (2001, 154) calculates the size of home ranges using variables like the number of months during the growing season when water remains stored in the soil, the number of millimeters of rainfall during the driest month of the year, and the standard deviation of mean monthly temperature readings. As I learn more about Minnesota's Early and Middle Holocene environments, I plan to develop more precise values (approximations) for this and other hunter-gatherer variables discussed in this section, whose values as cited here are taken from Binford (2001). For the importance of extensive mobility as a Middle Holocene adaptive strategy in another area north of the terrestrial plant threshold, see Lovis, Donahue, and Holman (2005).
34. Binford (2001), 228.
35. Ibid., 333, 340, and 269.
36. Ibid., 388.
37. Ibid., 383, 443.
38. Ibid., 188.
39. See Cleland (1982) for the increasing importance of fishing in the upper Great Lakes in the Late Archaic period and the changes in social practices that accompanied it. Many Old Copper implements may have been associated with the increased importance of fishing at this time.
40. Binford (2001), 165.

4. Southern Deer Hunters, Gardeners, and Bison Hunters

1. Neusius and Gross (2007, 452–559). Multiple reasons have been proposed for the adoption of pottery vessels throughout the world, including the preparation and serving of food, socioeconomic competition among "aggrandizing individuals," and as part of the emergence of prestige technologies (Rice 1999).
2. For La Moille Thick pottery, see Hudak and Johnson (1975) and Anfinson (1979e). For Black Sand pottery, see Griffin (1952), Munson (1986), and Farnsworth and Asch (1986). The regional variant of Marion culture in southwestern Wisconsin, the Indian Isle phase, dates to circa 300–100 BC, while the phase associated with Black Sand–like pottery, the Prairie phase, dates to circa 100 BC–AD 100 (Stoltman 1990). The presence of encrusted charred organic material on some Marion sherds indicates that they were most likely used as cooking vessels, but that does not exclude other uses and meanings for the vessels.
3. For an overview of Early Woodland archaeology in eastern North America, see Farnsworth and Emerson (1986).

4. For an overview of the Early Woodland period in southeastern Minnesota, see Arzigian (2008, 30–34).

5. Wilford (1954).

6. For a review of the Howard Lake phase, see Gibbon et al. (1993) and Arzigian (2008, 35–52). Besides southern Anoka County, Howard Lake phase settlement concentrations seem present around Swan Lake near Mankato and Lake Koronis near St. Cloud.

7. For a review of the Sorg phase and its ceramics, see E. Johnson (1959), Anfinson (1979h), and Arzigian (2008, 35–52).

8. According to Arzigian (2008, 48), "northern assemblages tend to be simpler and are considered 'Havana-related' or Havanoid." Local northern phases include the McGregor phase in northeast Iowa, the Nickerson phase in southeast Iowa and northwest Illinois, and at one time the Trempealeau in southwestern Wisconsin. Stoltman (2006) has argued in recent years, however, that the Havana-related material in southwestern Wisconsin is embedded in local Prairie phase and later Millville phase assemblages that have their own distinctive ceramics. Are Minnesota archaeologists creating "Havana" ceramic assemblage by picking Havana-related sherds out from what is in actuality a more mixed and complicated ceramic assemblage? The answer is yet another research priority in Minnesota archaeology. I follow tradition here in defining the Howard Lake and Sorg phases, but readers should be aware of this possible complication. For the lack of some typical Havana materials in Howard Lake assemblages, also see Anfinson (1979f, 96).

9. Gibbon (1998a, 347–48).

10. Seeman (1998, 371–73).

11. Mound 1 in the Howard Lake mound group was 125 feet long, 90 feet wide, and 19 feet high. Other large mounds in Anoka County associated with Havana-related pottery include 21AN2 by Centerville, which was 80 feet in diameter and 12 feet high, and 21AN10 by Boot Lake, which was 90 feet in diameter and 12 feet high (Winchell 1911, 280). Another mound near Centerville was 80 feet in diameter and 12 feet high. It is located on the east shore of Peltier Lake, directly across from several sites with Havana-related pottery (Winchell 1911, 282).

12. Wilford (1937); Anfinson (1979f, 95).

13. Wilford (1955); Harrison et al. (1977); Anfinson (1979f, 95); Arzigian and Stevenson (2003, 333–34).

14. Lewis (1896, 316); E. Johnson (1957); Arzigian and Stevenson (2003, 472–77).

15. Since both phases lie above the 42.6° latitude that Binford uses to separate plant-dependent populations to the south from terrestrial hunters to the north, I consider the phases apt models for what may have been taking place at the time in southeastern Minnesota.

16. This assumes that there were Havana-related assemblages unmixed with local wares in the Upper Mississippi River area. See note 8.

17. Stoltman (1990, 247) has argued that ceramics associated with the Millville phase were associated with Havana-related ceramics during the earlier phase. Again, see note 8. On Linn ware, also see Stoltman (2006).

18. Benn and Green (2000, 442).

19. Freeman (1969).

20. For overviews of the Fox Lake complex, see Anfinson (1997, 47–75) and Arzigian (2008, 63–74).

21. Anfinson (1997, 53–54).

22. For descriptions of Fox Lake ceramics, see Anfinson (1979g, 1997, 59–66) and Arzigian (2008, 66–68). Although a careful trait-by-trait comparison has not been carried out, Fox Lake ceramics appear very similar to ceramics in the Prairie phase of southwestern Wisconsin.

23. Anfinson (1997, 66–69); Arzigian (2008, 68).

24. For descriptions of these point types, see Justice (1987).
25. Anfinson (1997, 69–70); Arzigian (2008, 68–69).
26. Binford (2001, 163).
27. Ibid., 267.
28. Ibid., 439.
29. Ibid., 443–44.
30. Perkl (2009).
31. Binford (2001, 197, 442).
32. Ibid., 389, 390.
33. Perkl (2009).
34. In a delayed return subsistence system, food resources are processed and stored so that they can be consumed at some later time.
35. Binford (2001, 256–61, 430).
36. Ibid., 376.

5. Northern Hunters, Fishers, and Wild Rice Harvesters

1. For an overview of the Rum River phase and Elden Johnson's Mille Lacs cultural chronology, see Johnson (1984); also see Mather (2000b). The age range of the phase remains uncertain because of the few numbers of radiometric dates and their spread (Arzigian 2008, 39–40). Dates are 690 BC for the Morrison mound (21OT2), AD 150 for the Vanderbloom mound (21ML1), AD 240 to 450 for site 21ML102, and AD 350 to 605 for residues on Malmo vessels from the Malmo site (21AK1) (E. Johnson 1964; Trocki and Hudak 2005; Mather 2000a). Whether the Morrison mound is associated with Malmo pottery and/or the Rum River phase remains problematic. As Mather (2000a, 41) points out, "Johnson's concept of the Rum River Phase evolved from the Malmo Focus, as defined by Lloyd Wilford (1944, 1951[a])." It is worth noting here that Wilford (1944) first included the Havanoid Howard Lake ware in his definition of the Malmo focus, but he later reconsidered (Wilford 1951).
2. For overviews of archaeological investigations in the region, see Mather (2000a, 2000b). Also see Wilford (1941, 1944, 1955) and Wilford, Johnson, and Vicinus (1969).
3. Mather (2000a, 44–49).
4. Besides the Mille Lacs region, Malmo-like ceramics have been reported "westward across the Gull Lake area and westward to the lakes area in Ottertail County" (Hohman-Caine 1979, 137) and to the south as far as the Anoka Sand Plain. Hohman-Caine (ibid., 138) says, "It appears to have been general practice to simply group smooth body sherds and rims from central Minnesota under this label." Arzigian (2008, 40) adds, "This tendency might explain the broad distribution of 'Malmo' ceramics in the site database." For instance, while the form of the Graham Lake Mound vessel resembles typical Malmo jars (the restored vessel has a pointed base and no neck constriction), the pattern of decoration seems distinctive and may represent another regional variant of Initial Woodland jars.
5. Hohman-Caine (1979); Thomas (2000, 14.3–14.5).
6. Bakken (2000). Ongoing research by Bakken (2011) shows promise of improving our understanding of the pattern of use of raw materials over time in the Mille Lacs region.
7. Halloran, Johnson, and Malik (2000); Bakken (2000); Rothaus, Gold, and Mather (2005). For bone artifacts, see Mather, Wheland, and Nicholas (2000).
8. Jacob Brower excavated three mounds at the Malmo mound and village site (21AK1) in 1899, Bushnell excavated two in 1900, and G. Ekholm of the University of Minnesota excavated thirteen in 1936. Wilford excavated portions of the Anderson mound in a salvage operation in 1933,

and the Vanderbloom mound in 1952, both of which are now included in the Brower site (21ML1; Wilford, Johnson, and Vicinus 1969). Wilford also excavated within the Brower site habitation area in 1949.

9. Wilford, Johnson, and Vicinus (1969).

10. Aufderheide et al. (1994).

11. Wilford, Johnson, and Vicinus (1969, 19).

12. Gibbon (1975, 3).

13. Mather (2000a, 43).

14. Aufderheide et al. (1994).

15. Myster and O'Connell (1997, 280, 283).

16. For recent reviews of Hopewell and Havana-Hopewell, see Carr and Case (2005) and Charles and Buikstra (2006).

17. Possibly associated exotic materials include galena and obsidian and limestone temper on one vessel from the Malmo mound group (Rothaus, Gold, and Mather 2005, 59, 66, 73).

18. E. Johnson (1984). Also see Mather (1991, 1994). The source of this copper has not been established; I assume as an hypothesis that it was gathered from a larger geographical area than the Mille Lacs region.

19. Clark (1984).

20. Mather (2000a, 45); E. Johnson (1984).

21. Hohman-Caine and Goltz (1995, 127; 1999).

22. Hohman-Caine and Goltz (1995). Also see Birk (1979a) and Arzigian (2008, 21–23).

23. Holman-Caine and Goltz (1995); Arzigian (2008, 20–21).

24. Justin (1995, 5.6).

25. Holman-Caine and Goltz (1995). A reassessment by Holman-Caine and Goltz of the dating of Brainerd ware is under way at this writing.

26. Wright et al. (2004); Mulholland et al. (1996).

27. Mulholland et al. (1997b).

28. Hohman-Caine and Goltz (1995, 121–22; 1999, 19–21), Arzigian (2008, 23–24).

29. Arzigian and Stevenson (2003).

30. Other sites include Pimusche Boat Access (21BL88; Goltz 1993), Kitchie Bay (21BL273; Hohman-Caine and Goltz 1995), South Pike Bay (21CA38; Harrison 1988), Roosevelt Lake Narrows (21CA184; Justin 1995; Thompson 1995), Kelnhofer (21CA226; Hohman-Caine and Goltz 1995), Lake Carlos State Park (21DL2; Gonsior, George, and Allan 1999), LaSalle Creek (21HB26; Kluth and Kluth 1994), Third River Borrow Pit (21IC176; Mulholland et al. 1997b), North Twin Lake (21MH5; Michlovic and Sather 2000; Navarre, McCauley, and Hagglund 1994), and Blueberry Lake (21WD6; C. Johnson et al. 1995). This list is taken from Arzigian (2008, 20).

31. Hohman-Caine and Goltz (1995, 121–22; 1999).

32. For general overviews of Laurel, see Mason (1981), Rajnovich (2003), Reid and Rajnovich (1991), and J. V. Wright (1998). Laurel was first defined in print as a focus of the Rainy River aspect of the Woodland pattern by Lloyd Wilford in 1941 based in part on his excavations in the 1930s.

33. Laurel ceramics display relationships to North Bay in Wisconsin (Mason 1967, 1969), Saugeen in southern Ontario and Point Peninsula to the east (Stoltman 1973), and Havana-Hopewell to the south. Havana-Hopewell relationships are thought to be present in decorative attributes, such as dentate stamping, linear stamping, and bossing (Lugenbeal 1976). In general, however, Laurel ceramics are regarded as regional expressions of a ceramic continuum that runs north of the Great Lakes eastward to the Point Peninsula culture of New York State.

34. Radiocarbon determinations indicate a probable time span for Laurel ware in the Rainy River

region of 50/100 BC to AD 1000 (Lenius and Olinyk 1990, 83; Rapp et al. 1995, 8; Thomas and Mather 1996a, 18.3–18.4), though there is some uncertainty about the age range of the ware in the region (Arzigian 2008, 54–55). While some archaeologists limit the extent of Laurel in Minnesota to about AD 650/700, Lenius and Olinyk (1990, 81–82) extend its range to AD 1000, arguing that Laurel was contemporaneous with Blackduck between AD 700–1000 (see chapter 8). The Laurel archaeological culture or at least Laurel ceramics may persist in some areas of central Canada into the thirteenth century (Reid and Rajnovich 1991; Meyer et al. 2008).

35. In Minnesota Laurel sites are centered in the Rainy River drainage system, which defines the boundaries of the Rainy River region. However, small numbers of Laurel pottery sherds are also present throughout northern and central Minnesota. The following counties in the State Historic Preservation Office archaeology database (as of 2010) have sites that are reported to contain this ware (numbers in parentheses refer to number of sites reported to contain the ware as of 2009): Aitkin (1), Beltrami (7), Cass (10), Clay (1), Clearwater (1), Cook (7), Crow Wing (1), Itasca (11), Kittson (1), Koochiching (23), Lake (9), Marshall (2), Otter Tail (1), Pennington (2), Red Lake (1), Roseau (1), St. Louis (70), and Wadena (1?). For a recent overview of Laurel in Minnesota, see Arzigian (2008, 53–62). For a history of investigations in the region, see Thomas (1996a).

36. Dean Anderson (1979); Budak (1985, 1998); Lugenbeal (1976); Stoltman (1973); Thomas (1996b, 10.27–10.29); Wilford (1941). Arzigian (2008, 55) writes, "Ceramics are the most thoroughly studied of the Laurel artifact categories, and they have been the primary line of evidence for identifying Laurel components and phases." She adds, "There are differences in the literature in how specific ceramic attributes have been described, posing some problems for standardized typology" (ibid., 56).

37. Webster (1967, 1973); Hoppin and Mather (1996); Shen (1996); Arzigian (2008, 56–57).

38. Rapp, Allert, and Peters (1990). For worked bone, antler, and shell, see Webster (1973, 105–6) and Morey, Falk, and Semken (1996, 15.39–15.40). For copper, see Steinbring (1975). For other artifacts, see Rapp et al. (1995), Arzigian et al. (1994), and Thomas (1996c, 14.4).

39. Reid and Rajnovick (1985, 1991); Rapp et al. (1998, 12).

40. Despite the wide distribution of Laurel ceramics, Laurel burial mounds seem restricted to the Rainy River region of Minnesota and Ontario, and to Drummond Island near Sault Ste. Marie, Michigan (Rajnovich 2003, 7).

41. Torbenson, Langsjoen, and Aufderheide (1994). Wilford conducted excavations in Mound 4 in 1933 and in Mound 3 in 1956 (Wilford 1937, 1950a, 1950b, 1952a, 1952b), and Stoltman and Lugenbeal in the village area in 1970 and 1972, respectively (Lugenbeal 1976). Unexpectedly, the Grand Mound, which is about 25 feet high and 100 feet by 140 feet in width/length at its base, was discovered by Mike Budak, former site manager for the Minnesota Historical Society, to have a tail about 200 feet long (the mound is estimated to contain about 5,000 tons of earth) (Mather 2011). David Mather has suggested that the mound with tail represents muskrat imagery that is consistent with themes and symbolism in Algonquian origin narratives.

42. Torbenson, Aufderheide, and Johnson (1992, 513); Torbenson, Langsjoen, and Aufderheide (1994).

43. Ossenberg (1974).

44. Binford (2001, 214).

45. Ibid., 197.

46. Ibid., 381.

47. Extensification refers to the process of making something more extensive, in this case the use of equipment like canoes and sleds to expand the area in which daily or weekly subsistence pursuits could be carried out (think of how much farther an Inuit can travel in a day using a snowmobile as compared to a dogsled). See Binford (2001, 346–47).

48. Ibid., 417.
49. One possibility is that the burial mode itself was more widespread and had older roots than the Rum River phase itself.
50. Mather (1998).
51. Thompson (2000).
52. Mather (2000a, 23); Crawford, Smith, and Bowyer (1997). Matthew Boyd and his colleagues (2008) also report the presence of maize at many Middle and Late Woodland sites in the boreal forests north of Minnesota.
53. Ollendorf (2000); Valppu (2000).
54. Tieszen, Reinhard, and Foreshoe (1997a, 1997b).
55. Valppu (2000); Mather and Nicholas (2000).
56. Hohman-Caine and Goltz (1995, 127).
57. Kluth and Kluth (1994).
58. Hohman-Caine and Goltz (1999, 36).
59. Thompson, Mulholland, and Lindbeck (1995, 5.16).
60. Ibid., 5.31.
61. Hohman-Caine and Goltz (1995, 127); Yourd (1988).
62. Sayers, Thompson, and MacCore (2011); Gonsior, George, and Allan (1999).
63. Thomas and Mather (1996b, 5.10–5.11).
64. Yourd (1988); Anfinson, Michlovic, and Stein (1978).
65. Morey, Falk, and Semken (1996).
66. On the importance of gill nets in the Terminal/Late Woodland upper Great Lakes area, see Cleland (1982).
67. Valppu (1996, 16.2–16.3); Rapp, Allert, and Peters (1990, 235); Boyd et al. (2008).
68. Thompson (1996, 17.6).
69. For Native American adaptations in the boreal forests north of Minnesota, see Tanner (1979), Brightman (2002), and Lytwyn (2002).

6. Terminal Woodland Effigy Mound Builders and Bison Hunters

1. Theler and Boszhardt (2003, 122).
2. Anfinson (1979a, 76). Also see Arzigian (2008, 102).
3. Stoltman and Christiansen (2000). Also see Theler and Boszhardt (2003, 121–390), Arzigian (2008, 93–105), and various pages in Alex (2000, 115–37). I follow Dobbs and Anfinson's (1990, 62–67) suggestion to look to neighboring areas of Wisconsin and Iowa for models for lifeways and expected artifacts assemblages, including ceramics, for this area of Minnesota. Although known popularly as the driftless area, this area of Minnesota, while not covered with ice in all glaciations, was covered with glacial ice at times in the past, as evident in the presence of glacial till in areas. With this understanding, I continue to refer to this area as the driftless area, mainly because of a shared topography throughout what is popularly called the driftless area. This topography includes the presence of deeply carved river valleys and a general absence of inland lakes.
4. Stoltman (2003, 17); Stoltman and Christiansen (2000, 499).
5. Stoltman and Christiansen (2000, 500); Alex (2000, 124).
6. For overviews of the Effigy Mound culture, see Mallam (1976), Hurley (1986), Birmingham and Eisenberg (2000), and especially Rosebrough (2010). For the Effigy Mound culture in Minnesota, see Anfinson (1979a) and Arzigian (2008, 100–101).
7. Winchell (1911).
8. Arzigian (2008, 95–96); Anfinson (1979a).

9. Boszhardt (1996).

10. For descriptions of precontact stone spear and arrow points in the Midwest, see Justice (1987).

11. E. Johnson (1959).

12. Winchell (1911, 194–95).

13. Arzigian and Stevenson (2003, 487).

14. Benn and Green (2000, 469–72).

15. Ibid., 481–82.

16. For Illinois Canton pottery vessels, see Sampson (1988). For later Mississippian period vessels, see Benn (1989) and Hall (1991, 29).

17. Stoltman and Christiansen (2000, 518).

18. Anfinson (1997); Arzigian (2008, 75–84).

19. Anfinson (1979c; 1997, 76–77); Arzigian (2008, 76–78).

20. Arzigian (2008, 75).

21. Anfinson (1997, 71–72, 84–85); Arzigian (2008, 80–81).

22. Hudak (1974, 1976).

23. Anfinson (1997).

24. Myster and O'Connell (1997).

25. Sellars (1992a).

26. Alex (2000, 124).

27. Theler (1987); Arzigian (1993).

28. Theler and Boszhardt (2006, 460).

29. Scullin (1992). Also see Arzigian (2008, 97–99). Arzigian (2008, 99) writes, "Carbon isotopes of human bone from Millville (no corn), Aztalan (corn consumers), and Late Woodland burials indicate that some, although not all, Late Woodland people associated with Effigy Mound sites were consuming corn (Stoltman and Christiansen 2000, 512)."

30. Arzigian (1987, 229–31; 1993; 2008, 99).

31. Hurley (1986, 284–85). Also see Arzigian (2008, 101).

32. Theler and Boszhardt (2006, 460). Also see Benn (1983, 83).

33. Stoltman and Christiansen (2000, 519). See chapter 7.

34. Gibbon and Dobbs (1991); Gibbon (1972).

35. The discovery of Emergent Mississippian pottery (AD 1000–1050) in southwestern Wisconsin and the Mille Lacs region of Minnesota is one hint of this early interaction. See Stoltman, Benden, and Boszhardt (2008) and Gibbon (1994, 135).

36. Theler and Boszhardt (2006).

37. Fried (1975).

38. Anfinson (1997, 83); Arzigian (2008, 79–80).

39. Hunter (1992); Sellars (1992b, 179–80); Martin and Richmond (1992).

40. Anfinson (1997, 84).

7. First Tribes in Southern Minnesota

1. Wilford (1955, 140); Maxwell (1950).

2. For studies of the Silvernale phase, see Wilford (1985), Gibbon (1974, 1979), Gibbon and Dobbs (1991), Dobbs (1984a, 1987, 1989), Rodell (1991, 1997), Schirmer (2002), and Fleming (2009). Among the exotics, Fleming (2009, 216–17) reaffirms the presence of Cambria, Great Oasis, Mill Creek, and Middle Missouri ceramics in the locality.

3. Dobbs (1993, 6).

4. Thurston and O'Connell (1984).

5. Wilford (1945). For studies of Great Oasis in Minnesota, see Anfinson (1979d, 1997), Gibbon (1993), Henning and Henning (1978), and E. Johnson (1969).

6. For an overview of Great Oasis, see Alex (2000).

7. Alex and Tiffany (2000); Tiffany and Alex (2001).

8. For the Cambria phase, see Wilford (1945), Nickerson (1988), Knudson (1967), Watrall (1968), Anfinson (1997), Gibbon (1991), E. Johnson (1961, 1991), and Ready (1979).

9. E. Johnson (1991).

10. E. Johnson (1986, 4).

11. See Winchell (1911, 122).

12. For discussions of the Big Stone phase, see Anfinson (1987, 1997), Haug (1995), and Toom (2004).

13. See Hollinger (2005, 216–19, 230).

14. For overviews of the Oneota tradition, see Green (1995), Hollinger and Benn (1998), Gibbon (2001), and Hollinger (2005).

15. For excavation reports of Blue Earth phase sites in Minnesota, see Dobbs (1984b) and Gibbon (1973, 1979, 1983). Dobbs (1984b) and Gibbon (1983) concern sites along the Blue Earth River in south-central Minnesota; the Sheffield site (Gibbon 1973) is along the St. Croix River; Gibbon (1979) contains a report of excavations at the Bartron site in the Red Wing locality. For decades I have argued that the Oneota tradition seems to appear in the Red Wing locality by AD 1000/1050 or so. This conclusion was based on two early radiocarbon dates obtained by Elden Johnson for the Bartron site, the presence of Silvernale materials within a Bartron house, and the early presence of Oneota sites in eastern Wisconsin. Three recent studies show convincingly, however, that the Oneota tradition does not appear in the Red Wing locality until the early to mid-AD 1200s: an unpublished typological study of Silvernale and Oneota pottery in the locality by George Halley strongly suggests a transformation of Silvernale pottery to Oneota pottery; a stratigraphic study of ceramics in the successive building stages of several houses in the locality by Edward Fleming (2009) demonstrates that high-rim Oneota-like pottery appears with the waning of Silvernale pottery; and a suite of five radiocarbon dates obtained by Ronald Schirmer on Oneota materials in the locality firmly date them to the AD 1200s.

16. Dobbs and Shane (1982).

17. Dobbs (1984b).

18. Dobbs and Shane (1982, 68).

19. For an overview of the Orr phase, see Betts (1998). Oneota sites in this area of extreme southeastern Minnesota and northeastern Iowa and the adjacent La Crosse area of Wisconsin are concentrated in three localities—La Crosse, Upper Iowa, and Riceford Creek—in what is called the La Crosse region. In the Willey and Phillips taxonomic system, a region covers a larger geographic space than a locality and may, as here, include two or more aggregations of sites in localities.

20. See Griffin (1937), Mott (1938), Wedel (1959, 1986), and Wilford (1955, 142). See Betts (1998, 233–34) for recent thoughts on the ethnicity of the Orr phase. Since the movements of the Otoe are less well confirmed, I continue to associate the Orr phase with the Ioway for convenience here, keeping in mind, though, that "ethnically distinct groups may share a material culture while maintaining their identity through other means" (Betts 1998, 234; also see Gibbon 1995). For cautions about the Orr phase-Ioway association, see Hollinger (2005, 291).

21. See Betts (1998, 231–33) for the age range of the Orr phase. In Minnesota, an uncorrected radiocarbon date of 220±62 BP has been reported for the Hogback site (as reported in Betts 1998), and an uncorrected date of 200±50 BP for the historic component at the Farley Village (Gallagher 1990).

22. See Alex (2000, 217–18).

23. For excavation reports on Minnesota Orr phase sites, see Wilford (1952c), Wilford and Brink (1974), and Gallagher (1990). See Anfinson (1979b) for an overview of the Orr phase in Minnesota. Following excavations at the Farley Village site by Mississippi Valley Archaeological Center crews in 1989 and 1991, Farley Village is now "the most thoroughly investigated Orr phase site" (Betts 1998, 231; also see Gallagher 1990). The Yucatan Fort site was fortified with an earthen enclosure. Hollinger (2005, 241) suggests that at "least two additional sites in southeastern Minnesota may have been Classic Horizon Oneota [AD 1400–1650] fortifications (Sasso 1989, 386); Winchell 1911, 82, 85)."

24. Blue (1996); Wilford and Brink (1974).

25. Wilford (1955, 141). The Rushford site (21FL9) is an example of an Orr phase mound site in Minnesota. Orr burials are also occasionally intrusive into earlier Woodland mounds (Anfinson 1979b, 157).

26. Wilford (1955, 141).

27. For the case for disease, see Green (1993) and Betts (2000, 2006), who both also review proposed nondisease explanations for population decline in the La Crosse locality, for movement westward across the Mississippi River, or for both events. Of course, warfare, climate change, and the pull of bison herds to the west may have been contributing factors to these events. Hollinger (2005) documents the prevalence of conflict in the Midwest in the late prehistoric period. Although Betts (2000, 2006) favors a Great Lakes trade route origin for epidemic disease in the La Crosse region, epidemic disease was spreading into the interior of North America from the Southwest and Lower Mississippi River regions as well.

28. See Wedel (1986). Betts (1998, 234) mentions that groups of Ottawa, Huron, Kickapoo, and Miami passed through or resided in the La Crosse region in the seventeenth century due to social strife to the east. Their presence may have been a factor as well in the Ioway's westward movement at the end of the seventeenth century.

29. Binford (2001, 188, 196, 314).

30. Ibid., 55.

31. Ibid., 222, 401, 396.

32. Pratt (1994).

33. See Gibbon (1974) and Gibbon and Dobbs (1991). Elden Johnson (1991) proposes a Woodland origin for Cambria, and others have suggested that Great Oasis also emerged from a Woodland base (Alex 2000, 148; Anfinson 1997, 92). However, a DNA study of the Schild people of the Lower Illinois valley, which was also a peripheral region to the Mississippian center at Cahokia, indicates that "some degree of immigration (at least of females) into the Lower Illinois Valley occurred during the Emergent Mississippian period" (Raff 2008, 25). She adds that this "migration would likely have created interregional kinship and political ties, perhaps 'giving northern families direct access to Cahokian culinary practices, pottery technologies, agricultural knowledge, and bloodlines' (Pauketat 2004, 171)" (25). The discovery of small amounts of Emergent Mississippian pottery in the Upper Mississippi valley (Stoltman, Benden, and Boszhardt 2008) and in Mille Lacs region sites (Gibbon 1994, 135) suggests that a similar process of limited in-migration may have taken place in Minnesota.

34. Fried (1975).

35. Glenn (1974). However, this individual may not be representative of the Silvernale phase population, since the skeleton was recovered from a probable refuse pit, a common way of disposing of captive individuals upon their death (Hollinger 2005).

36. M. Peterson (1964).

37. Gibbon (1974); E. Johnson (1991).

38. Boszhardt (2004). Also see Theler and Boszhardt (2000, 2006) for a model of the emergence of the Oneota.

39. Emerson (1997); Pauketat and Emerson (1991).

40. Boszhardt (2004); Hollinger (2005, 216–219, 230).

41. Binford (2001, 461).

42. Griffin (1960); Penman (1988). Also see Watrall (1974) for a climatic deterioration explanation for the northwestward movement of the Cambria population.

43. Baerreis and Bryson (1965).

44. Anfinson and Wright (1990), for example, do not find a correlation in Minnesota between major climatic transitions and marked episodes of culture change. But see Kidder (2006) for a Lower Mississippi valley example of such a correlation. Kidder (2006, 195) argues that global "climatic changes led to greatly increased flood frequencies and magnitudes in the Mississippi River watershed" that were "one cause of major cultural reorganization at the end of the Archaic throughout much of eastern North America."

8. First Tribes in Central and Northern Minnesota

1. For overviews of the St. Croix complex and its ceramic assemblages, see George (1979b), Ready and Anfinson (1979c), E. Johnson (1984), Gibbon and Caine (1980), Hohman-Caine (1974, 1983), Mather (2000a), Mather and Abel (2000), and Arzigian (2008, 85–92). Anfinson (2006) includes this portion of the archaeological record in central Minnesota in a Central Minnesota Transitional Woodland complex. In the Mille Lacs region, the St. Croix complex includes both the Isle phase and the Vineland phase.

2. E. Johnson (1984). In his study of Mille Lacs region ceramics, Matt Thomas (2000) includes both St. Croix and Onamia pottery in an Onamia series because of their many shared similarities. I follow his recommendation here.

3. Bakken (2000). In his recent PhD dissertation, Bakken (2011) raises the possibility that raw material use patterns may differ between the Initial and Terminal Woodland periods: Initial Woodland use may be more like its use during the earlier Archaic period, and Terminal Woodland use may reflect the adoption of new provisioning strategies.

4. E. Johnson (1984). Also see Arzigian (2008, 88–89).

5. Hohman-Caine (1983); Arzigian and Stevenson (2003).

6. Myster and O'Connell (1997, 224).

7. E. Johnson (1973). For a critique of the concept of an Arvilla burial complex, see Syms (1982).

8. Taxonomic concepts like *phase* and *focus* assume the presence of bounded (or clumped) communities that can be distinguished by differences in their material culture. The suggestion here is that the material culture of small band-level societies in the north woods of Minnesota and northward may be better represented by clines than by clumps, for the underlying social reality seems to have been contiguous, small-scale, widespread band groups that interacted closely with their nearest neighbors in a pattern that was repeated across large geographical areas.

9. For overviews of Blackduck, Kathio, and Clam River in Minnesota, see Wilford (1955), Lugenbeal (1976), Thomas and Mather (1996b), Anfinson (2006), and Arzigian (2008, 106–25). Anfinson (2006) splits Blackduck into two cultural complexes, a Blackduck-Kathio (BDK) that includes Blackduck, Kathio, and Clam River ceramics (as well as Lugenbeal's [1976] Early Blackduck and Thomas and Mather's [1996b, 5.17] Blackduck Configuration), and a Rainy River Late Woodland (RRLW) that includes Late Blackduck, Selkirk, and Duck Bay ceramics (it approximates Late Blackduck [Lugenbeal 1976] and the Rainy River Composite of Lenius and Olinyk [1990]).

10. For Blackduck, Kathio, and Clam River ceramics in Minnesota, see Thomas (1996b, 2000), Ready and Anfinson (1979a), George (1979a), Lugenbeal (1976, 1978, 1979), and Arzigian (2008, 109–13).

11. Evans (1961a, 1961b). Also see Arzigian (2008, 113–14).
12. E. Johnson (1993).
13. See Arzigian (2008, 109) for a recent review of the chronology of Blackduck and Kathio.
14. See ibid., 117–18, for a summary of mortuary practices and ideology.
15. See Myster and O'Connell (1997, 288–91) for a summary.
16. Torbenson, Langsjoen, and Aufderheide (1996, 72).
17. Myster and O'Connell (1997, 289).
18. Torbenson, Langsjoen, and Aufderheide (1996).
19. Johnson and Ready (1992).
20. Ossenberg (1974).
21. Evans (1961a).
22. Johnson, Harrison, and J. Schaaf (1977). Also see Thomas and Mather (1996b, 5.14) on regional population increases.
23. E. Johnson (1979).
24. For overviews of the Psinomani complex, see Gibbon (1994, 2003) and Arzigian (2008, 126–47). For descriptions of Sandy Lake pottery, see Cooper and Johnson (1964), Birk (1979b), L. Peterson (1986), and Arzigian (2008, 130–33). The complex was originally called the Wanikan culture (Birk 1977), which is an Ojibwa word for a pit or hole in the ground. The name was changed to Psinomani, which is the Dakota word for "wild rice gatherer" (Gibbon 1994), to better reflect the complex's likely Dakota connection.
25. For a description of Ogechie ware and for its distribution, see Ready and Anfinson (1979b) and Holley and Michlovic (2010). Also see Birk (1977, 28), Michlovic (1982, 63), and Gibbon (1995).
26. Arzigian (2008, 143–45).
27. Since a report of these excavations has not been prepared, the artifact and feature associations of these structures remain unknown. My suggestion that they are storage bins is only speculative. A map of the palisade structure prepared by Elden Johnson and his students label them winter dwellings, though in conversation Johnson mentioned that they could be storage facilities.
28. Michlovic (1987); Michlovic and Schneider (1993).
29. For a recent review, see Arzigian (2008, 128–29).
30. Birk (1977, 31); Aufderheide et al. (1994); Arzigian and Stevenson (2003, 101–2); Arzigian (2008, 137–38).
31. Myster and O'Connell (1997).
32. Lenius and Olinyk (1990).
33. Ibid., 82. Also see Anfinson (2006), who places Blackduck, Selkirk, and Duck Bay ceramics into a Rainy River Late Woodland.
34. Lenius and Olinyk (1990, 84).
35. E. Johnson (1984).
36. Aufderheide et al. (1994).
37. Mather (2000a, 68).
38. E. Johnson (1984, 1985).
39. Mather (1991, 1994); Justin and Schuster (1994, 83).
40. Lothson (1972).
41. E. Johnson (1991).
42. Mather and Cummings (2010). Recent radiocarbon dates run by Patricia Emerson, head archaeologist at the Minnesota Historical Society, date the palisade at the Cooper site in the same general late prehistoric/early historic age range.
43. As stressed earlier, component mixing in shallow sites, poor preservation of subsistence materials like animal bone, and the lack of flotation and other fine-scale collecting techniques in early

excavations make the interpretation of the archaeological record in central and northern Minnesota less than straightforward. For an evaluation of some of these suggestions and a review of the data, see Arzigian (2008, 85–147).

44. E. Johnson (1985, 161).

45. For a review of subsistence and settlement data for the Psinomani complex, see Arzigian (2008, 134–37, 141–45); for floral resources, see Bailey (1997), Schaaf (1981), E. Johnson (1985, 160), Lucking (1973, 50–51), Birk and Johnson (1992, 227), Thompson, Mulholland, and Lindbeck (1995, 5.15), and Valppu (2000, 2010). Despite the problems of component mixing, Arzigian (2008, 136) concludes that "wild rice exploitation is likely to have been central to Psinomani culture." For faunal resources, see E. Johnson (1985) and Mather, Wheland, and Nicholas (2000) for the Mille Lacs region. For a Psinomani-related site in the Red River area, see Michlovic (1987). Mather (2005, 163, 175) and Hohman-Caine and Goltz (1998) describe a specialized fishing camp at the Third River Bridge site (21IC46) in the Headwaters Lakes region. Mather and Abel (2000) conclude that the Cooper, Wilford, and Vineland Bay sites in the Mille Lacs region were most likely permanently occupied, as suggested by Whelan (1990).

46. For an overview of subsistence and settlement data in the Early and Middle Terminal Woodland periods in central and northern Minnesota, see Arzigian (2008, 89–92, 114–17, 120–23). Also see Gibbon and Caine (1980), Hohman-Caine (1983, 255), Forsberg and Dobbs (1997, 39), Mulholland (2000, 5), Rapp et al. (1995), Morey, Falk, and Semken (1996, 15.3), Lugenbeal (1976, 369–76), Michlovic (1979, 34, 2005), Valppu and Rapp (2000), and Dobbs and Anfinson (1990, 230). Matthew Boyd and his colleagues have demonstrated that after AD 1000, maize has a consistent presence in Late (Terminal) Woodland components in the subarctic boreal forest north of Minnesota (Boyd et al. 2008; Boyd and Surette 2010).

47. Binford (2001, 276).

48. In this regard, see Cleland (1982): "Late Woodland sites [in the northern Great Lakes] show evidence of occupation by much larger groups than Middle Woodland sites. This is thought to be the result not only of a larger total population but also of a new labor requirement. Both of these factors are the direct result of yet another innovation, which is hypothesized to have appeared in conjunction with gill nets: the preservation of large quantities of fish by freezing or freezing and drying." Cleland adds: "Another and perhaps more important consideration than increased size of fall sites is the need for a larger labor force to preserve the catch. Obviously, the short fishing season and the huge volume of the catch prescribes a large labor force to clean fish, gather firewood, build smoking racks, sustain fires, turn the smoking fish, and pack the preserved fish" (779).

49. Binford (2001, 460).

50. Ibid., 254.

51. Ibid., 430.

52. Ibid., 299.

53. Hennepin (1938, 104–23).

54. Binford (2001, 433).

55. Gibbon (2003, 44–45).

56. The date when Ogechie ceramics first appear in central Minnesota remains a research objective. If they are a northern version of protohistoric Orr phase ceramics, as frequently mentioned (Ready and Anfinson 1979b), then they may be more closely related to the protohistoric Bradbury phase than earlier Psinomani phases. I assume, however, that Ogechie ware is more diverse in origin and appears in central Minnesota soon after the emergence of Oneota in the southern part of the state.

Conclusion

1. If this statement is not clear enough, let me stress further and more emphatically that the lifeways that I identify in this book are based for the most part on flimsy archaeological evidence, for the basic focus of Minnesota archaeologists has been and continues to be on cultural historical pursuits, such as descriptions of pottery types and the contents recovered through archaeological excavations, most often in a mitigation context. This is true as well of much of my own archaeological research. The conclusions reached in this book require testing, then, but no more than does any other approach that attempts to re-create the lifeways of people who lived in the past through the medium of the archaeological record.

2. I concentrate fairly exclusively on Bodley's perspective in the last two sections of this chapter for three reasons. First, he provides extensive descriptions of societies in each of the three worlds he identifies: the tribal world, the imperial world, and the commercial world. His book is a handy reference, then, for readers interested in the range of human societies present in the past and today. Second, unlike many descriptions of the development of human societies through time, he presents reasons for the transformation of one world into another. And third, I find his approach useful (and convincing) as a framework for studying and understanding the development of human societies through time. Of course, like all frameworks of study, his ideas must be challenged and tested.

3. See Scarre (2005) for a description of the emergence and spread of human beings throughout the world.

4. Bodley (2005, 1–163). For a more explicitly archaeological review of the evolution of early human societies, see Johnson and Earle (2000).

5. Bodley (2005, 525).

6. Ibid., 21.

7. Ibid., 22.

8. Ibid., 25.

9. Ibid., 22.

10. For a very accessible overview of the reasons societies collapse, see Diamond (2005).

11. Bodley (2005, 23).

12. Ibid., 21.

13. Ibid., 22.

14. Ibid., 520.

15. Ibid., 23.

16. Friedman (2009, 56).

17. Bodley (2005, 13–28). Also see Bodley (1999).

18. For a discussion of this process, see Kuper (1988).

19. Bodley (2005, 27).

20. Ibid., 3.

21. Ibid., 18.

Aaseng, N.E., J.C. Almendinger, R.P. Dana, B.C. Delaney, H.L. Dunevitz, K.A. Rusterholz, N.P. Sather, and D.S. Wovcha. 1993. *Minnesota's Native Vegetation: A Key to Natural Communities.* Minnesota Department of Natural Resources, Natural Heritage Program, Biological Report 20: L1–111, St. Paul.

Alex, Lynn M. 2000. *Iowa's Archaeological Past.* University of Iowa Press, Iowa City.

Alex, Lynn M., and Joseph A. Tiffany. 2000. A Summary of the DeCamp and West Des Moines Great Oasis Burial Sites in Central Iowa. *Midcontinental Journal of Archaeology* 25 (2): 313–51.

Allan, S. 1993. *Final Report on the Data Recovery Investigation of the Cedar Creek Site, 21AK58, a Multicomponent Habitation Site.* Archaeology Department, Minnesota Historical Society, St. Paul. Report prepared for the Minnesota Department of Transportation, St. Paul.

Anderson, David G., and Michael K. Faught. 2000. Paleoindian Artefact Distributions: Evidence and Implications. *Antiquity* 74: 507–13.

Anderson, Dean. 1979. Laurel. In *A Handbook of Minnesota Prehistoric Ceramics,* ed. Scott F. Anfinson, 121–35. Occasional Publications in Minnesota Anthropology, No. 5. Minnesota Archaeological Society, Fort Snelling.

Anderson, Duane C., and H.A. Semken Jr., eds. 1980. *The Cherokee Excavations: Holocene Ecology and Human Adaptations in Northwestern Iowa.* Academic Press, New York.

Anfinson, Scott F. 1979a. Effigy Mound Phase. In *A Handbook of Minnesota Prehistoric Ceramics,* ed. Scott F. Anfinson, 73–78. Occasional Publications in Minnesota Anthropology, No. 5. Minnesota Archaeological Society, Fort Snelling.

———. 1979b. Orr Phase. In *A Handbook of Minnesota Prehistoric Ceramics,* ed. Scott F. Anfinson, 137–61. Occasional Publications in Minnesota Anthropology, No. 5. Minnesota Archaeological Society, Fort Snelling.

———. 1979c. Lake Benton Phase. In *A Handbook of Minnesota Prehistoric Ceramics,* ed. Scott F. Anfinson, 109–14. Occasional Publications in Minnesota Anthropology, No. 5. Minnesota Archaeological Society, Fort Snelling.

———. 1979d. Great Oasis Phase. In *A Handbook of Minnesota Prehistoric Ceramics,* ed. Scott F. Anfinson, 87–94. Occasional Publications in Minnesota Anthropology, No. 5. Minnesota Archaeological Society, Fort Snelling.

———. 1979e. La Moille Thick. In *A Handbook of Minnesota Prehistoric Ceramics,* ed. Scott F. Anfinson, 115–20. Occasional Publications in Minnesota Anthropology, No. 5. Minnesota Archaeological Society, Fort Snelling.

———. 1979f. Howard Lake Phase. In *A Handbook of Minnesota Prehistoric Ceramics*, ed. Scott F. Anfinson, 95–101. Occasional Publications in Minnesota Anthropology, No. 5. Minnesota Archaeological Society, Fort Snelling.

———. 1979g. Fox Lake Phase. In *A Handbook of Minnesota Prehistoric Ceramics*, ed. Scott F. Anfinson, 79–86. Occasional Publications in Minnesota Anthropology, No. 5. Minnesota Archaeological Society, Fort Snelling.

———. 1979h. Sorg Phase. In *A Handbook of Minnesota Prehistoric Ceramics*, ed. Scott F. Anfinson, 197–202. Occasional Publications in Minnesota Anthropology, No. 5. Minnesota Archaeological Society, Fort Snelling.

———. 1987. The Prehistory of the Prairie Lake Region in the Northeastern Plains. PhD diss., Department of Anthropology, University of Minnesota, Minneapolis.

———. 1990. Archaeological Regions in Minnesota and the Woodland Period. In *The Woodland Tradition in the Western Great Lakes*, ed. Guy E. Gibbon, 135–66. Publications in Anthropology, No. 4. University of Minnesota, Minneapolis.

———. 1997. *Southwestern Minnesota Archaeology: 12,000 Years in the Prairie Lake Region*. Minnesota Prehistoric Archaeology Series, No. 14. Minnesota Historical Society, St. Paul.

———. 2006. Woodland Historic Contexts in Minnesota. Manuscript on file, Office of the State Archaeologist, St. Paul.

Anfinson, Scott F., Michael Michlovic, and Julie Stein. 1978. *The Lake Bronson Site (21KT1): A Multicomponent Prehistoric Site on the Prairie-Woodland Border in Northwestern Minnesota*. Occasional Publications in Minnesota Anthropology, No. 3. Minnesota Archaeological Society, Fort Snelling.

Anfinson, Scott F., and H. E. Wright Jr. 1990. Climatic Change and Culture in Prehistoric Minnesota. In *The Woodland Tradition in the Western Great Lakes: Papers Presented to Elden Johnson*, ed. Guy E. Gibbon, 213–32. University of Minnesota Publications in Anthropology, No. 4. Minneapolis.

Artz, Joe A. 1995. Geologic Contexts of the Early and Middle Holocene Archaeological Record in North Dakota and Adjoining Areas of the Northern Plains. In *Archaeological Geology of the Archaic Period in North America*, ed. E. A. Bettis III, 67–86. Geological Society of America Special Paper 297. Boulder, Colo.

Arzigian, Constance. 1987. The Emergence of Horticultural Economies in Southwestern Wisconsin. In *Emergent Horticultural Economies of the Eastern Woodlands*, ed. William Keegan, 217–42. Occasional Paper, No. 7. Center for Archaeological Investigations, Southern Illinois University, Carbondale.

———. 1993. An Analysis of Prehistoric Subsistence Strategies in the Driftless Area, Southwestern Wisconsin. PhD diss., Department of Anthropology, University of Wisconsin–Madison.

———. 2008. *Minnesota Statewide Multiple Property Documentation Form for the Woodland Tradition*. Report submitted to the Minnesota Department of Transportation, St. Paul (posted on Minnesota Department of Transportation's Web site).

Arzigian, Constance, and Katherine Stevenson. 2003. *Minnesota's Indian Mounds and Burial Sites: A Synthesis of Prehistoric and Early Historic Archaeological Data*. Publication 1. Office of the State Archaeologist, St. Paul, Minnesota.

Arzigian, Constance, Dean Wilder, James Gallagher, and James Theler. 1994. *McKinstry Site Re-evaluation: Final Report*. Reports of Investigations No. 175. Mississippi Valley Archaeology Center, University of Wisconsin-La Crosse. Submitted to the Minnesota Department of Transportation. Copy on file, Office of the State Archeologist, St. Paul.

Aufderheide, A. C., E. Johnson, and O. Langsjoen, with G. Lothson and J. Streiff. 1994. Health, Demography, and Archaeology of the Mille Lacs Native American Mortuary Populations. Memoir 28, *Plains Anthropologist* 39: 251–375.

Babbitt, F. E. 1884. Vestiges of Glacial Man in Minnesota. *American Naturalist* 18 (6/7): 594–605, 697–708.

Baerreis, David A., and Reid A. Bryson. 1965. Climatic Episodes and the Dating of the Mississippian Cultures. *The Wisconsin Archeologist* 46: 203–20.

Bailey, Thomas. 1997. Evidence for Tobacco Use at the Wilford Site (21ML12), Mille Lacs County, Minnesota. Master's thesis, Interdisciplinary Archaeological Studies, University of Minnesota, Minneapolis.

Baker, R. G., E. A. Bettis, R. F. Denniston, L. A. Gonzalez, L. E. Strickland, and J. R. Kreig. 2002. Holocene Paleoenvironments in Southeastern Minnesota: Chasing the Prairie-Forest Ecotone. *Palaeogeography, Palaeoclimatology, Palaeoecology* 177 (1): 103–22.

Bakken, Kent. 2000. Lithic Technologies and Raw Materials Economies in Mille Lacs Area Archaeological Sites, East Central Minnesota. In *The Lake Onamia–Trunk Highway 169 Data Recovery Project, Mille Lacs County, Minnesota,* ed. D. Mather and E. Abel, 15.1–15.39. Loucks Project Report 96506-1. Loucks & Associates, Inc., Maple Grove. Report prepared for the Minnesota Department of Transportation, St. Paul.

———. 2011. Lithic Raw Material Use Patterns in Minnesota. PhD diss., Department of Anthropology, University of Minnesota, Minneapolis.

Benchley, Elizabeth D., Blane Nansel, Clark A. Dobbs, Susan M. Thurston Myster, and Barbara H. O'Connell. 1997. *Archeology and Bioarcheology of the Northern Woodlands.* A volume in the Central and Northern Plains Archeological Overview, Arkansas Archeological Survey Research Series 52.

Benn, David W. 1979. Some Trends and Traditions in Woodland Cultures of the Quad-State Region in the Upper Mississippi River Basin. *The Wisconsin Archeologist* 60 (1): 47–82.

———. 1983. Diffusion and Acculturation in Woodland Cultures on the Western Prairie Peninsula. In *Prairie Archaeology: Papers in Honor of David Baerreis,* ed. Guy E. Gibbon, 75–86. University of Minnesota Publications in Anthropology, No. 3, Minneapolis.

———. 1989. Hawks, Serpents, and Bird-Men: Emergence of the Oneota Mode of Production. *Plains Anthropologist* 43: 233–60.

Benn, David W., and William Green. 2000. Late Woodland Cultures in Iowa. In *Late Woodland Societies: Tradition and Transformation across the Midcontinent,* ed. T. E. Emerson, D. L. McElrath, and A. C. Fortier, 429–96. University of Nebraska Press, Lincoln.

Bettis, E. Arthur, III, and Edwin R. Hajic. 1995. Landscape Development and the Location of Evidence of Archaic Cultures in the Upper Midwest. In *Archaeological Geology of the Archaic Period in North America,* ed. E. A. Bettis III, 87–113. Geological Society of America Special Paper 297. Boulder, Colo.

Betts, Colin Matthew. 1998. The Oneota Orr Phase: Space, Time, and Ethnicity. *The Wisconsin Archeologist* 79: 225–35.

———. 2000. Symbolic, Cognitive, and Technological Dimensions of Orr Phase Oneota Ceramics. PhD diss., University of Illinois at Urbana-Champaign.

———. 2006. Pots and Pox: The Identification of Protohistoric Epidemics in the Upper Mississippi Valley. *American Antiquity* 71 (2): 233–59.

Beyers, J. M. 1989. *Northwoods Wildlife: A Watcher's Guide to Habitats.* Northwoods Press, Minocqua, Wis.

Binford, Lewis R. 2001. *Constructing Frames of Reference: An Analytical Method for Archaeological Theory Building Using Ethnographic and Environmental Data Sets.* University of California Press, Berkeley.

Birk, Douglas A. 1977. The Norway Lake Site: A Multicomponent Woodland Complex in North Central Minnesota. *The Minnesota Archaeologist* 36 (1): 16–45.

———. 1979a. Brainerd Ware. In *A Handbook of Minnesota Prehistoric Ceramics,* ed. Scott F. Anfinson, 45–50. Occasional Publications in Minnesota Anthropology, No. 5. Minnesota Archaeological Society, Fort Snelling.

———. 1979b. Sandy Lake Ware. In *A Handbook of Minnesota Prehistoric Ceramics,* ed. Scott F. Anfinson, 175–82. Occasional Publications in Minnesota Anthropology, No. 5. Minnesota Archaeological Society, Fort Snelling.

Birk, Douglas A., and Elden Johnson. 1992. The Mdewakanton Dakota and Initial French Contact. In *Calumet and Fleur-de-Lys: Archaeology of Indian and French Contact in the Midcontinent,* ed. John A. Walthall and Thomas E. Emerson, 203–40. Smithsonian Institution Press, Washington, DC.

Birmingham, Robert A., and Leslie E. Eisenberg. 2000. *Indian Mounds of Wisconsin.* University of Wisconsin Press, Madison.

Bleed, Peter. 1969. *The Archaeology of Petaga Point: The Preceramic Component.* Minnesota Prehistoric Archaeology Series, No. 2. Minnesota Historical Society, St. Paul.

Blue, K. B. 1996. Osteological Analysis of Human Remains from the Hogback Site (21HU01). Unpublished manuscript on file at the Department of Anthropology, Hamline University, St. Paul.

Bodley, John H. 1999. Socioeconomic Growth, Culture Scale, and Household Well-Being: A Test of the Power-Elite Hypothesis. *Current Anthropology* 40 (5): 595–620.

———. 2005. *Cultural Anthropology: Tribes, States, and the Global System.* 4th ed. McGraw-Hill Higher Education, New York.

Bonnichsen, R., B. T. Lepper, D. Stanford, and M. R. Waters. 2006. *Paleoamerican Origins: Beyond Clovis.* Center for the Study of First Americans, College Station, Tex.

Boszhardt, Robert F. 1996. Angelo Punctated: A Late Woodland Ceramic Type in Western Wisconsin. *Journal of the Iowa Archeological Society* 43: 129–37.

———. 2004. The Late Woodland and Middle Mississippian Component at the Iva Site, La Crosse County, Wisconsin, in the Driftless Area of the Upper Mississippi River Valley. *The Minnesota Archaeologist* 63: 60–85.

———. 2006. Triangular Cross-Section Adzes from the Upper Mississippi River Valley: The Liska Cache. *The Minnesota Archaeologist* 64: 60–85.

Boyd, Matthew, and Clarence Surette. 2010. Northernmost Precontact Maize in North America. *American Antiquity* 75 (1): 117–33.

Boyd, Matthew, Tamara Varney, Clarence Surette, and Jennifer Surette. 2008. Reassessing the Northern Limit of Maize Consumption in North America: Stable Isotope, Plant Macrofossil, and Trace Element Content of Carbonized Food Residue. *Journal of Archaeological Science* 35 (9): 2545–56.

Brightman, Robert A. 2002. *Grateful Prey: Rock Cree Human-Animal Relationships.* Canadian Plains Research Center, University of Regina, Regina.

Brower, J. V., and D. I. Bushnell. 1900. *Memoirs and Explorations in the Basin of the Mississippi: Mille Lacs.* Vol. 3. Report to the Minnesota Historical Society, St. Paul.

Brown, James A., and R. Vierra. 1983. What Happened in the Middle Archaic? Introduction to an Ecological Approach to Koster Site Archaeology. In *Archaic Hunters and Gatherers in the American Midwest,* ed. J. Phillips and J. A. Brown, 165–95. Academic Press, New York.

Bryson, R. A. 1998. Climatic Episodes (Holocene). In *Archaeology of Prehistoric Native America: An Encyclopedia,* ed. Guy Gibbon, 158–60. Garland Publishing, New York.

Bryson, R. A., and F. K. Hare, eds. 1974. *Climates of North America.* World Survey of Climatology, vol. 11. Elsevier Scientific Publishing Co., New York.

Bryson, R. A., and Katherine McEnaney DeWall, eds. 2007. *A Paleoclimatology Workbook: High Resolution, Site-Specific, Macrophysical Climate Modeling.* The Mammoth Site of Hot Springs, S. Dak.

Budak, Michael K. 1985. Laurel Ceramics: A Pointed Question. *The Minnesota Archaeologist* 44 (2): 31–40.

———. 1998. Laurel Ceramics. *Bulletin of Primitive Technology* 15: 12–17.

Camill, P., C. E. Umbanhower Jr., R. Teed, C. E. Geiss, J. Aldinger, L. Dvorak, J. Kenning, J. Limmer, and K. Walkup. 2003. Late-Glacial and Holocene Climatic Effects on Fire and Vegetational Dynamics at the Prairie-Forest Ecotone in South-Central Minnesota. *Journal of Ecology* 91 (5): 822–36.

Carr, Christopher, and D. Troy Case. 2005. *Gathering Hopewell: Society, Ritual, and Ritual Interaction.* Kluwer Academic/Plenum Publishers, New York.

Charles, Douglas K., and Jane E. Buikstra, eds. 2006. *Recreating Hopewell.* University of Florida Press, Gainesville.

Clark, F. 1984. Knife River Flint and Interregional Exchange. *Midcontinental Journal of Archaeology* 9 (2): 173–98.

Clark, J. S., E. C. Grimm, J. Lynch, and P. G. Mueller. 2001. Effects of Holocene Climate Changes of C_4 Grassland/Woodland Boundary in the Northern Plains, USA. *Ecology* 82: 620–36.

Cleland, Charles E. 1982. The Inland Shore Fishery of the Northern Great Lakes: Its Development and Importance in Prehistory. *American Antiquity* 47 (4): 761–84.

Cooper, Leland R., and Elden Johnson. 1964. Sandy Lake Ware and Its Distribution. *American Antiquity* 26 (4): 474–79.

Costello, D. F. 1980. *The Prairie World.* University of Minnesota Press, Minneapolis.

Crawford, Gary W., David Smith, and Vandy Bowyer. 1997. Dating the Entry of Corn (Zea Mays) into the Lower Great Lakes Region. *American Antiquity* 62 (1): 112–19.

Daniel, G., and J. Sullivan. 1981. *The Northwoods of Michigan, Wisconsin, Minnesota, and Southern Ontario.* Sierra Club Books, San Francisco.

Diamond, Jared. 2005. *Collapse: How Societies Choose to Fail or Succeed.* Viking, New York.

Dillehay, Thomas D. 2001. *Settlement of the Americas: A New Prehistory.* Basic Books, New York.

Dobbs, Clark A. 1984a. Excavations at the Bryan Site: 1983–1984. *The Minnesota Archaeologist* 43: 49–58.

———. 1984b. Oneota Settlement Patterns in the Blue Earth River Valley, Minnesota. PhD diss., Department of Anthropology, University of Minnesota, Minneapolis.

———. 1987. *Archaeological Excavations at the Bryan Site (21GD4), Goodhue County, Minnesota: 1983 and 1984.* Reports of Investigations, No. 8. Institute for Minnesota Archaeology, Minneapolis.

———. 1989. *Cataloguing and Preliminary Analysis of Archaeological Materials Obtained from the Bryan Site (21GD4), Goodhue County, MN.* Reports of Investigations, No. 63. Institute for Minnesota Archaeology, Minneapolis.

———. 1993. A Pilot Study of High Precision Radiocarbon Dating at the Red Wing Locality. Paper presented at the 58th Annual Meeting of the Society for American Archaeology, St. Louis, Mo., April 14–18, 1993. Available at www.fromsitetostory.org/sources/papers/rwlradiocarbondating.

Dobbs, Clark A., and Scott Anfinson. 1990. *Outline of Historic Contexts for the Prehistoric Period (ca. 12,000 BP–AD 1700).* Reports of Investigations No. 37. Institute for Minnesota Archaeology, Minneapolis.

Dobbs, Clark A., and O. C. Shane III. 1982. Oneota Settlement Patterns in the Blue Earth River Valley, Minnesota. In *Oneota Studies*, ed. Guy Gibbon, 55–68. Publications in Anthropology, No. 1. University of Minnesota, Minneapolis.

Dyke, A. S., and V. K. Prest. 1986. Late Wisconsinian and Holocene History of the Laurentide Ice Sheet. *Géographie Physique et Quaternaire* 41: 237–64.

Emerson, Thomas E. 1997. *Cahokia and the Archaeology of Power.* University of Alabama Press, Tuscaloosa.

Emerson, Thomas E., Dale L. McElrath, and Andrew C. Fortier, eds. 2009. *Archaic Societies: Diversity and Complexity across the Midcontinent.* State University of New York Press, Albany.

Evans, G. Edward. 1961a. A Reappraisal of the Blackduck Focus or Headwaters Lakes Aspect. Master's thesis, Department of Anthropology, University of Minnesota, Minneapolis.

——. 1961b. Ceramic Analysis of the Blackduck Ware and Its General Cultural Relationships. *Minnesota Academy of Science, Proceedings* 29: 33–54.

Eyre, S. R. 1968. *Vegetation and Soils: A World Picture.* 2nd ed. Aldine, Chicago.

Fagan, Brian M. 2005. *Ancient North America: The Archaeology of a Continent.* 4th ed. Thames and Hudson, New York.

Farnsworth, Kenneth B., and David L. Asch. 1986. Early Woodland Chronology, Artifact Styles, and Settlement Distribution in the Lower Illinois Valley Region. In *Early Woodland Archeology,* ed. Kenneth B. Farnsworth and Thomas E. Asch, 326–457. Center for American Archeology, Kampsville Seminars in Archeology No. 2.

Farnsworth, Kenneth B., and Thomas E. Emerson, eds. 1986. *Early Woodland Archeology.* Center for American Archeology, Kampsville Seminars in Archeology No. 2.

Fiedel, Stuart J. 2002. Initial Human Colonization of the Americas: An Overview of the Issues and the Evidence. *Radiocarbon* 44 (2): 407–36.

Fiske, Timothy, and Gary Hume. 1963. The Voight Site. *Minnesota Archeological Newsletter* 5: 1–11.

Fleming, Edward. 2009. Community and Aggregation in the Upper Mississippi River Valley: The Red Wing Locality. PhD diss., Department of Anthropology, University of Minnesota, Minneapolis.

Florin, Frank. 1996. Late Paleo-Indians of Minnesota and Vegetation Changes from 10,500-8000 BP. 2 vol. Master's thesis, Interdisciplinary Archaeological Studies, University of Minnesota, Minneapolis.

Forester, R. M., L. D. DeLorme, and J. P. Bradbury. 1987. Mid-Holocene Climate in Northern Minnesota. *Quaternary Research* 28: 263–72.

Forsberg, Drew, and Clark Dobbs. 1997. *Archaeological Data Recovery at Site 21AN106, Anoka County, Minnesota.* Reports of Investigation 395. Institute for Minnesota Archaeology, Minneapolis. Copy on file, Office of the State Archaeologist, St. Paul.

Fowles, Severin M. 2002. From Social Type to Social Process: Placing "Tribe" in a Historical Framework. In *The Archaeology of Tribal Societies,* ed. William A. Parkinson, 13–33. Archaeological Series 15, International Monographs in Prehistory, Ann Arbor, Mich.

Freeman, Joan A. 1969. The Millville Site, a Middle Woodland Village in Grant County, Wisconsin. *The Wisconsin Archeologist* 50: 37–88.

Fried, Morton A. 1975. *The Notion of Tribe.* Cummings, Menlo Park, Calif.

Friedman, Thomas L. 2009. *Hot, Flat, and Crowded: Why We Need a Green Revolution—And How It Can Renew America.* Picador/Farrar, Straus and Giroux, New York.

Gallagher, J. P. 1990. *The Farley Village Site 21HU2, An Oneota/Ioway Site in Houston County, Minnesota.* Reports of Investigation No. 117. Mississippi Valley Archaeology Center, University of Wisconsin–La Crosse, La Crosse.

George, Douglas. 1979a. Clam River Ware. In *A Handbook of Minnesota Prehistoric Ceramics,* ed. Scott F. Anfinson, 67–72. Occasional Publications in Minnesota Anthropology, No. 5. Minnesota Archaeological Society, Fort Snelling.

——. 1979b. St. Croix Series. In *A Handbook of Minnesota Prehistoric Ceramics,* ed. Scott F. Anfinson, 169–74. Occasional Publications in Minnesota Anthropology, No. 5. Minnesota Archaeological Society, Fort Snelling.

Gibbon, Guy E. 1972. Cultural Dynamics and the Development of the Oneota Life-Way in Wisconsin. *American Antiquity* 37 (2): 166–85.

———. 1973. *The Sheffield Site: An Oneota Site on the St. Croix River.* Minnesota Prehistoric Archaeology Series No. 10. Minnesota Historical Society, St. Paul.

———. 1974. A Model of Mississippian Development and Its Implications for the Red Wing Area. In *Aspects of Upper Great Lakes Anthropology: Papers in Honor of Lloyd A. Wilford,* ed. Elden Johnson, 129–37. Minnesota Prehistoric Archaeology Series, No. 11. Minnesota Historical Society, St. Paul.

———. 1975. The Brower Site: A Middle Woodland Mound and Camp Site on Lake Onamia. *The Minnesota Archaeologist* 34 (3–4): 1–43.

———. 1979. *The Mississippian Occupation of the Red Wing Area.* Minnesota Prehistoric Archaeology Series No. 13. Minnesota Historical Society, St. Paul.

———. 1983. The Blue Earth Phase of Southern Minnesota. *Journal of the Iowa Archeological Society* 30: 1–84.

———. 1991. Middle Mississippian Presence in Minnesota. In *Cahokia and the Hinterlands: Middle Mississippian Cultures of the Midwest,* ed. T. E. Emerson and R. B. Lewis, 207–20. University of Illinois Press, Urbana and Chicago.

———. 1993. The Middle Missouri Tradition in Minnesota. In *Prehistory and Human Ecology of the Western Prairies and Northern Plains: Papers in Honor of Robert A. Alex,* ed. J. A. Tiffany, 169–88. Memoir 27. Plains Anthropological Society, Lincoln, Neb.

———. 1994. Cultures of the Upper Mississippi River Valley and Adjacent Prairies in Iowa and Minnesota. In *Plains Indians, AD 500–1500, The Archaeological Past of Historic Groups,* ed. K. H. Schlesier, 128–48. University of Oklahoma Press, Norman.

———. 1995. Oneota at the Periphery: Trade, Political Power, and Ethnicity in Northern Minnesota and on the Northeastern Plains in the Late Prehistoric Period. In *Oneota Archaeology Past and Future Research,* ed. William Green, 175–99. Report 20, Office of the State Archaeologist, University of Iowa, Iowa City.

———. 1998a. Various in *Archaeology of Prehistoric Native America: An Encyclopedia,* ed. Guy Gibbon. Garland, New York.

———. 1998b. Old Copper in Minnesota: A Review. *Plains Anthropologist* 43 (163): 27–50.

———. 2001. Oneota. In *Encyclopedia of Prehistory,* vol. 6: *North America,* 389–407. Kluwer Academic/Plenum Publishers, New York.

———. 2003. *The Sioux: The Lakota and Dakota Nations.* Basil Blackwell, New York.

———. 2007. McKern's Science. *The Wisconsin Archeologist* 85 (2): 18–23.

Gibbon, Guy E., Gwen Bennett, K. Anne Ketz, and Thomas W. Bailey. 1993. *Phase III Data Recovery Operations at Site 21AN17, Anoka County, Minnesota.* BRW, Inc. Prepared for the Anoka County Highway Department. Copy on file, Office of the State Archaeologist, St. Paul.

Gibbon, Guy E., and Christy A. H. Caine. 1980. The Middle to Late Woodland Transition in Eastern Minnesota. *Midcontinental Journal of Archaeology* 5 (1): 57–72.

Gibbon, Guy E., and Clark A. Dobbs. 1991. The Mississippian Presence in the Red Wing Area. In *New Perspectives on Cahokia: Views from the Periphery,* ed. James B. Stoltman, 281–306. Monographs in World Archaeology, No. 2. Prehistory Press, Madison, Wis.

Glenn, Elizabeth J. 1974. *Physical Affiliations of the Oneota Peoples.* Report No. 7. Office of the State Archaeologist, University of Iowa, Iowa City.

Goldberg, Paul, David T. Nash, and Michael D. Petraglia, eds. 1993. *Formation Processes in Archaeological Context.* Prehistory Press, Madison, Wis.

Goltz, Grant. 1993. *Pimushe Lake Boat Access Site Evaluation.* Blackduck Ranger District, Chippewa National Forest. Soils Consulting, Longville, Minn.

Gonsior, LeRoy, Douglas George, and Stacy Allan. 1999. *Archaeological Investigations of the Lake*

Carlos State Park Beach Site (21DL2), Lake Carlos State Park, Douglas County, Minnesota. Minnesota Department of Natural Resources, Minnesota Historical Society. Copy on file, Office of the State Archaeologist, St. Paul.

Grayson, Donald K. 1991. Late Pleistocene Mammalian Extinctions in North America: Taxonomy, Chronology, and Explanations. *Journal of World Prehistory* 5: 193–231.

Green, William. 1993. Examining Protohistoric Depopulation in the Upper Midwest. *The Wisconsin Archeologist* 74: 290–323.

——, ed. 1995. *Oneota Archaeology: Past, Present, and Future.* Office of the State Archaeologist Report No. 20. University of Iowa, Iowa City.

Griffin, James B. 1937. The Archaeological Remains of the Chiwere Sioux. *American Antiquity* 2: 180–81.

——. 1952. Some Early and Middle Woodland Pottery Types in Illinois. In *Hopewellian Communities in Illinois,* ed. T. Deuel, 93–129. Illinois State Museum, Scientific Papers 5.

——. 1960. A Hypothesis for the Prehistory of the Winnebago. In *Culture History: Essays in Honor of Paul Radin,* ed. Stanley Diamond, 807–65. Columbia University Press, New York.

Grimm, E. C. 1983. Chronology and Dynamics of Vegetation Change in the Prairie-Woodland Region of Southern Minnesota, USA. *New Phytologist* 93: 311–50.

——. 1984. Fire and Other Factors Controlling the Big Woods Vegetation of Minnesota in the Mid-nineteenth Century. *Ecological Monographs* 54 (3): 291–311.

Gruchow, Paul. 2009. *Journal of a Prairie Year,* 2nd ed. Milkweed Editions, Minneapolis.

Hall, Robert. 1991. Cahokia Identity and Interaction Models of Cahokia Mississippian. In *Cahokia and the Hinterlands: Middle Mississippian Cultures of the Midwest,* ed. Thomas E. Emerson and R. B. Lewis, 3–34. University of Illinois Press, Urbana.

Halloran, Teresa, Elden Johnson, and Riaz Malik. 2000. Groundstone. In *The Lake Onamia–Trunk Highway 169 Data Recovery Project, Mille Lacs County, Minnesota,* ed. D. Mather and E. Abel, 16.1–16.37. Loucks Project Report 96506-1. Loucks & Associates, Inc., Maple Grove. Report prepared for the Minnesota Department of Transportation, St. Paul.

Harrison, Christina. 1988. *Report on Evaluation for National Register Significance of the Cultural Resource Site(s) at South Pike Bay Campground, Cass County, Minnesota.* Prepared for Chippewa National Forest. Archaeological Research Services, Minneapolis.

Harrison, Christina, Mike Budak, Martha Hopeman, and Brad Johnson. 1977. *21AN1 The Howard Lake Mounds (with associated habitation material).* Minnesota Historical Society field check 10.10–11.1977. Report on file, Minnesota Historical Society, Fort Snelling, St. Paul.

Harrison, Christina, E. Redepenning, C. L. Hill, G. (Rip) Rapp Jr., S. E. Aschenbrenner, J. K. Huber, and S. C. Mulholland. 1995. *The Paleo-Indians of Southern St. Louis Co., Minnesota.* Monograph 4, Interdisciplinary Archaeological Studies, University of Minnesota. Kendall/Hunt Publishing Co., Dubuque, Iowa.

Haug, J. K. 1995. The Hartford Beach Site (Again). *Newsletter of the South Dakota Archaeological Society* 25 (4): 1–2.

Haynes, Gary. 2002. *The Early Settlement of North America: The Clovis Era.* Cambridge University Press, New York.

Heinselman, Miron L. 1996. *The Boundary Waters Ecosystem.* University of Minnesota Press, Minneapolis.

Hennepin, Louis. 1938. *Father Louis Hennepin's Description of Louisiana, Newly Discovered to the Southwest of New France by Order of the King.* Edited and translated by Marion E. Cross. University of Minnesota Press, Minneapolis.

Henning, Dale R., and E. R. Henning. 1978. Great Oasis Ceramics. In *Some Studies of Minnesota*

Prehistoric Ceramics: Papers Presented at the First Council for Minnesota Archeology Symposium, 1976, ed. A. R. Woolworth and M. A. Hall, 12–26. Occasional Publications in Minnesota Anthropology, No. 2. Minnesota Archaeological Society, Fort Snelling.

Hill, Christopher L. 2007. Geoarchaeology and Late Glacial Landscapes in the Western Lake Superior Region, Central North America. *Geoarchaeology* 22 (1): 15–47.

Hohman-Caine, Christy. 1974. The Archaeology of the Snake River Region in Minnesota. In *Aspects of Upper Great Lakes Anthropology,* ed. Elden Johnson, 55–63. Prehistoric Archaeology Series, Minnesota Historical Society, St. Paul.

Hohman-Caine [Caine], Christy. 1979. Malmo-Kern Series. In *A Handbook of Minnesota Prehistoric Ceramics,* ed. Scott F. Anfinson, 137–41. Occasional Publications in Minnesota Anthropology, No. 5. Minnesota Archaeological Society, Fort Snelling.

———. 1983. Normative Typology and Systemic Stylistic Approaches to the Analysis of North Central Minnesota Ceramics. PhD diss., Department of Anthropology, University of Minnesota, Minneapolis.

Hohman-Caine, Christy, and Grant E. Goltz. 1995. Brainerd Ware and the Early Woodland Dilemma. *The Minnesota Archaeologist* 54: 109–29.

———. 1998. A Spring Piscary in the Headwaters Region: The Third River Bridge Site. Unpublished manuscript, Hamline University, St. Paul. Copy on file, State Historic Preservation Office, St. Paul.

———. 1999. *Final Report: The Shingobee Island Site (21-CA-28).* Prepared by Soils Consulting, Longville, Minn. Copy on file, Office of the State Archaeologist, St. Paul.

Holley, George R., and Michael G. Michlovic. 2010. Oneota in the Northeastern Plains. *The Minnesota Archaeologist* 69: 13–44.

Hollinger, R. Eric. 2005. Conflict and Culture Change in the Late Prehistoric and Early Historic American Midcontinent. PhD diss., Department of Anthropology, University of Illinois at Urbana-Champaign.

Hollinger, R. Eric., and David W. Benn, eds. 1998. Oneota Taxonomy: Papers from the Oneota Symposium of the 54th Plains Anthropological Conference, 1996. *The Wisconsin Archeologist* 79 (2).

Hoppin, Art, and David Mather. 1996. Lithic Analysis. In *McKinstry Site (21KC2): Final Report of Phase III Investigations for Mn/DOT S.P. 3604–44, Replacement of T.H. 11 Bridge 5178 over the Little Fork River, Koochiching County, Minnesota,* ed. Matthew Thomas and David Mather, chapter 12. Loucks Project Report 93512. Copy on file, Office of the State Archaeologist, St. Paul.

Howard, C. D. 1990. The Clovis Point: Characteristics and Type Description. *Plains Anthropologist* 35 (129): 255–62.

Hruby, Thomas Homer. 1977. *Lithic Analysis of the Anderson Site, 21AN8.* Plan B Master of Arts paper, Center for Ancient Studies, University of Minnesota.

Hudak, G. Joseph. 1974. The Pedersen Site (21LN2), Lincoln County, Minnesota. Master's thesis, Department of Anthropology, University of Nebraska, Lincoln.

———. 1976. *Woodland Ceramics from the Pedersen Site.* Scientific Publications of the Science Museum of Minnesota, New Series, 3–2.

Hudak, G. Joseph, Elizabeth Hobbs, Allyson Brooks, Carol Ann Sersland, and Crystal Phillips. 2002. *Mn/Model Final Report 2002: A Predictive Model of Precontact Archaeological Site Location for the State of Minnesota.* Minnesota Department of Transportation, St. Paul.

Hudak, G. Joseph, and Elden Johnson. 1975. *An Early Woodland Pottery Vessel from Minnesota.* Scientific Publications of the Science Museum of Minnesota, New Series 2–4.

Hunter, Andrea. 1992. Paleobotanical Remains from the Johnsrud Site. In *Archeological Investigations in the Vicinity of Lake Oscar, Douglas County, Minnesota. S.P. 2101-18 (T.H. 27),* ed. Jonathan

Sellars, 157–69. Prepared for the Minnesota Department of Transportation. Bear Creek Archaeology. Copy on file, State Archaeologist Office, St. Paul.

Hurley, William M. 1986. The Late Woodland Stage: Effigy Mound Culture. In *Introduction to Wisconsin Archaeology,* ed. W. Green, J. B. Stoltman, and A. B. Kehoe, 283–301. *The Wisconsin Archeologist* 67.

Irwin, H. T., and H. M. Wormington. 1970. Paleo-Indian Tool Types in the Great Plains. *American Antiquity* 35: 24–34.

Jenks, Albert E. 1936. *Pleistocene Man in Minnesota: A Fossil Homo Sapiens.* University of Minnesota Press, Minneapolis.

———. 1937. *Minnesota's Browns Valley Man and Associated Burial Artifacts.* American Anthropological Association, *Memoirs,* No. 49.

Jenks, Albert E., and Lloyd A. Wilford. 1938. Sauk Valley Skeleton. *Texas Archeological and Paleontological Society Bulletin* 10: 136–68.

Johnson, Allen W., and Timothy Earle. 2000. *The Evolution of Human Societies: From Foraging Group to Agrarian State.* 2nd ed. Stanford University Press, Stanford, Calif.

Johnson, Craig, with Stacey Buck, Chandra Maki, and Rebecca St. George. 1995. *Archaeological Data Recovery at the Blueberry Lake Site (21WD6), Wadena County, Minnesota.* Prepared for Blueberry Township by BRW, Inc. Copy on file, Office of the State Archaeologist, St. Paul.

Johnson, Elden. 1957. *Hopewell Burial Mounds, Indian Mounds Park-St. Paul.* Park Leaflet 3. St. Paul Science Museum, St. Paul.

———. 1959. *Spring Lake Archaeology: The Sorg Site.* Science Bulletin 3–3. St. Paul Science Museum.

———. 1961. Cambria Burial Mounds in Big Stone County. *The Minnesota Archaeologist* 23 (3): 51–81.

———. 1964. Twenty New Radiocarbon Dates from Minnesota Archaeological Sites. *The Minnesota Archaeologist* 26 (2): 34–49.

———. 1969. Decorative Motifs on Great Oasis Pottery. *Plains Anthropologist* 14 (46): 272–76.

———. 1971. The Northern Margin of the Prairie Peninsula. *Journal of the Iowa Archaeological Society* 18: 13–21.

———. 1973. *The Arvilla Complex: Based on Field Notes by Lloyd A. Wilford.* Minnesota Prehistoric Archaeology Series, No. 9. Minnesota Historical Society, St. Paul.

———. 1979. *Cultural Resources Investigations of the Reservoir Shorelines: Gull Lake, Leech Lake, Pine River, and Lake Pokegama.* Report submitted to the U.S. Army Corps of Engineers, St. Paul District. Copy on file, Office of the State Archaeologist, St. Paul.

———. 1984. *Cultural Resource Survey of the Mille Lacs Area.* University of Minnesota, Minneapolis. Report prepared for the Minnesota Historical Society, St. Paul.

———. 1985. The 17th Century Mdewakanton Dakota Subsistence Mode. In *Archaeology, Ecology, and Ethnohistory of the Prairie-Forest Border Zone of Minnesota and Manitoba,* ed. J. Spector and E. Johnson, 154–66. J & L Reprints, Lincoln.

———. 1986. Cambria and Cahokia's Northwestern Periphery. Paper presented at the 51st annual meeting of the Society for American Archaeology, New Orleans, April 23–26.

———. 1991. Cambria and Cahokia's Northwestern Periphery. In *New Perspectives on Cahokia: Views from the Periphery,* ed. James B. Stoltman, 307–18. Prehistory Press, Madison, Wis.

———. 1993. Snake River Pit Houses. *The Minnesota Archaeologist* 52: 52–59.

Johnson, Elden, C. Harrison, and J. Schaaf. 1977. *Cultural Resources Investigations of the Lands Adjacent to Lake Winnibigoshish.* Report submitted to the U.S. Army Corps of Engineers, St. Paul District. Copy on file, Office of the State Archaeologist, St. Paul.

Johnson, Elden, and Timothy Ready. 1992. Ceramic Funerary Masks from McKinstry Mound 2. *Midcontinental Journal of Archaeology* 17 (1): 16–45.

Justice, Noel D. 1987. *Stone Age Spear and Arrow Points of the Midcontinental and Eastern United States: A Modern Survey and Reference.* Indiana University Press, Bloomington.

Justin, Michael A., ed. 1995. *Archaeological Data Recovery at the Roosevelt Lake Narrows Site, Cass County, Minnesota.* Woodward-Clyde Report 93e209. Report prepared for the Minnesota Department of Transportation. Copy on file, Office of the State Archaeologist, St. Paul.

Justin, Michael A., and Lynn Schuster. 1994. The Basswood Shores Site, 21DL90: A Late Woodland Habitation. *The Minnesota Archaeologist* 53: 77–85.

Kidder, Tristram R. 2006. Climate Change and the Archaic to Woodland Transition (3000–2500 cal BP) in the Mississippi River Basin. *American Antiquity* 71 (2): 195–231.

Kluth, Rose, and David Kluth. 1994. *Phase II Archaeological Evaluation of Site No. HB-CSAH 9-A, Hubbard County, Minnesota.* Leech Lake Heritage Sites program, Cass Lake.

Knudson, R. A. 1967. Cambria Village Ceramics. *Plains Anthropologist* 12 (37): 247–99.

Kuper, Adam. 1988. *The Invention of Primitive Societies: Transformations of an Illusion.* Routledge, New York.

Larson, G., and R. J. Schaetzl. 2001. Origin and Evolution of the Great Lakes. *Journal of Great Lakes Research* 27: 518–46.

Lehmer, Donald J. 1971. *Introduction to Middle Missouri Archeology.* Anthropological Papers, 1. U.S. Department of the Interior, National Park Service, Washington, DC.

Lenius, B. J., and D. M. Olinyk. 1990. The Rainy River Composite: Revisions to Late Woodland Taxonomy. In *The Woodland Tradition in the Western Great Lakes: Papers Presented to Elden Johnson,* ed. Guy Gibbon, 77–112. Publications in Anthropology, No. 4. University of Minnesota, Minneapolis.

Lewis, T. H. 1896. Mounds and Stone Cists at St. Paul, Minnesota. *American Antiquarian and Oriental Journal* 18 (5): 314–20.

Logan, W. D. 1976. *Woodland Complexes in Northeastern Iowa.* National Park Service, Publications in Archaeology 15.

Lothson, Gordon A. 1972. Burial Mounds of the Mille Lacs Lake Area. Master's thesis, Department of Anthropology, University of Minnesota, Minneapolis.

Lovis, William A., Randolph E. Donahue, and Margaret B. Holman. 2005. Long-Distance Logistical Mobility as an Organizing Principle among Northern Hunter-Gatherers: A Great Lakes Middle Holocene Settlement System. *American Antiquity* 70 (4): 669–93.

Lucking, L. J. 1973. Subsistence Ecology of the Cooper Site with an Addendum on Bone Artifacts. Master's thesis, Department of Anthropology, University of Minnesota, Minneapolis.

Lugenbeal, Edward N. 1976. The Archaeology of the Smith Site: A Study of the Ceramics and Culture History of Minnesota Laurel and Blackduck. PhD diss., Department of Anthropology, University of Wisconsin, Madison.

———. 1978. The Blackduck Ceramics of the Smith Site (21KC3) and Their Implications for the History of Blackduck Ceramics and Culture in Northern Minnesota. *Midcontinental Journal of Archaeology* 3 (1): 45–68.

———. 1979. Blackduck Ware. In *A Handbook of Minnesota Prehistoric Ceramics,* ed. Scott F. Anfinson, 23–37. Occasional Publications in Minnesota Anthropology, No. 5. Minnesota Archaeological Society, Fort Snelling.

Lynch, Wayne, and Aubrey Lang. 2001. *The Great Northern Kingdom: Life in the Boreal Forest.* Fitzhenry & Whiteside, Markham, Ont.

Lytwyn, Victor P. 2002. *Muskekowuck Athinuwick Original People of the Great Swampy Land.* University of Manitoba Press, Manitoba.

Madson, John. 1995. *Where the Sky Began: Land of the Tallgrass Prairie.* University of Iowa Press, Iowa City.

Malik, Riaz, and Kent Bakken. 1999. Bradbury Brook (21ML42): A Late Paleoindian Lithic Workshop in East-Central Minnesota. *The Minnesota Archaeologist* 58: 134–71.

Mallam, R. C. 1976. *The Iowa Effigy Mound Tradition: An Interpretive Model.* Office of the State Archaeologist Report 9. University of Iowa, Iowa City.

Martin, Terrance, and John Richmond. 1992. Animal Remains Recovered from Three Prehistoric Sites in the Vicinity of Lake Oscar. In *Archeological Investigations in the Vicinity of Lake Oscar, Douglas County, Minnesota. S.P. 2101-18 (T.H. 27),* ed. Jonathan Sellars, 170–74. Prepared for the Minnesota Department of Transportation. Bear Creek Archaeology. Copy on file, State Archaeologist Office, St. Paul.

Mason, Ronald J. 1967. The North Bay Component at the Porte des Morts Site, Door County, Wisconsin. *The Wisconsin Archeologist* 48 (4): 267–345.

———. 1969. Laurel and North Bay: Diffusional Networks in the Upper Great Lakes. *American Antiquity* 34 (3): 295–302.

———. 1981. *Great Lakes Archaeology.* Academic Press, New York.

Mather, David. 1991. Toward a Cultural Landscape in the Mille Lacs Region: Trunk Highway 169 Survey and Site Evaluation in the Vicinity of Lake Onamia. *The Minnesota Archaeologist* 50 (1): 31–46.

———. 1994. *Cultural Resource Survey and Evaluation Report: MnDOT S.P. 4812-49 for Reconstruction of T.H. 169 from 2.0 Miles South of Onamia to 0.2 Mile South of the North T.H. 27 Junction, Mille Lacs County.* Minnesota Trunk Highway Archaeological Reconnaissance Study, Minnesota Historical Society, St. Paul. Report prepared for the Minnesota Department of Transportation, St. Paul.

———. 1998. *Faunal Remains from Funerary Contexts from the Gull Lake Dam Mounds (21CA37).* Loucks Project Report 97512. Loucks & Associates, Inc., Maple Grove. Report prepared for the U.S. Army Corps of Engineers, St. Paul District.

———. 2000a. *Archaeological Overview of the Mille Lacs Locality.* Loucks Project Report 96506–2. Loucks & Associates, Inc., Maple Grove. Report prepared for the Minnesota Department of Transportation, St. Paul.

———. 2000b. History of Archaeological Investigations in the Mille Lacs Region. In *The Lake Onamia–Trunk Highway 169 Data Recovery Project, Mille Lacs County, Minnesota,* ed. David Mather and E. J. Abel, chapter 4. Loucks Project Report 96506–1. Loucks & Associates, Inc., Maple Grove. Report prepared for the Minnesota Department of Transportation, St. Paul.

———. 2005. Zooarchaeology of the Third River Bridge Site (21IC46), a Late Woodland Fishing Camp in Itasca County, Minnesota. *The Minnesota Archaeologist* 64: 155–84.

———. 2011. Grand Mound National Historic Landmark Nomination (NPS Form 10-900). (The nomination was approved on June 23, 2011.)

Mather, David, and E. J. Abel, eds. 2000. *The Lake Onamia–Trunk Highway 169 Data Recovery Project, Mille Lacs County, Minnesota.* Loucks Project Report 96506–1. Loucks & Associates, Inc., Maple Grove. Report prepared for the Minnesota Department of Transportation, St. Paul.

Mather, David, and Jim Cummings. 2010. *Kathio Archaeology Day Public Research Program: The Petaga Point Site (21ML11), Mille Lacs Kathio State Park (Interim Project Report for 2006–2009).* State Historic Preservation Office, Minnesota Historical Society, St. Paul, and Mille Lacs Kathio State Park, Onamia.

Mather, David, and S. Nicholas. 2000. The Van Grinsven Site (21ML37). In *The Lake Onamia–Trunk Highway 169 Data Recovery Project, Mille Lacs County, Minnesota,* ed. D. Mather and E. Abel, 9.1–9.7. Loucks Project Report 96506–1. Loucks & Associates, Inc., Maple Grove. Report prepared for the Minnesota Department of Transportation, St. Paul.

Mather, David, Mary Wheland, and Sara Nicholas. 2000. Mille Lacs Regional Zooarchaeology. In *The Lake Onamia-Trunk Highway 169 Data Recovery Project, Mille Lacs County, Minnesota*, ed. D. Mather and E. Abel, 17.1–17.10. Loucks Project Report 96506–1. Loucks & Associates, Inc., Maple Grove. Report prepared for the Minnesota Department of Transportation, St. Paul.

Maxwell, Moreau S. 1950. A Change in the Interpretation of Wisconsin's Prehistory. *Wisconsin Magazine of History* 33: 427–43.

McKern, Will C. 1939. The Midwestern Taxonomic Method as an Aid to Archaeological Culture Study. *American Antiquity* 4 (4): 301–13.

Meltzer, David J. 2010. *First Peoples in a New World: Colonizing Ice Age America*. University of California Press, Berkeley.

Meltzer, David J., and J. I. Mead. 1985. Dating Late Pleistocene Extinctions: Theoretical Issues, Analytical Bias, and Substantive Results. In *Environments and Extinctions: Man in Late Glacial North America*, ed. J. I. Mead and D. J. Meltzer, 145–74. Center for the Study of Early Man, Orono, Maine.

Meyer, David, Peggy McKeand, J. Michael Quigg, and Gary Wowchuk. 2008. The River House Complex: Middle Woodland on the Northwestern Periphery. *Canadian Journal of Archaeology* 32: 43–76.

Michlovic, Michael G. 1979. *The Dead River Site (21OT51)*. Minnesota Archaeological Society, St. Paul.

———. 1982. Report on the Red River Archaeological Survey in Norman County, Minnesota. *The Minnesota Archaeologist* 41 (2): 53–69.

———. 1986. The Archaeology of the Canning Site. *The Minnesota Archaeologist* 45 (1): 1–36.

———. 1987. The Archaeology of the Mooney Site (21NR29). *The Minnesota Archaeologist* 46 (2): 39–64.

———. 2005. A Prairie Blackduck Site in Northwestern Minnesota. *The Minnesota Archaeologist* 64: 49–84.

Michlovic, Michael G., and Dean Sather. 2000. *Analysis of Cultural Materials from the North Twin Lake Site (21MH5), Mahnomen County, Minnesota*. Archaeology Laboratory, Moorhead State University, Moorhead, Minnesota. Copy on file, State Historic Preservation Office, St. Paul.

Michlovic, Michael G., and F. Schneider. 1993. The Shea Site: A Prehistoric Fortified Village on the Northeastern Plains. *Plains Anthropologist* 38 (143): 117–37.

Moore, John H. 1994. Putting Anthropology Back Together Again: The Ethnogenetic Critique of Cladistic Theory. *American Anthropologist* 96 (4): 925–48.

Morey, Darcy, Carl Falk, and Holmes Semken Jr. 1996. Vertebrate Remains from the McKinstry Site. In *McKinstry Site (21KC2): Final Report of Phase III Investigations for Mn/DOT S.P. 3604-44, Replacement of T.H. 11 Bridge 5178 over the Little Fork River, Koochiching County, Minnesota*, ed. Matthew Thomas and David Mather, chapter 15. Loucks Project Report 93512. Copy on file, Office of the State Archaeologist, St. Paul.

Morrow, Juliet, and T. A. Morrow. 1999. Geographic Variation in Fluted Projectile Points: A Hemispheric Perspective. *American Antiquity* 64 (2): 215–31.

Mott, Mildred. 1938. The Relation of Historic Indian Tribes to Archaeological Manifestations in Iowa. *Iowa Journal of History and Politics* 36: 227–314.

Mulholland, Susan C. 2000. The Arrowhead since the Glaciers: The Prehistory of Northeastern Minnesota. *The Minnesota Archaeologist* 59: 1–10.

Mulholland, Susan C., and Stephen L. Mulholland. 2002. A Folsom Site in Northeastern Minnesota. *Current Research in the Pleistocene* 19: 68–70.

Mulholland, Susan C., S. L. Mulholland, G. R. Peters, J. K. Huber, and H. D. Mooers. 1997a. Paleo-Indian Occupations in Northeastern Minnesota: How Early? *North American Archaeologist* 18: 371–400.

Mulholland, Susan C., Stephen L. Mulholland, Jennifer Shafer, and George Rapp Jr. 1997b. *Mitigation of the Third River Borrows Pit Site (21-IC-0176, 09-03-01-0355), Blackduck District, Chippewa National Forest, Itasca County, Minnesota.* Archaeometry Laboratory, University of Minnesota, Duluth. Prepared for Itasca County Highway Department and Chippewa National Forest. Copy on file, Office of the State Archaeologist, St. Paul.

Mulholland, Susan C., Stephen L. Mulholland, Jennifer R. Shafer, S. H. Valppu, and George Rapp Jr. 1996. *Evaluation of Two Sites on the Dixon Lake Road/Third River, Blackduck District, Chippewa National Forest, Itasca County, Minnesota.* Archaeometry Laboratory Report No. 96–24. University of Minnesota, Duluth.

Munson, Patrick J. 1986. Black Sand and Havana Tradition Ceramic Assemblages and Culture History in the Central Illinois River Valley. In *Early Woodland Archeology,* ed. Kenneth B. Farnsworth and Thomas E. Asch, 280–300. Center for American Archeology, Kampsville Seminars in Archeology No. 2.

Myster, Susan M. T. 2001. Ten Thousand Years of Population Relationships at the Prairie-Woodland Interface: Cranial Morphology in the Upper Midwest and Contiguous Areas of Manitoba and Ontario. PhD. diss., University of Tennessee, Knoxville.

Myster, Susan M. T., and Barbara O'Connell. 1997. Bioarchaeology. In *Archeology and Bioarcheology of the Northern Woodlands,* ed. E. Benchley, B. Nansel, C. Dobbs, S. M. Thursten Myster, and B. O'Connell, 215–302. A volume in the Central and Northern Plains Archeological Overview, Arkansas Archeological Survey Research Series 52. USACERL Special Report 97/100. U.S. Army Corps of Engineers Construction Engineering Research Laboratory, U.S. Department of Defense Legacy Resource Management Program.

Navarre, G., T. McCauley, and K. Hagglund. 1994. *Phase 1 Archaeological Survey of the North Twin Lake Road Reconstruction Project and Phase 11 Evaluation of Site 21MH05.* U.S. Department of the Interior, Bureau of Indian Affairs, Minneapolis Area Office.

Neusius, Sarah W., and G. Timothy Gross. 2007. *Seeking Our Past: An Introduction to North American Archaeology.* Oxford University Press, New York.

Nickerson, W. B. 1988. Archaeological Evidences in Minnesota. *The Minnesota Archaeologist* 47 (2): 4–40.

O'Connell, Barbara, and Susan Myster. 1996. Paleoindian and Early Archaic Human Remains in Minnesota. Paper presented at the Plains Anthropological Conference, Iowa City.

Odell, George H. 1998. Atlatl. In *Archaeology of Prehistoric America: An Encyclopedia,* ed. Guy Gibbon, 35–36. Garland Publishing, New York.

Ojakangas, R. W., and C. L. Matsch. 1982. *Minnesota's Geology.* University of Minnesota Press, Minneapolis.

Ollendorf, Amy L. 2000. Paleoecology of the Mille Lacs Locality. In *The Lake Onamia–Trunk Highway 169 Data Recovery Project, Mille Lacs County, Minnesota,* ed. D. Mather and E. Abel, 12.1–12.21. Loucks Project Report 96506–1. Loucks & Associates, Inc., Maple Grove. Report prepared for the Minnesota Department of Transportation, St. Paul.

Ossenberg, N. S. 1974. Origins and Relationships of Woodland Peoples: The Evidence of Cranial Morphology. In *Aspects of Upper Great Lakes Anthropology: Papers in Honor of Lloyd A. Wilford,* ed. Elden Johnson, 15–39. Minnesota Prehistoric Archaeology Series No. 11. Minnesota Historical Society, St. Paul.

Owen, Roger C. 1965. The Patrilocal Band: A Linguistically and Culturally Hybrid Social Unit. *American Anthropologist* 67: 675–90.

Patterson, Carrie J. 1997. *Contributions to the Quaternary Geology of Southwestern Minnesota.* Minnesota Geological Survey, University of Minnesota, St. Paul.

Pauketat, Timothy R. 2004. *Ancient Cahokia and the Mississippians*. Cambridge University Press, Cambridge.

Pauketat, Timothy R., and Thomas E. Emerson. 1991. The Ideology of Authority and the Power of the Pot. *American Anthropologist* 93: 919–41.

Penman, J. T. 1988. Neo-boreal Climatic Influences on the Late Prehistoric Agricultural Groups in the Upper Mississippi Valley. *Geoarchaeology* 3: 139–45.

Perkl, Bradley. 2009. The Late Archaic-Early Woodland Transition in Southeastern Minnesota. PhD diss., Interdisciplinary Archaeological Studies, University of Minnesota, Minneapolis.

Peterson, Barbara B. 2011. *Peopling of the Americas, Currents, Canoes, and DNA*. Nova Science Publishers, Hauppauge, N.Y.

Peterson, Lynelle A. 1986. An Attribute Study of Sandy Lake Ware from Norman County and Northcentral Minnesota. Master's thesis, Department of Anthropology, University of Nebraska, Lincoln.

Peterson, Martin Q. 1964. The Estimation of Relationship and Biological Distance between Selected Minnesota Prehistoric Groups. Master's thesis, Department of Anthropology, University of Minnesota, Minneapolis.

Phillips, B. A. M. 1993. A Time-Space Model for the Distribution of Shoreline Archaeological Sites in the Lake Superior Basin. *Geoarchaeology* 8 (2): 87–107.

Pielou, E. C. 1988. *The World of Northern Evergreens*. Cornell University Press, Ithaca, N.Y.

——. 1991. *After the Ice Age: The Return of Life to Glaciated North America*. University of Chicago Press, Chicago.

Powell, J. F., and D. G. Steele. 1994. A Multivariate Craniometric Analysis of North American Paleoindian Remains. *Current Research in the Pleistocene* 9: 59–62.

Pratt, Daniel R. 1994. A Carbon Isotope Analysis of Fifty-Nine Burials from the Upper Mississippi River Valley. Master's thesis, Interdisciplinary Archaeological Studies, University of Minnesota, Minneapolis.

Raff, Jennifer Anne. 2008. An Ancient DNA Perspective on the Prehistory of the Lower Illinois Valley. PhD diss., Departments of Biology and Anthropology, Indiana University, Bloomington.

Rajnovich, Margaret Grace. 2003. The Laurel World: Time-Space Patterns of Ceramic Styles and Their Implications for Culture Change in the Upper Great Lakes in the First Millennium AD. PhD diss., Department of Anthropology, Michigan State University, East Lansing.

Rapp, George, James Allert, and Gordon Peters. 1990. The Origins of Copper in Three Northern Minnesota Sites: Pauly, River Point, and Big Rice. In *The Woodland Tradition in the Western Great Lakes: Papers Presented to Elden Johnson*, ed. Guy Gibbon, 233–38. Publications in Anthropology 4, University of Minnesota, Minneapolis.

Rapp, George, Susan Mulholland, Stephen Mulholland, Zhichun Jing, Doris Stoessel, Christopher Hill, Orrin Shane, Seppo Valppu, James Huber, James Stoltman, and Jennifer Shafer. 1995. *Final Report: Hannaford Data Recovery Project, Koochiching County, Minnesota*. Archaeometry Laboratory Report Number 95-31. Submitted to the Minnesota Department of Transportation. Copy on file, Office of the State Archaeologist, St. Paul.

Rapp, George, with Doris Stoessel, Edith Dunn, Martin Engseth, and Mary Pulford. 1998. *The Woodland Period: Native Americans of the Rainy River Region*. Archaeometry Laboratory, University of Minnesota, Duluth.

Ready, T. 1979. Cambria Phase. In *A Handbook of Minnesota Prehistoric Ceramics*, ed. Scott F. Anfinson, 51–65. Occasional Publications in Minnesota Anthropology, No. 5. Minnesota Archaeological Society, Fort Snelling.

Ready, T., and Scott Anfinson. 1979a. Kathio Series. In *A Handbook of Minnesota Prehistoric Ceramics*, ed. Scott F. Anfinson, 103–7. Occasional Publications in Minnesota Anthropology, No. 5. Minnesota Archaeological Society, Fort Snelling.

———. 1979b. Ogechie Series. In *A Handbook of Minnesota Prehistoric Ceramics,* ed. Scott F. Anfinson, 143–48. Occasional Publications in Minnesota Anthropology, No. 5. Minnesota Archaeological Society, Fort Snelling.

———. 1979c. Onamia Series. In *A Handbook of Minnesota Prehistoric Ceramics,* ed. Scott F. Anfinson, 149–55. Occasional Publications in Minnesota Anthropology, No. 5. Minnesota Archaeological Society, Fort Snelling.

Reid, C. S. "Paddy," and Grace Rajnovich. 1985. Laurel Architecture: Five Case Studies. *The Minnesota Archaeologist* 44 (2): 5–30.

———. 1991. Laurel: A Re-evaluation of the Spatial, Social and Temporal Paradigms. *Canadian Journal of Archaeology* 15: 193–234.

Rice, Prudence M. 1999. On the Origins of Pottery. *Journal of Archaeological Method and Theory* 6 (1): 1–54.

Robertson, James A., William A. Lovis, and John R. Halsey. 1999. The Late Archaic: Hunter-Gatherers in an Uncertain Environment. In *Retrieving Michigan's Buried Past: The Archaeology of the Great Lakes State,* ed. John R. Halsey, 95–124. Bulletin 64, Cranbrook Institute of Science, Bloomfield Hills, Mich.

Rodell, Roland. 1991. The Diamond Bluff Complex and Cahokia Influence in the Red Wing Locality. In *New Perspectives on Cahokia: Views from the Periphery,* ed. James B. Stoltman, 253–80. Monographs in World Archaeology, No. 2. Prehistory Press, Madison, Wis.

———. 1997. The Diamond Bluff Site Complex: Time and Tradition in the Northern Mississippi Valley. PhD diss., Department of Anthropology, University of Wisconsin–Milwaukee.

Rosebrough, Amy L. 2010. Every Family a Nation: A Deconstruction and Reconstruction of the Effigy Mound "Culture" of the Western Great Lakes of North America. PhD diss., Department of Anthropology, University of Wisconsin–Madison.

Rothaus, Richard, Debra Gold, and David Mather. 2005. *Mille Lacs Indian Museum Data Recovery Project (21ML06– Indian School Site).* Copy on file, Office of the State Archaeologist, St. Paul.

Sahlins, M. 1968. *Tribesmen.* Prentice-Hall, Englewood Cliffs, N.J.

———. 2004. *Stone Age Economics.* Routledge, New York.

Salzer, Robert J. 1974. The Wisconsin North Lakes Project: A Preliminary Report. In *Aspects of Upper Great Lakes Anthropology: Papers in Honor of Lloyd A. Wilford,* ed. Elden Johnson, 40–54. Minnesota Prehistoric Archaeology Series 11. Minnesota Historical Society, St. Paul.

Sampson, Kelvin W. 1988. Conventionalized Figures on Late Woodland Ceramics. *The Wisconsin Archeologist* 69: 163–88.

Sassaman, Kenneth E., and David G. Anderson, eds. 1996. *Archaeology of the Mid-Holocene Southeast.* University of Florida Press, Gainesville.

Sasso, Robert F. 1989. Oneota Settlement Practices in the La Crosse Region: An Analysis of the Coon Creek Drainage in the Driftless Area of Western Wisconsin. PhD diss., Department of Anthropology, Northwestern University, Evanston, Ill.

Sayers, June, Robert Thompson, and Robert MacCore. 2011. Phytoliths from Food Residue Provide the Oldest Date for the Use of Wild Rice in Minnesota. Paper presented at 2011 GSA Annual Meeting in Minneapolis, 9–12 October 2011.

Scarre, Chris, ed. 2005. *The Human Past: World Prehistory and the Development of Human Societies.* Thames & Hudson, New York.

Schaaf, Jeanne. 1981. A Method for Reliable and Quantifiable Subsampling of Archaeological Features for Flotation. *Midcontinental Journal of Archaeology* 6: 219–48.

Schiffer, Michael B. 1996. *Formation Processes of the Archaeological Record.* University of Utah Press, Salt Lake City.

Schirmer, Ronald C. 2002. Plant-Use Systems and Late Prehistoric Culture Change in the Red Wing Locality. PhD diss. Interdisciplinary Archaeological Studies, University of Minnesota, Minneapolis.

Schroeder, Sissel. 2007. Evidence for Paleoindians in Wisconsin and at the Skare Site. *Plains Anthropologist* 52 (201): 63–91.

Scullin, M. 1992. Cambria, Easternmost of the Western or Westernmost of the Eastern? Cahokia State Agricultural Extension Office, Occasional Papers No. 3. Available online at: http://www.mnsu.edu/emuseum/offices/scullin/Cambria.Pc92.9711.html, accessed April 2009.

Seeman, Mark F. 1998. Hopewell Interaction Sphere. In *Archaeology of Prehistoric Native America: An Encyclopedia,* ed. Guy Gibbon, 371–73. Garland Publishing, New York.

Sellars, Jonathan. 1992a. The Lake Oscar Sites in Cultural Context. In *Archeological Investigations in the Vicinity of Lake Oscar, Douglas County, Minnesota. S.P. 2101-18 (T.H. 27),* ed. Jonathan Sellars, 175–88. Prepared for the Minnesota Department of Transportation. Bear Creek Archaeology. Copy on file, Office of the State Archaeologist, St. Paul.

———, ed. 1992b. *Archeological Investigations in the Vicinity of Lake Oscar, Douglas County, Minnesota. S.P. 2101-18 (T.H. 27).* Prepared for the Minnesota Department of Transportation. Bear Creek Archaeology. Copy on file, Office of the State Archaeologist, St. Paul.

Service, Elman R. 1979. *The Hunters.* 2nd ed. Prentice-Hall, Englewood Cliffs, N.J.

Shane, O.C., III. 1991. Final Report to the Minnesota Historical Society for Contract 90-C2443: Radiocarbon Assays of Bone from the Browns Valley Skeleton. Ms. on file, Science Museum of Minnesota, St. Paul.

Shay, C.T. 1971. *The Itasca Bison Kill Site: An Ecological Analysis.* Minnesota Prehistoric Archaeology Series, No. 6. Minnesota Historical Society, St. Paul.

Shen, Chen. 1996. Use-Wear Analysis of Chipped Stone Artifacts. In *McKinstry Site (21KC2): Final Report of Phase III Investigations for Mn/DOT S.P. 3604-44, Replacement of T.H. 11 Bridge 5178 over the Little Fork River, Koochiching County, Minnesota,* ed. Mathew Thomas and David Mather, chapter 13. Loucks Project Report 93512. Copy on file, Office of the State Archaeologist, St. Paul.

Shuman, B.P., J. Bartlein, N. Logar, P. Newby, and T. Webb III. 2002. Parallel Climate and Vegetation Responses to the Early Holocene Collapse of the Laurentide Ice Sheet. *Quaternary Science Reviews* 21: 1793–1802.

Steinbring, Jack. 1974. The Preceramic Archaeology of Northern Minnesota. In *Aspects of Upper Great Lakes Anthropology: Papers in Honor of Lloyd A. Wilford,* ed. Elden Johnson, 64–73. Minnesota Prehistoric Archaeology Series, No. 11. Minnesota Historical Society, St. Paul.

———. 1975. Taxonomic and Associational Considerations of Copper Technology during the Archaic Tradition. PhD diss. University of Minnesota, Minneapolis.

Stoltman, James B. 1973. *The Laurel Culture in Minnesota.* Minnesota Historical Society, St. Paul.

———. 1986. The Archaic Tradition. In Introduction to Wisconsin Archaeology, ed. W. Green, J.B. Stoltman, and A.B. Kehoe, 207–38. *The Wisconsin Archeologist* 67 (3–4).

———. 1990. The Woodland Tradition in the Prairie Du Chien Locality. In *The Woodland Tradition in the Western Great Lakes: Papers Presented to Elden Johnson,* ed. Guy Gibbon, 239–59. University of Minnesota Publications in Anthropology, No. 4. Minneapolis.

———. 1997. The Archaic Tradition. In Wisconsin Archaeology, ed. R.A. Birmingham, C.I. Mason, and J.B. Stoltman. *The Wisconsin Archeologist* 78 (1/2): 112–39.

———. 2003. *Phase II Archaeological Investigations of the Tillmont Site (47 CR 460): A Stratified Prehistoric Site in the Upper Mississippi Valley.* Report prepared for the St. Paul District, U.S. Army Corps of Engineers. Copy on file, State Historic Preservation Office, Madison, Wis.

———. 2006. Reconsidering the Context of Hopewell Interaction in Southwestern Wisconsin. In *Recreating Hopewell,* ed. Douglas K. Charles and Jane E. Buikstra, 310–27. University Press of Florida, Gainesville.

Stoltman, James B., Danielle M. Benden, and Robert F. Boszhardt. 2008. New Evidence in the Upper Mississippi Valley for Premississippian Cultural Interaction with the American Bottom. *American Antiquity* 73 (2): 317–36.

Stoltman, James B., and George W. Christiansen. 2000. The Late Woodland Stage in the Driftless Area of the Upper Mississippi Valley. In *Late Woodland Societies: Tradition and Transformation across the Midcontinent,* ed. T. E. Emerson, D. L. McElrath, and A. C. Fortier, 497–524. University of Nebraska Press, Lincoln.

Syms, E. Leigh. 1977. Cultural Ecology and Ecological Dynamics of the Ceramic Period in Southwestern Manitoba. *Plains Anthropologist,* Memoir 12, vol. 22, no. 76, pt. 2. Plains Anthropological Society, Lincoln, Neb.

———. 1982. The Arvilla Burial Complex: A Re-assessment. *Journal of the North Dakota Archaeological Association* 1: 135–66.

Tanner, Adrian. 1979. *Bringing Home Animals: Religious Ideology and Mode of Production of the Mistassini Cree.* St. Martin's Press, New York.

Teller, J. T. 1987. Proglacial Lakes and the Southern Margin of the Laurentide Ice Sheet. In *North America and Adjacent Oceans during the Last Deglaciation,* ed. W. F. Ruddiman and H. E. Wright Jr., 39–69. Geological Society of America, Boulder, Colo.

Teller, J. T., and L. Clayton, eds. 1983. *Glacial Lake Agassiz.* Geological Association of Canada Special Paper 26. Department of Geology, Memorial University of Newfoundland, St. John's.

Tester, John R. 1995. *Minnesota's Natural Heritage: An Ecological Perspective.* University of Minnesota Press, Minneapolis.

Theler, James L. 1987. *Woodland Tradition Economic Strategies: Animal Resource Utilization in Southwestern Wisconsin and Northeastern Iowa.* Report 17. Office of the State Archaeologist, University of Iowa, Iowa City.

Theler, James L., and Robert F. Boszhardt. 2000. The End of the Effigy Mound Culture: The Late Woodland to Oneota Transition in Western Wisconsin. *Midcontinental Journal of Archaeology* 25: 289–312.

———. 2003. *Twelve Millennia: Archaeology of the Upper Mississippi River Valley.* University of Iowa Press, Iowa City.

———. 2006. Collapse of Crucial Resources and Culture Change: A Model for the Woodland to Oneota Transformation in the Upper Midwest. *American Antiquity* 71 (3): 433–72.

Thomas, Matthew. 1996a. History of Archaeological Investigations. In *McKinstry Site (21KC2): Final Report of Phase III Investigations for Mn/DOT S.P. 3604-44, Replacement of T.H. 11 Bridge 5178 over the Little Fork River, Koochiching County, Minnesota,* ed. Matthew Thomas and David Mather, chapter 8. Loucks Project Report 93512. Copy on file, Office of the State Archaeologist, St. Paul.

———. 1996b. Ceramic Analysis. In *McKinstry Site (21KC2): Final Report of Phase III Investigations for Mn/DOT S.P. 3604-44, Replacement of T.H. 11 Bridge 5178 over the Little Fork River, Koochiching County, Minnesota,* ed. Matthew Thomas and David Mather, chapter 10. Loucks Project Report 93512. Copy on file, Office of the State Archaeologist, St. Paul.

———. 1996c. Native Copper, Fire-Cracked Rock, Groundstone, and Ochre and Unmodified Stone. In *McKinstry Site (21KC2): Final Report of Phase III Investigations for Mn/DOT S.P. 3604-44, Replacement of T.H. 11 Bridge 5178 over the Little Fork River, Koochiching County, Minnesota,* ed. Matthew Thomas and David Mather, chapter 14. Loucks Project Report 93512. Copy on file, Office of the State Archaeologist, St. Paul.

——. 2000. The Prehistoric Ceramic Record of the Mille Lacs Region. In *The Lake Onamia–Trunk Highway 169 Data Recovery Project, Mille Lacs County, Minnesota*, ed. D. Mather and E. Abel, 14.1–14.64. Loucks Project Report 96506-1. Loucks & Associates, Inc., Maple Grove. Report prepared for the Minnesota Department of Transportation, St. Paul.

Thomas, Matthew, and David Mather, eds. 1996a. *McKinstry Site (21KC2): Final Report of Phase III Investigations for Mn/DOT S.P. 3604-44, Replacement of T.H. 11 Bridge 5178 over the Little Fork River, Koochiching County, Minnesota*. Loucks Project Report 93512. Copy on file, Office of the State Archaeologist, St. Paul.

——. 1996b. Regional Culture History. In *McKinstry Site (21KC2): Final Report of Phase III Investigations for Mn/DOT S.P. 3604-44, Replacement of T.H. 11 Bridge 5178 over the Little Fork River, Koochiching County, Minnesota*, ed. Matthew Thomas and David Mather, chapter 5. Loucks Project Report 93512. Copy on file, Office of the State Archaeologist, St. Paul.

Thompson, Robert. 1995. Ceramic Artifacts. In *Archaeological Data Recovery at the Roosevelt Lake Narrows Site, Cass County, Minnesota*, ed. Michael Justin, chapter 9. Woodward-Clyde Report 93e209, prepared for Minnesota Department of Transportation. Copy on file, State Historic Preservation Office, St. Paul.

——. 1996. Phytolith Analysis of Selected Ceramic Sherds. In *McKinstry Site (21KC2): Final Report of Phase III Investigations for Mn/DOT S.P. 3604-44, Replacement of T.H. 11 Bridge 5178 over the Little Fork River, Koochiching County, Minnesota*, ed. Matthew Thomas and David Mather, chapter 17. Loucks Project Report 93512. Copy on file, Office of the State Archaeologist, St. Paul.

——. 2000. Phytolith Analysis of Selected Ceramic Sherds from the Mille Lacs Region. In *The Lake Onamia–Trunk Highway 169 Data Recovery Project, Mille Lacs County, Minnesota*, ed. D. Mather and E. Abel, 19.1–19.10. Loucks Project Report 96506-1. Loucks & Associates, Inc., Maple Grove. Report prepared for the Minnesota Department of Transportation, St. Paul.

Thompson, Robert, Susan Mulholland, and James Lindbeck. 1995. Paleoethnobotany of the Roosevelt Lake Narrows Site. In *Archaeological Data Recovery at the Roosevelt Lake Narrows Site, Cass County, Minnesota*, ed. Michael Justin, chapter 5. Woodward-Clyde Report 93e209. Report prepared for the Minnesota Department of Transportation. Copy on file, Office of the State Archaeologist, St. Paul.

Thurston, S., and B. H. O'Connell. 1984. Report on Human Skeletal Material Goodhue County, Bryan Site (21GD04). Manuscript on file, Department of Anthropology, Hamline University, St. Paul.

Tieszen, Larry L., Karl J. Reinhard, and Dawn L. Foreshoe. 1997a. Stable Isotopes in the Central and Northern Great Plains. In *Bioarcheology of the North Central United States*, ed. Douglas W. Owsley and Jerome C. Rose, 329–36. A volume in the Central and Northern Plains Archeological Overview, Arkansas Archeological Survey Research Series 49. USACERL Special Report 97/4. U.S. Army Corps of Engineers Construction Engineering Research Laboratory, U.S. Department of Defense Legacy Resource Management Program.

——. 1997b. Application of Stable Isotopes in the Analysis of Dietary Patterns in the Central and Northern Great Plains. In *Bioarcheology of the North Central United States*, ed. Douglas W. Owsley and Jerome C. Rose, 329–36. A volume in the Central and Northern Plains Archeological Overview, Arkansas Archeological Survey Research Series 49. USACERL Special Report 97/4. U.S. Army Corps of Engineers Construction Engineering Research Laboratory, U.S. Department of Defense Legacy Resource Management Program.

Tiffany, Joseph A., and Lynn M. Alex. 2001. *Great Oasis Archaeology: New Perspectives from the DeCamp and West Des Moines Burial Sites in Central Iowa*. Memoir 33. *Plains Anthropologist* 46 (178).

Toom, Dennis L. 2004. Northeastern Plains Village Complex Timelines and Relations. *Plains Anthropologist* 49 (191): 281–97.

Torbenson, Michael, Arthur Aufderheide, and Elden Johnson. 1992. Punctured Human Bones of the Laurel Culture from Smith Mound Four, Minnesota. *American Antiquity* 57 (3): 506–14.

Torbenson, Michael, Odin Langsjoen, and Arthur Aufderheide. 1994. Laurel Culture Human Remains from Smith Mounds Three and Four. *Plains Anthropologist* 39 (150): 429–44.

———. 1996. Human Remains from McKinstry Mound Two. *Plains Anthropologist* 39 (150): 71–92.

Trocki, Patricia, and Curtis Hudak. 2005. *Phase I Archaeological Survey and Phase II Evaluation of 23 Archaeological Sites along the T.H. 169 Corridor Project South of CSAH 21/Timber Trails Road, Mille Lacs County, Minnesota (S.P. 4814-49)*. Prepared for the Minnesota Department of Transportation by Foth and Van Dyke. Copy on file, State Historic Preservation Office, St. Paul.

Upham, Warren. 1902. Man in the Ice Age at Lansing, Kansas, and Little Falls, Minnesota. *American Geologist* 30: 135–50.

———. 1916. The Work of N. H. Winchell in Glacial Geology and Archaeology. *Economic Geology* 11 (1): 62–73.

Valppu, Seppo H. 1996. Plant Macrofossil Analysis. In *McKinstry Site (21KC2): Final Report of Phase III Investigations for Mn/DOT S.P. 3604-44, Replacement of T.H. 11 Bridge 5178 over the Little Fork River, Koochiching County, Minnesota,* ed. Matthew Thomas and David Mather, chapter 16. Loucks Project Report 93512. Copy on file, Office of the State Archaeologist, St. Paul.

———. 2000. Archaeobotanical Analysis. In *The Lake Onamia–Trunk Highway 169 Data Recovery Project, Mille Lacs County, Minnesota,* ed. D. Mather and E. Abel, 18.1–18.12. Loucks Project Report 96506-1. Loucks & Associates, Inc., Maple Grove. Report prepared for the Minnesota Department of Transportation, St. Paul.

———. 2010. Archaeobotanical Analysis: Petaga Point 21-ML-11 Archaeological Site, Mille Lacs Kathio State Park, Mille Lacs County, Minnesota. In *Kathio Archaeology Day Public Research Program: The Petaga Point Site (21ML11), Mille Lacs Kathio State Park (Interim Project Report for 2006–2009),* ed. David Mather and Jim Cummings, Appendix A. State Historic Preservation Office, Minnesota Historical Society, St. Paul, and Mille Lacs Kathio State Park, Onamia.

Valppu, Seppo H., and George Rapp. 2000. Paleoethnobotanical Context and Dating of the Laurel Use of Wild Rice: The Big Rice Site. *The Minnesota Archaeologist* 59: 81–87.

van der Valk, A. 1989. *Northern Prairie Wetlands.* Iowa State University Press, Ames.

Waters, Thomas F. 1977. *The Streams and Rivers of Minnesota.* University of Minnesota Press, Minneapolis.

———. 1987. *The Superior North Shore.* University of Minnesota Press, Minneapolis.

Watrall, Charles R. 1968. An Analysis of the Bone, Stone, and Shell Materials from the Cambria Focus. Master's thesis, Department of Anthropology, University of Minnesota, Minneapolis.

———. 1974. Subsistence Pattern Change at the Cambria Site: A Review and Hypothesis. In *Aspects of Upper Great Lakes Anthropology: Papers in Honor of Lloyd A. Wilford,* ed. Elden Johnson, 138–42. Minnesota Prehistoric Archaeology Series, No. 11. Minnesota Historical Society, St. Paul.

Webster, David L. 1967. Mounds of the Rainy River: An Examination of the Laurel Focus of Minnesota. Master's thesis, Department of Anthropology, University of Minnesota, Minneapolis.

———. 1973. Nonceramic Artifacts from Laurel Culture Sites Excavated Prior to 1961. In *The Laurel Culture in Minnesota,* ed. James B. Stoltman, 94–111. Minnesota Historical Society, St. Paul.

Wedel, Mildred M. 1959. Oneota Sites on the Upper Iowa River. *Missouri Archaeologist* 21 (2–4): 1–181.

———. 1986. Peering at the Ioway Indians through the Mist of Time: 1650–circa 1700. *Journal of the Iowa Archeological Society* 33: 1–74.

Whelan, M. 1990. Late Woodland Subsistence Systems and Settlement Size in the Mille Lacs Area. In *The Woodland Tradition in the Western Great Lakes: Papers Presented to Elden Johnson,* ed. Guy Gibbon, 55–75. Publications in Anthropology 4, University of Minnesota, Minneapolis.

Wilber, Ken. 2000. *A Brief History of Everything.* Rev. ed. Shambhala, Boston.

Wilford, Lloyd A. 1937. Minnesota Archaeology, with Special Reference to the Mound Area. PhD diss., Department of Anthropology, Harvard University.

———. 1941. A Tentative Classification of the Prehistoric Cultures of Minnesota. *American Antiquity* 6 (3): 231–49.

———. 1944. The Prehistoric Indians of Minnesota: The Mille Lacs Aspect. *Minnesota History* 25: 329–41.

———. 1945. Three Village Sites of the Mississippi Pattern in Minnesota. *American Antiquity* 11: 32–40.

———. 1950a. The Prehistoric Indians of Minnesota: The McKinstry Mounds of the Rainy River Aspect. *Minnesota History* 31: 231–37.

———. 1950b. The Prehistoric Indians of Minnesota: Some Mounds of the Rainy River Aspect. *Minnesota History* 31: 163–67.

———. 1951. The Prehistoric Indians of Minnesota: The Mille Lacs Aspect. *The Minnesota Archaeologist* 17 (3): 9–16.

———. 1952a. McKinstry Mounds of the Rainy River Aspect. *The Minnesota Archaeologist* 18 (2): 10–14.

———. 1952b. The Prehistoric Indians of Minnesota: Some Mounds of the Rainy River Aspect. *The Minnesota Archaeologist* 18 (1): 4–9.

———. 1952c. The Wilsey Burial Site. Unpublished manuscript on file in the University of Minnesota archives at the Minnesota Historical Society, St. Paul.

———. 1954. The La Moille Rock Shelter. *The Minnesota Archaeologist* 19 (2): 17–21.

———. 1955. A Revised Classification of the Prehistoric Cultures of Minnesota. *American Antiquity* 21 (2): 131–43.

———. 1960. The First Minnesotans. In *Minnesota Heritage,* ed. L. M. Brings, 40–79. T. S. Denison, Minneapolis.

———. 1985. The Bryan Site: A Prehistoric Village in Southern Minnesota. *The Minnesota Archaeologist* 43 (2): 21–36.

Wilford, Lloyd A., and John W. Brink. 1974. Hogback: A Protohistoric Oneota Burial Site. *The Minnesota Archaeologist* 33 (1, 2).

Wilford, Lloyd A., E. Johnson, and J. Vicinus. 1969. *Burial Mounds of Central Minnesota: Excavation Reports.* Minnesota Prehistoric Archaeology Series, No. 1. Minnesota Historical Society, St. Paul.

Willey, Gordon R., and Philip Phillips. 1958. *Method and Theory in American Archaeology.* University of Chicago Press, Chicago.

Winchell, Newton H. 1878. *Sixth Annual Report of the Geological and Natural History Survey of Minnesota.* Johnson, Smith, and Harrison, Minneapolis.

———. 1903. Was Man in America in the Glacial Period? Presidential Address, Geological Society of America, Dec. 30, 1902. *Bulletin of the Geological Society of America* 14: 133–52.

———. 1911. *The Aborigines of Minnesota.* Minnesota Historical Society, St. Paul.

Wittry, Warren L. 1957. A Preliminary Study of the Old Copper Complex. *The Wisconsin Archeologist* 38 (4): 204–21.

Wright, H. E., Jr. 1971. Retreat of the Laurentide Ice Sheet from 14,000 to 9,000 Years Ago. *Quaternary Research* 1: 316–30.

———. 1972a. Quaternary History of Minnesota. In *Geology of Minnesota: A Centennial Volume in Honor of George M. Schwartz,* ed. P. K. Sims and G. B. Morey, 515–47. Minnesota Geological Survey, St. Paul.

———. 1972b. Physiography of Minnesota. In *Geology of Minnesota: A Centennial Volume in Honor of George M. Schwartz,* ed. P. K. Sims and G. B. Morey, 561–78. Minnesota Geological Survey, St. Paul.

———. 1976a. Ice Retreat and Revegetation of the Western Great Lakes Region. In *Quaternary Stratigraphy of North America,* ed. W. C. Malaney, 119–32. Dowden, Hutchison, and Ross, Stroudsberg, Penn.

———. 1976b. The Dynamic Nature of Holocene Vegetation. *Quaternary Research* 6: 581–96.

Wright, H. E., Jr., B. A. Coffin, and N. Aaseng, eds. 1992. *The Patterned Peatlands of Minnesota.* University of Minnesota Press, Minneapolis.

Wright, H. E., Jr., Ivanka Stefanova, Jian Tin, Thomas A. Brown, and Feng Sheng Hu. 2004. A Chronological Framework for the Holocene Vegetational History of Central Minnesota: The Steel Lake Pollen Record. *Quaternary Science Reviews* 23: 611–26.

Wright, J. V. 1998. Laurel. In *Archaeology of Prehistoric Native America: An Encyclopedia,* ed. Guy Gibbon, 451–53. Garland Publishing, New York.

Yahner, R. H. 1995. *Eastern Deciduous Forest.* University of Minnesota Press, Minneapolis.

Yourd, W. 1988. The Antiquity and Distribution of Wild Rice in Lake Marquette, North-Central Minnesota: Implications for Regional Archaeology and the Natural History of Wild Rice. Master's thesis, Center for Ancient Studies, University of Minnesota, Minneapolis.

GUY GIBBON is professor emeritus of archaeology in the Department of Anthropology at the University of Minnesota.